JOURNALS FROM A WARRIOR'S MOTHER

RAINBOWS AND BRAINSTORMS
Collector's Edition

Navigating through Brain
Surgery and Depression amid
the Arrival of Rainbow Babies

Chrissy L. Whitten

Illustrated by Tammy S. Edwards,
Piper Whitten, and Daphne Whitten

Copyright © 2024 by Chrissy L. Whitten
www.chrissylwhitten.com

All rights reserved. No part of this publication may be reproduced, distributed, or transmitted in any form or by any means, without prior written permission.

Publisher's Note: This is a narrative nonfiction memoir. The events and conversations contained in this book have been documented to the best of the author's ability.

All Scripture quotations marked (NIV) are taken from the Holy Bible, New International Version®, NIV®. Copyright © 1973, 1978, 1984, 2011 by Biblica, Inc.™ Used by permission of Zondervan. All rights reserved worldwide. www.zondervan.com. The "NIV" and "New International Version" are trademarks registered in the United States Patent and Trademark Office by Biblica, Inc.™

Cover design by Tammy S. Edwards & Chrissy L. Whitten
Illustrations on pages 18, 112, 134, 178, 184, 197, 214, 228, 236, 248, 254, 258, 280, 330, 356, 439 © 2024 by Piper A. Whitten
Illustrations on pages 177, 183, 185, 213, 231, 234, 344, 401 © 2024 by Daphne M. Whitten
Remaining illustrations copyright © 2024 by Tammy S. Edwards, tammyedwards63@yahoo.com
Photographs on pages 82, 93, 312 by Kelli Marone, NILMDTS Affiliated Photographer. Photograph on page 30 by Jeannette Adamyk. Photographs on pages 40, 402, 457 by Chera Myers, Bluebird Photography. Photographs on pages 126 and 426 by Stephanie Dooley. Photograph on page 394 by Brandy Moton Photography. Photograph on page 450 by daniilantiq2010/stock.adobe.com. Remaining photographs by Chrissy L. Whitten.
Edited by Staci D. Mauney, prestigeprose.com
Formatted by Danelle G. Young, danelleyoung.com
Book Layout © 2016 BookDesignTemplates.com

Rainbows & Brainstorms/ Chrissy L. Whitten. — 1st ed.
ISBN 978-1-7365322-6-3 (Paperback)
ISBN 978-1-7365322-7-0 (e-book)
ISBN 978-1-7365322-8-7 (Collector's Edition)
Library of Congress Control Numbers: 2024900622 and 2024900621 (Collector's Edition)

DEDICATION

God,

Less of me and more of You! Making my way through this major book project has been grueling on myself, my family, and my warrior tribe. Thank you for never giving up on me. You continue to meet me where I am without question. Three books down and one more to go for this series!

Michael, Lilian Grace, Piper Allegra, and Daphne Mae,

I don't know what I would do without our little family. Thanks for giving me breaks and adding joy to this crazy journey. You make my life full and worth all the storms that have led us to the beautiful rainbows and sunshine!

Warrior Tribe,

You all haven't flinched. Thank you for the countless hours you've put into each book. We are seventy-five percent there! It's a true honor to serve beside each of you.

Family, friends, and divine appointments,

Your prayers and encouragement mean everything to me. You show up for me at the perfect moment. May you all be blessed and find joy!

Chrissy and Rachel finishing the inaugural race
that honored Lilian Grace's memory

INTRODUCTION

The Fight, my first book in this series, is Lilian's story—her birth, life, departure, and the months that followed. *The Fall to the Climb*, my second book in this series, brought you along my grief journey as I tried to work through my first year without her. In this book (number three), I welcome my second baby, experience brain surgery, and deliver my third baby.

You will pick up where book two ends. I had grieved for a full year following Lilian's death. Revising these journal entries helped me process my grief journey as mountains and storms continue to come into my life daily. No one is exempt from the hardships and sorrows of life.

May God bring you joy, affirmations, and strength as you read through my story. As before, I provide songs, Scriptures, and inspirational thoughts in these entries. I hope you continue to swim no matter how rough the waters get in your storms. God always provides.

My big takeaway from this book is that each storm has a beautiful rainbow. I'm blessed to watch my two biggest rainbows learn, grow, and prosper. The ocean theme of this book was inspired by Lilian Grace's three-month birthday. I hope you find peace while learning about the symbolism of the art on the cover and inside the pages.

Welcome (back) to book number three. Though my work on the Journals from a Warrior's Mother series has been challenging and tiresome, I love seeing God shine brightly through it. He continues to rock my world wherever He takes me. He's embedded in my heart and brain a desire to keep moving forward. If one more person reads my story, then I am successful. Jesus left the ninety-nine for the one. I will not give up. I will continue to be less for Him to be more of my story.

May you feel joy in all you do. Thank you for supporting me by reading this book. You are worth everything. You have a purpose! Let His light shine brightly in the storms of your life.

Love,
Chrissy

CONTENTS

DEDICATION	3
INTRODUCTION	5
LILIAN'S CARINGBRIDGE	11
187 › Being Real	13
188 › Conference Project	19
189 › Human	23
190 › Mighty Mouse	29
191 › I Look to You	35
192 › Rainbow Baby #1	37
193 › Lift My Hands	45
194 › Be My Strength	49
195 › Hold My Heart	51
196 › Not Alone	55
197 › Fall Apart	59
198 › Survivors	63
199 › Strong Enough	75
200 › Change This Heart	79
201 › Angel by Your Side	83
202 › Break Through	87
203 › Broken	89
204 › Weeps for You	91
205 › Piper's 103-Day Milestone	95
206 › Race Details	99
207 › So Small	101
208 › Footprints & New Days	105
209 › Reality	109
210 › Time	113
211 › Reopen	119
212 › Feet over Heart	127
213 › Never Easier	131
214 › Wander with Focus	135
215 › Beam Me Up	141

216 › Ticktock _____ 149
217 › Three-Year Angelversary _____ 155
218 › Worn Yet Calling Me Higher _____ 163
CHRISSY'S CARINGBRIDGE _____ 167
1 › The Journey Changes _____ 169
2 › My Cup _____ 179
3 › Going into Brain Surgery _____ 181
4 › Surgery Update _____ 183
5 › Recovery Update _____ 185
6 › His Warrior Princess _____ 187
7 › Update from Leslie _____ 189
8 › Amazing Grace _____ 193
9 › Short & Sweet _____ 197
10 › Meal Train _____ 199
11 › Scripture for Healing & Hope _____ 201
12 › Home Sweet Home _____ 209
13 › My Doctor Rocks _____ 211
14 › Calling All Christians _____ 215
15 › Born for This _____ 217
16 › O Holy Night _____ 219
17 › Ten-Year Wedding Anniversary _____ 223
18 › Let Go, Let God _____ 229
19 › He Never Lets Go _____ 233
20 › Pathology Results _____ 235
21 › Tired _____ 237
22 › Wake Up _____ 239
LILIAN'S CARINGBRIDGE _____ 244
219 › Missing Lilian _____ 245
CHRISSY'S CARINGBRIDGE _____ 248
23 › Video Update _____ 249
24 › In the End _____ 255
25 › Truth Is Truth _____ 259
26 › Holding Tight to His Hand _____ 263
27 › Walk on the Water _____ 273
28 › Waking Up _____ 281
29 › Seven-Weeks Post-Brain Surgery ____ 283

30 › Eight-Weeks Post-Brain Surgery	289
31 › Nine-Weeks Post-Brain Surgery	293
32 › Eleven-Weeks Post-Brain Surgery	297
33 › Finally, an Update	301
LILIAN'S CARINGBRIDGE	311
220 › Even If	313
CHRISSY'S CARINGBRIDGE	316
34 › I Can Just Be Me	317
35 › Good News	321
36 › Heaven or Bust	331
37 › Both Sides	341
38 › Hope & Strength in the ER	345
39 › Quick Update	351
40 › Miracles Grow	353
41 › Reset & Reach Up	357
42 › Warrior Princess Angel Run	361
43 › My Celebration of Life Wishes	365
44 › It's Time!	371
45 › Twenty-Week Scan Praise	373
46 › Gestational Diabetes	375
47 › Update & Baby Sprinkle	377
48 › Car Wreck	381
49 › Thankful	385
50 › One-Year Post-Brain Surgery	391
51 › C-section Date	395
52 › Looking Back	397
53 › Rainbow Baby #2	403
54 › He Makes Me Brave	409
55 › Time Flies	413
56 › Extended Deadline	419
57 › Daphne's 103-Day Milestone	421
A NOTE FROM THE AUTHOR	425
BOOK COVER LEGEND	427
MEMORY VERSES	441
PLAYLIST	451
ACKNOWLEDGEMENTS	455

ABOUT THE AUTHOR	457
MORE FROM CHRISSY L. WHITTEN	459
REVIEW PLEA	461
COMING SOON	462

LILIAN'S CARINGBRIDGE

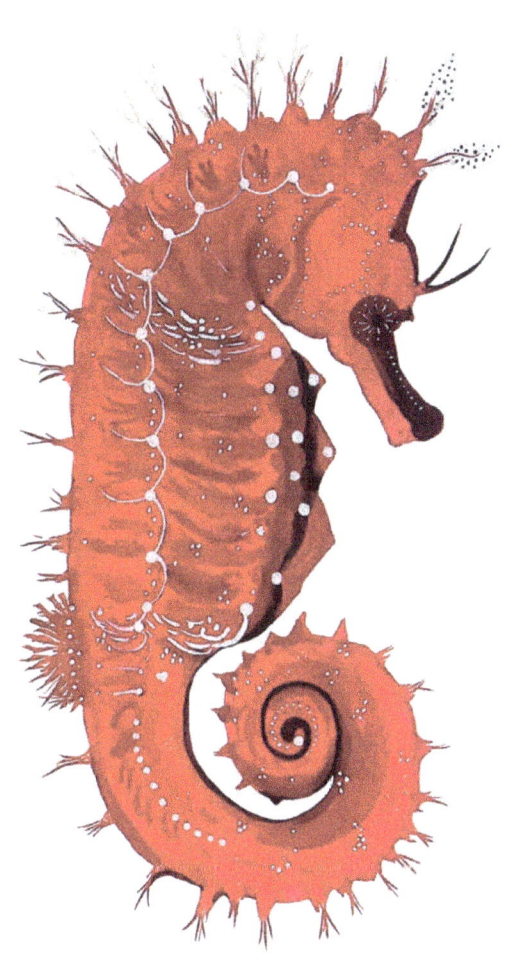

The Children's Hospital at St. Francis

AUGUST 21, 2011

187 › Being Real

I wanted to listen to a song while typing this entry, so I played "What If We Were Real" by Mandisa—it was a total God thing. I'm still here, writing on Lilian Grace's CaringBridge site! I thought I was possibly done journaling, but God decided not yet. I love how He works!

Sunday at church, we had a phenomenal sermon about how Jesus gave His life in place of ours. We don't ever have to face a death penalty because Jesus died in my place. It's incredible to remember such a truth. Not only did the sermon and special prayer time following church get me thinking, but I was also inspired by more thought-provoking moments when I went to the movies with my hubby.

I'm sharing the realness of my thoughts as people got saved this morning at church. Pastor Matt (Blair) gave a wonderful picture of God celebrating with the angels above, which led me to a wonderful daydream. I pictured sweet Lilian Grace, four days short of fifteen months, nestled in my great-grandmother's arms—clapping her hands with a big ol' gorgeous grin to celebrate those getting saved!

Tears flow now as I picture it again. My child is being cared for in a way that I never could have done here on earth. She had an incredible purpose here that meant something. She lived and fought so people could grow, choose, or discover their faith. This momma's heart sings praise a million times over to our heavenly Father while knowing His plans keep outperforming mine. The number one reason Lilian came was to awaken my spirit and realign me with my heavenly Father's purposes!

> *My child is being cared for in a way that I never could have done here on earth.*

After our movie, I took time to analyze and debrief my life as of late. I've been scrapbooking pieces I saved from years past and am placing them in chronological order. Both the paperwork and pictures create a time capsule that brings up memories both cherished and appreciated. What have I discovered the most from all the pieces?

I'm remembering how things really were and not what I had settled on at the time. I'm being more real than I've ever been before. I've even corrected memories that had been lost in translation over the years. Guess what? It feels good to fix broken and delusional memories. God truly keeps blessing me with a crazy, full life. For most of it, I've been the biggest dork I've ever met. I've been God's biggest dork, which makes me feel pretty dang special. I'm real and owning it.

I joked with Michael and asked him how in the world he could still be with me or want me. Though he gave joking remarks, the words he has written over the years reveal the real answer to my inquiry. He saw God through the holes and my dorky ways. I'm glad he did.

I've discovered the most by looking at myself as a baby, child, teenager, young lady, adult, and woman. In many of the pictures, I've found myself displaying a Chrissy who was behind, stressed out, and overwhelmed. Don't get me wrong—it wasn't all negative. There was evidence in some photos that I was radiating extreme happiness, yet the other ones hit me harder with a heavy dose of reality.

When I get behind, I can fall short—causing chaos and unhappiness. Pictures prove that I tried to be strong and camouflage my true self, yet I was drowning in perfectionism and people pleasing. I wasn't a good chameleon, because I looked exhausted with my messy hair and no makeup status time after time. I was a hot mess—trying to do it all!

Today, I can honestly say that I've gotten my act together this summer by decluttering, reshaping, reforming, and rediscovering. These small acts of obedience have been one of the best gifts I could receive from my heavenly Father. It's been rough through all the tears and bitterness/anger. God has encouraged me numerous times to slow down to get my act together. I always seem to take it for granted with statements like I didn't make time; it really could wait for another day; it's not that important right now; or I had too much other stuff to do.

I never thought that all the piled boxes and unfinished projects would be such blockers and weights in my life, emotionally and physically—getting in my way, weighing me down—until now. Going through the boxes by reducing, discarding, shredding, and giving away has finally—yes, FINALLY—happened and helped! God has blessed me with goodness during this period of brokenness where I finally caught up with myself after all these years. In taking this wonderful time, I've discovered Him completely through His love, comfort, joy, and happiness to gain a deeper understanding!

I wish I'd slowed down time after time to relish each amazing God-given moment. I did enjoy many, yet the letters, papers, and pictures showed space for a deeper enjoyment at the time. I've never seen it more clearly than I do now. Stopping to be real has made a difference.

I can't wait until the last project is complete so I can focus on the present ones that will follow. I don't want to be a prisoner of my past or my craziness to overbook myself nor procrastinate to the extent that I can't bask in the moment. I desire to be completely caught up and ready for whatever God has planned for me or that the dang devil throws at me. I want to be real by being present! I want to be able to feel at the exact moment life happens while readily armed to conquer it all!

PRAISE GOD, my daughter's life gave me this opportunity to become who I need to be. I can get out of the way and do the one thing I've read about all the years of my life—to do God's will by expanding His kingdom.

All the surgeries plus recovery time, internships far away, and time off from work life never woke me up enough to produce follow through. My daughter was the ultimate alarm. God made sure meeting her would make going backward impossible. My complete self was broken. He knew she would make the impossible possible so I could live the life He intended for me.

Do I wish I could have grasped this sooner? You bet! Many times, I'd start out with an amazing amount of steam—bulldozing to change and make myself better. Without fail, I'd get in the way and old habits would return. But now I'm doing the opposite. I'm trusting God completely—no matter the storm that comes and tries to drag me down or push me backward. Old habits are fading and replaced by new, positive ones! HALLELUJAH!

I have the best Pilot, not copilot, there ever will be. He is taking me on one adventure after another. I am not perfect nor will I ever be here on earth. I'm finally at a place in my life where my brain has room to think, breathe, and live—enjoying life like never before. I'm hoping by the time "The Who" gets here that I'll have my slate cleared to be ready for them! I'm so excited I could run a marathon! I get to live this life. It feels magnificent! Even through the bad times when I'm not on my game, it still feels good!

Here's to hoping you get to experience this adventure feeling caught up, and all those bags you've been dragging around disappear. May God help you clean out, adjust, and make you the "you" He meant for you to be. May you not build the roadblocks back up. May we all have a journey where we are awake for each day without all the crazy distractions destroying our present or future.

The journey will always have its ups and downs. What if we were real, present, and able to tackle any or all as a whole person? It would be worth trying to see how it plays out. I love you all.

AUGUST 23, 2011

188 › Conference Project

Hello, ladies! I hope this finds you healthy and prosperous. I know many of you have been praying and thinking about attending the Women of Faith Conference—Over the Top on November 11–12, 2011. Now is the time to make the decision to purchase your $89 ticket. You have until Thursday, September 2, 2011, to claim your ticket by paying a $45 (nonrefundable) deposit. The balance will be due by Friday, September 30, 2011. Here are two options for sending your money:[1]

Option 1
Please put the following information on a piece of paper: Name, Address, Email, Phone number, Church

Mail this information and your $45 deposit (that will reserve your ticket) or $89 (if you're paying in full) with check payable to: Solace Church, Women of Faith Conference Nov 2011, 6607 West 42nd St, Tulsa, Oklahoma 74107.

* Make sure to put "Women of Faith Conference Nov 2011" in the memo of your check. When the tickets come in, I'll mail them to you.

Option 2
You can pay by credit card when registering as a group member

---

[1] Note from author: This is old information.

on the GPS Women of Faith website (full payment will be charged):

Go to the GPS home page, gps.womenoffaith.com,[2] click on "FIND A GROUP," and enter the following information:

Name/Keyword: Solace Church
Group City: Tulsa
Group State: Oklahoma
Group Zip: 74107
Event State: Oklahoma and click "SEARCH," click on the group name (underlined in blue) in the search results, and click on "JOIN GROUP."

Fill out your registration form and click save. You will receive an email confirmation with your username/password. Once you are approved by your Group Leader, you will receive an email. Proceed to the GPS login and make payment for your ticket by credit card.

You will have to pay the whole amount at this time. Currently, there are forty-five tickets left. Whatever tickets aren't accounted for on September 2, 2011, will be relinquished back to the Women of Faith organization. This means that you may not be able to sit with the group if you try to buy a ticket later through Women of Faith. This is very important to decide right now. Here is the conference information:

What: Women of Faith Conference—Over the Top

Go to http://www.womenoffaith.com/events/2011-events/

---

[2] Note from author: This registration link is no longer active.

oklahoma-city/[3] *to see the promotional video. Make sure to register in only one of the two ways mentioned above.*

Where: Oklahoma City Arena

When: Friday, November 11, 2011, 10:00 a.m.–3:30 p.m., 7:00–10:00 p.m., and Saturday, November 12, 2011, 9:00 a.m.–5:00 p.m.

Meals provided with your ticket: Box lunches for both days

Speakers: Patsy Clairmont, Marilyn Meberg, Sandi Patty, and Lisa Whelchel

Dramatist: Deborah Joy Winans

Musical Guests: Amy Grant and Mandisa

Special Guest: Andy Andrews

Go to http://www.womenoffaith.com/events/line-up/ [4] *to find out more about the speakers and guests.*

---

[3] Note from author: This registration link is no longer active.
[4] Note from author: This registration link is no longer active.

AUGUST 26, 2011

189 › Human

I had a tough day yesterday. I still find myself having bad days, even during the good times. Why was it tough? Lilian Grace came into the world fifteen months ago. Wow! It's been fifteen months since my life changed forever after my eternal lightboard lit up. I remember taking a quick glance at her and saying that I would quit everything because she is all I need! Funny how a tiny person can have such a major impact on you in a nanosecond. I got Lilian's third picture book done this week involving birthdays, holidays, and special celebrations. It's the best one thus far. I'm sure I'll say that about each completed book. Glancing at all the pictures, I can't help but let the tears flow as I see so much life being lived in those 103 days.

I've always been a girl who doesn't like to regret or miss out on life—FOMO (fear of missing out). I thank God He made me this way. The pictures give you all the snapshots—all the craziness. There are sad, happy, crazy, and more precious ones that no money could ever buy. I was excited when Michael finally looked at the picture books without me and commented on how much he loved them!

I got to share them with a couple of my dear friends last night. It made this momma's heart and soul so happy to be a normal mommy by proudly showing off my baby girl. It's hard when I don't have her here to show off, since we, as humans, need tangible things in front of us. What makes me really overwhelmed with joy? When I get to talk about her—remembering all the goodness from her life. There's an abundance to tell, even with her short-lived life.

After experiencing a rough day, life took a turn for the better. This morning—I believe God is taking care of me—I got a call from a company wanting all the information about the Warrior Princess Foundation. They want to give a donation following an upcoming fundraiser. I'm crying just thinking about it. I know it's the company my dad works for, but he didn't ask them to do this. Today, they decided to talk to him about doing this amazing gesture. It was a much-needed surprise, which is blessing me beyond measure!

I know many people haven't forgotten Lilian, but it was extremely comforting to know she is still vibrant and imbedded in others' lives—especially ones not related or majorly connected. When she is remembered, people can't help but think of our heavenly Father. This brings me more pride in my daughter than anything else—her mission lives on! I pray "The Who" finds their own godly mission and lives it out fully, just as their big sister did so gracefully!

When she is remembered, people can't help but think of our heavenly Father. This makes me so proud . . . her mission lives on!

This reminded me that we have changed the address for the Warrior Princess Foundation—which just happened this week. Remember that all donations are tax deductible after we officially became a 501(c)(3) organization.

I have another couple of weeks before I start hitting the ground running with updates, a new foundation website, and major information about the Second Annual 2012 Warrior Princess Trail Run. I've been planning and can't wait to share. Actually, I can give you a small hint—we will be visited by an extra special guest star, who will take pictures with all the kiddos who attend the race. Let's just say, she is enchanting with her wings!

Now for updates about "The Who":

I am borderline gestational diabetic, which means a new diet has been implemented. I give it up to all those who have suffered with gestational diabetes or diabetes. If I go off the plan, I'm miserably sick. Sickness has existed the entire pregnancy. Up until this point, my nausea medicine could lighten the sorrow. Now the medicine is not cutting it if I go off the diet even slightly. Plus, the baby is bigger than Lilian Grace ever thought about being. I don't know how big, but I can feel that they are bigger.

Lilian Grace came eight weeks early plus was two weeks behind on growth. I never got to experience the full third trimester. Now I see that I really wasn't missing any fun at all. I'm buckled up, though, and ready to conquer however many weeks remain—minimum of eight if I go full term. That is not too much. To be honest, my prayers have included requests for time to speed up to the birth day, then slow down. Is it the end of October yet?

In my grieving process, the closer we get to the birth of our next child, the harder it is for me. The anxieties that well up are ridiculous and tiresome—constantly causing me to be aware and process each one. The unknown scares me to death. I'm happy God has my back and everything else is in His hands. I've been saying my prayers. I know He has prepared me to raise this lil miracle for however long He intends.

I looked at my CaringBridge guestbook with tears welling. Two friends, Teresa (Kellogg) and Kevin (Hackett), along with others, were very encouraging with their precise, solid truths. God does have a glorious plan that I get to live out, because He decided I was capable through His strengths and abilities! WOW!

Keep those needed prayers coming daily, because life is hard and knocks us down over and over. Missing Lilian Grace will always be part of Michael's and my daily walk. Our connection to our firstborn never fades, as God designed it that way. We will always love her no matter the time, the day, or the year. It's something a griever lives with until they die. This isn't a terrible thing but a reality that's unfixable. I know this now more than ever, especially after communicating with and watching other grievers.

We are stamped differently because our hearts are no longer what they were before the loss. I do love my new heart even though I still see the areas God is fixing—and trust me, those parts need a major overhaul. I feel stronger, wiser, and more emotional these days. My trust has a long way to go. I know if I keep working and processing that my brokenness will be healed as well.

We have fewer than eight weeks until we are honored to meet the next miracle God is entrusting us with—to borrow, love, teach, and share our lives with. It's not fully sunk in. The baby keeps the realities alive though. The kicks, turns, and punches—whatever other crazy trapeze act is going on inside me—remind me often they exist. I have a big grin with tears streaming as I ponder. Sorrow and happiness go hand in hand, but my God is Big! I'm buckled up—waiting for this new chapter to begin.

All in all, I am only human. There's a perfect song called "Human" by Natalie Grant and Jordin Sparks. Being human is what really makes us special, so why try to be something we are not? Be who you were meant to be by being human! God only asks that we be, grow, live, and love! We have one life to show His love and light up the darkest times. We are all human, so take a deep breath and know He has a purpose for your life. You are needed right now. Love you all! The song is a must-hear on YouTube!

Peace, remembrance, and happiness

AUGUST 30, 2011

190 › Mighty Mouse

God, I keep asking myself, "Who am I that You would care and still want me in Your army?" There are times—in abundance—where I fail miserably, yet You continue to love and want me. I was reminded last night and this morning of what it feels like to miss an opportunity You had planned for me. In the past, failing at a mission didn't hurt like this.

Normally, I would carry on while shrugging my shoulders and saying, "Oh well, I missed that one." Now it's a different story. When I recognize that God has called me to do something and I don't, my heart breaks. I know I'm not perfect, but I do not want to go through the motions anymore in my life. By not doing what I am called to do, my emotions are magnified, and my heart is heavily burdened. I acknowledge that my weakness in people pleasing got in the way once again.

I constantly struggle with this weakness, but I will not let it win. The most important thing in learning of a missed God opportunity is that His love is unconditional, and He can use others when I don't follow through.

Perfection and holding the world in my hands was not in His original design. I'm merely a warrior in God's army, who understands being called is an honor. An obedience check is in order! When I do step up and out of His way, God shines and gets to work in a tangible way.

When we are obedient in taking His call by listening to His voice and following through when He has laid something or someone on our hearts—His plans succeed—we all benefit! Are you being obedient? Did you make the call when someone popped into your head? Did you write that letter, text, etc., with those encouraging words burning in your heart? Did you follow through with an obligation that He led you to sign up for? Did you pray for them when they crossed your mind?

What triggered all this? Little "Mighty Mouse" Caleb passed away last night. His mother, Jeannette (Adamyk), has been a warrior for Michael, Lilian, and me. She was one of the top trisomy 18 mommies to step up and give me hours of time away from her lil man to help us with our fight. She has been obedient in God's journey by listening and stepping out, even if she didn't have the energy or drive. I am forever thankful and blessed by her obedience. Her ultimate sacrifices helped give us 103 more days after Lilian's first breath!

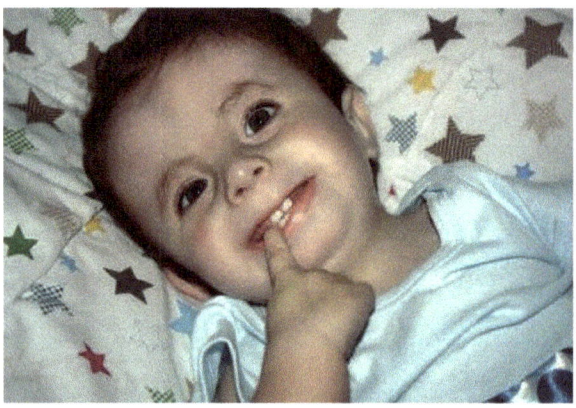

Mighty Mouse and his famous smile

She and I spent many hours having long conversations. I have learned a multitude from her godly, shining attitude and character. Jeannette, her hubby, and two other boys have a long journey ahead where God will start to heal the wounds and mend the broken pieces. This journey is not for everyone! We are a pack of travelers who will forever miss those we lost but continue to grow in strength. God provides everything to the grievers as long as we are willing to trust and let Him lead the way. All He wants as our heavenly Daddy is to hold us and make all the hurt, pain, sorrow, and boo-boos melt away.

Though I have been truly blessed with all of you as supporters, I have also been extremely blessed to meet the super warriors God created and reformed. Just this morning, I was encouraged by hearing God's prompting and calling one of them. She is incredible. If you don't have godly warriors in your inner circle, then you are missing out on one of the greatest gifts God can give you.

Because of that call, I've been prayed over, gotten to pray, and heard the verse God stored up for me to equip me for today's battle. He gave me tangible love and peace through her words and everlasting support. I pray that each of us have super warriors to lift us up and that we reciprocate for them—a two-way street. This life has huge burdens and losses. The only way I can get through such a trek is to face the truth, name all those fears, and cast them out. I can place the good, the bad, and the indifferent—the pain, losses, disappointments, and worries—into His hands!

My heart breaks more after hearing about how the Adamyk's journey has changed. I lift them, their supporters, and their grief up to my heavenly Father. Caleb has completed his earthly mission. He is a true Warrior Prince, just as Lilian Grace is a Warrior Princess. Their lives have touched thousands from all over the world.

Caleb fought his battles and lived his mission with the biggest grin on his face and in his heart. God has shined because Caleb was willing to fulfill God's glorious mission. For twenty-nine months with an imperfectly functioning heart, Caleb battled hard every day until his last. Praise God that Caleb's family has trusted God and lived this journey, rocking it out loud! They have no clue just how far the fingerprints of God have gone through their journey or how much farther His prints will reach now! Thank you for your obedience in fighting daily and showing us how to live every moment by thinking outside the box!

Here's a perfect verse for all of us that my amazing friend gave me during our conversation this morning:

Memory Verse 1

🗡 *"It is God who arms me with strength and keeps my way secure" (2 Samuel 22:33).*

We all need to remember these wise words given in this verse. Life doesn't stop knocking us down and trying to keep us from living out God's will for each of us. Equip yourself with His Word and surround yourself with His warriors—gain strength. I always say to my ladies at The Phoenix Experience, when life is painful and you're hurting, say the following: *we can do this; it'll be okay; it's good for you!* God turns all the pain into goodness and changes His kingdom for the better! His love is shown through our journeys. Love you all!

At church this past Sunday, we sang a beautiful praise song, "With Everything" by Hillsong, that is very fitting. Hope is needed to fuel yourself for the journey. May God's glorious ways and light be seen in everything that we do. He is King, and He is worthy to be praised. Be the light!

Is your life allowing others to praise Him and appreciate

His glory? It's never too late. Let your heart cry out and allow Him to make everything good.

With everything I have I praise God for another miracle that is almost here!

SEPTEMBER 5, 2011

191 › I Look to You

As I visited the children's hospital, I discovered that it's been exactly thirteen months since Lilian Grace earned her wings. This wasn't planned. Lil Paxton is back in the hospital, and I was hanging out with his momma, Bri. I got to visit many of Lilian Grace's wonderful nurses and staff—especially her godmother, Amy (Goforth). God made it a special time—a wonderful, unexpected blessing!

In a weird place all day, I struggled to understand and accept what this anniversary means to me. I don't know if the timing of each month will ever really change. Our brains are good about being wrapped up and distracted by other stuff, but our hearts and souls never forget. I somehow take comfort in that—a security of not forgetting her. I spoke with a trisomy 18 mommy who just lost her little boy last night. Though it breaks my heart, I look to God, rejoicing that He has a splendid plan while providing comfort to everyone.

"I Look to You" by Selah is an incredible song describing my and many others' roads along the grieving journey. Looking to God is my only hope, and He is the strength that has truly gotten me this far. I do feel like the best version of myself after the brokenness and the healing work over the past thirteen months. God really has been rewiring, molding, and reshaping me. I can't wait to see how much better He puts me back together through more active grieving and healing on this journey—what we put in, we will get out!

> *I do feel like the best version of myself after the brokenness and the healing work.*

Just when I think I can't go on or want to quit, l look to Him and know He is my true strength. I will carry on—no matter the depth of pain, the level of fear, or the endless unknowns. He will get me through anything and everything. Remember that if He is for us, no one can be against us!

If you find yourself on the ground, look to Him. Let Him pick you back up and dust you off. Lean on Him. Trust Him! You got this as long as you have Him. He wants to make the best version of you that there ever could be. I wish it were simple for the transition and transformation. As far as I can see, it never will be a simple process or understanding—nothing worth changing ever is! Love you all!

NOVEMBER 21, 2011

192 › Rainbow Baby #1

Seventy-seven days have passed since my journal entry. Did I plan to stop writing on CaringBridge? Yes. Did I think I'd write another entry after my last one? No. Did I feel like it was time to do another entry? Yes. Here I am posting another one after months of not. I played "Jar of Hearts" by Christina Perri first before writing because it's been on my mind to create and post many entries previously. Somehow, though, those thoughts never made the cut until now.

Why? Well, this song is like me talking to death, sorrow, pain, and disappointment—you get my drift. They seem to be collecting hearts. When Lilian Grace took her last breath, my heart went into a jar. I've had to learn to live life half alive. There are many days I struggle with handling all the emotions while thinking I'm going to completely lose myself or life as I know it.

In death—my child's death—I have explained away to justify or comfort others. I've repeatedly said similar statements when my daughter's soul departed, like "Part of me went with her," and the brokenness has been—at times—too much to bear. Looking back at almost sixteen months of living and walking this grieving journey, I wonder what in the world happened during this time period. I'm glad I documented this season with pictures, for the most part, and journal entries. I'm not sure I could completely give accounts of everything I've gotten to do in this healing process. God has been overwhelmingly generous with me and my healing.

I've traveled all over the country, from as far west as east and north to south. Each trip represented a healing segment. I didn't comprehend the importance of each trip until I looked back at the pictures and remembered the buckets of tears, the pain I felt, and the healing that occurred regardless of the state or purpose of the trip—on a plane or in a car. God made each one meaningful and helpful.

Just when I think I'm okay, God reminds me of the pain so I can be ready to do more of His purpose for my own life. I get the opportunity to meet so many broken people. For the most part, I'm in the right emotional state to connect with and help them along their grieving journey. I couldn't be used without being molded into the appropriate tool my heavenly Father needs me to be. I've been burnished to shiny silver and molded into the perfect shape of clay. To reach this state, I had to go through my version of life and experiences, in order to be a person He can use at any given moment—ready, willing, and able.

I am thankful when I look back at all the past events and experiences in my life. I praise God for taking, changing, adjusting, altering, correcting, keeping, providing, and comforting me. I've had the pleasure of God showing me glimpses of how life could have been if my path would have forked differently on the roads I've traveled. I remember crying many tears over experiences, relationships, jobs, etc., that didn't work out. Now I see it all differently. They were the building blocks, fires, shapers, and molders. Without them, I wouldn't be Chrissy!

God always has the best plan for me as He gives me exactly what and who I need through it all—the good, the bad, and the ugly. He does it every single day when I choose to keep living for Him. By choosing Him, the devil gets scared or disgusted with what God can do when I step aside.

The devil tries to tear me down by distracting, destroying, and almost killing me, but through Christ I can do all things. The devil doesn't have a chance, as I continue to choose God in both sunny skies and terrible storms.

Even when my attitude and words are negative, God continues to let me live out His will. He makes sure I am placed where needed in order to fulfill His purposes—no one else can give me this. I am worthy, strong, courageous, a champion, a warrior, and successful because of Him—His strength and abilities in me! With an infinite amount of thank yous and love, I thank God for life—this life with all my past, present, and future.

Since I became pregnant with "The Who" in 2011, I can officially announce that she—yes, she—has finally joined our family and the world. She was born on Wednesday, October 19, 2011, at 7:51 p.m., weighing 6 lbs., 6 oz. and measuring eighteen inches long. Her name is Piper Allegra Whitten.

How she got her name:

Piper: To play on a pipe
We want her to always remember to keep playing life into a beautiful song no matter what comes her way. She is meant to be whatever God has in store for her. Many trials will come and go, so it's important to play on!

Allegra: Happy, Jaunty
We wanted Lilian Grace and her sister to have something in common, so we chose Allegra for the middle name. If you move the E to the end and put a C for Christ in the center, you get "All Grace." We believe that His grace makes us who we are today!

Piper and her big sissy's urn

Piper is perfect in every way! Up to this point, part of her existence has been to keep me active in my grieving journey. I continue to be on a dual journey: one of complete, utter happiness and the other crying, feeling, mending, and healing from my loss. When I have my moments of sadness or the healing aches and pains magnify, I explain to my second daughter what her mommy is going through. I need her to know she can survive anything as long as she has God! He's the only antidote to all that life throws at us.

Parents who have lost a child ask what it's like to have another child enter your life after one has died. It's hard because my grief has magnified since Piper got here. Many assumed having Piper would make things better, but—in truth—it's made it harder. She will make it better one day, but I have to do the work to get there. This means surviving many days with sorrow and tears.

Lilian Grace and Piper Allegra look so much alike. I have to make sure I'm not in the dream world where I visit Lilian Grace so often. Even at Piper's first church service, I felt like saying, "Welcome back, Lilian Grace." I do know Piper is her own self—not Lilian Grace—but Piper has her big sissy's personality, spirit, characteristics, looks, and behaviors. I catch moments where I can't even breathe—the tears flow, and I have to pull myself together.

I find myself reliving moments when triggered by certain people or places. It all comes flooding back vigorously, but I have to let myself work through it—tears and all. There were amazing moments and also bitter ones. I sometimes wish I could erase it all and make it go away. I'd make people grow, change, improve, be more disciplined, accept what can't be undone, and progress forward by not looking back, but I wouldn't be who I am today if I altered the slightest thing. I can happily say with flowing tears that I'm better for it all.

God always knows what He's doing. I look forward to what will come and am confident I'll get through it because of Him and His glorious ways. We are not guaranteed a life without pain and sorrow until we die and get to live in eternity with Him. Both my girls have an earthly purpose, and Lilian Grace lived hers out—even if for a short 103 days. I do look forward to watching Piper live out hers. I know my girls are not entirely the same, but at this stage, it's hard to see their differences. I may not understand it, but I trust God in how He has made this journey for us. I appreciate how He made the girls so similar!

Having a child after losing one—well, I'll just say it—it's harder than I'd like to admit, yet it is rewarding and comforting. It's like going through a divorce or losing a spouse and trying to start a new relationship. You have a past. You had a person. But they aren't with you any longer. You must figure out how to live without them—they're in the past—and in the present create more memories that are vastly different than you dreamed or hoped for.

Memories are forever etched in our hearts, minds, and souls. No one can replace a person—whether they were good, bad, or indifferent. A person is a person! Like Dr. Suess says, it does not matter how small! Piper won't ever replace Lilian Grace. She will add to our life by filling it with her own experiences and ways. There won't be a day that goes by that I don't think of my first baby girl, with whom I got to experience motherhood for the first time. Even with Lilian's challenges, she gave me everything a mother could ever hope for by lighting up my life and electrifying my purpose. It beats anything the world has to offer. She blew me away, just as Piper is now. I think personal assistant is a better name for motherhood.

I, like many, would give anything for Lilian Grace to be here with us. Experiencing Piper's many firsts that we never got to do with her big sissy and celebrating her one month of life last Saturday, my soul ached. The broken pieces have been slowly coming back together as my soul mends. Missing Lilian Grace hasn't lessened; it's only grown. I pictured Lilian Grace walking all over the place with giggles and smiles for her little sissy's big moments. The tears freely rolled. If Lilian Grace were here, I know she would have had limitations. It's a hurtful happiness to imagine her normal. The thought of Lily being here to experience these moments with us on earth, instead of from heaven's view, is mind-blowing.

Not getting over her and the pain that hasn't lessened brings more tears. But I've gotten better at living with a mix of pain and happiness. It's ultimately a bittersweet adventure. I praise God for perspective, grace, and mercy. If I didn't have His perspective, I'd be in my own padded room—shut off from the world and not living out His will. I'm not sure how this grieving journey will go. I do know when I'm actively participating, I see Him changing me and other people through wonderful moments. I got chosen for a journey that I wouldn't wish on anyone—no matter how I feel about them. He doesn't choose sporadically though, I know. I hope to step up and get this journey right more times than I get it wrong.

As I compare pictures of Lilian Grace and Piper, a smile of joy laced with sorrow appears on my face. I will watch Piper grow, and hopefully, I will see her live a full life—as will I. Visualizing a dream of what would have been for Lilian Grace brings bittersweet feelings. I'm thankful to be chosen to borrow another of His children, especially a baby girl! I need people to understand that Piper isn't Michael's and my introduction to parenthood, motherhood, or fatherhood. Our first-time experiences were with Lilian Grace. Yes, Piper will give us many more experiences. However, Lilian Grace gets credit for making us the parents we are today. Without her influence, we wouldn't appreciate the small things as much as the big ones. We will take little for granted and relish it all.

Lilian Grace gets credit for finally breaking me so I could be better, more alive, and focused on what God has in store for me. She forever changed everything for me, especially when I held her for the last time. I had a miracle in my arms, then she had to depart. I didn't think I would survive, but I knew I had to fight with everything that's in me—He's not finished with me. How do I know this? He would have taken me instead when I begged Him to switch places with her.

I've lived thirty-three years with many hard missions completed for Him. I've been blessed to see people healed, humbled, and saved in my lifetime. I've been lucky to pray, praise, and sing all about His glory. I've been on one path and rerouted or directed to another. Every person I've met has been purposeful—some encourage and strengthen me, others test me, and many more brighten my days. Some I've simply learned a lesson from no matter the outcome. Everyone helped make me who I am and is a special part of my journey.

He still has more for me until He calls me home! Lilian Grace lived her life out for a short time yet made a godly and pure imprint on all. I hope to do the same. Are you living out His will that He fashioned just for you? If not, it's never too late! Drop to your knees, open your ears and heart, get out of His way, and let Him lead. You will never be the same again—living a blessed and enriched life! Love you all!

Hope you have an amazing Thanksgiving, Christmas, and New Year!

JANUARY 17, 2012

193 › Lift My Hands

Twelve days to go . . .

A little before four this morning, God woke me up to feed Piper and to start searching for a song I remembered—which led to multiple songs. On my phone in the notes section, I typed each song title. At first, I didn't realize that it would later prompt me to write another CaringBridge journal entry.

When I recognized what was happening, I made sure to keep going until I couldn't. When my phone froze, I decided perhaps God had given me enough songs meant for future use. I've discovered that the combination of my crazy emotions and easily flowing tears are due to Piper approaching 103 days of life. Michael and I have been super emotional, and now I know why. I remain amazed at how the heart doesn't need a date or schedule to know when something is coming. It reacts to another form of time on the journey—the scars are an alarm!

I can tell you without a calendar how close we are getting. I've had a heavier heart for myself and those around me. Tears flow while my heart aches for us all. I struggle believing all that we've gotten to do with Piper in the same amount of time compared to her big sister. Lilian Grace's days alive were filled with wires, medicines, surgeries, and survival. Piper's life has been filled with laughter, joy, and adventures with no strings or wires attached—just living.

I am blessed with anything and everything we get to do, even with the minor adjustments we've made due to respiratory syncytial virus (RSV) season. My heart breaks more for my first daughter, who had to live in a bubble with a major time limit. YET God reminds me that Lilian Grace is with Jesus, where we all hope to be when our bodies and life on earth expire. My heart rejoices for Lilian knowing she's in better hands yet breaks knowing Piper will have to face problems—not so good ones that can hurt her—that I can't control. I pray (just like any other parent) that the bad won't ever happen. Sadly, I know life happens—no exemptions.

It's messed up how my heart reacts. It feels what it feels while acting out a *Matrix* movie—all over the place with action-packed chaos. My anxieties have increased as we approach three-and-a-half months. I've noticed I dive into busyness to avoid milestones—happy or not. The heart likes to protect itself, so it's been doing a single-person boot camp to prepare. I've been worn out from the tears, lack of sleep, and the side effects. I trust God in whatever He wants. I do hope His plan is for us to see Piper Allegra grow and prosper in life through His kingdom's work. There's always that nagging fear she can be taken at any moment—healthy or not. The loss of Lilian Grace could have been the end for everything in my life, but God didn't leave me there.

I say all this to share that everything we go through can be scary and unpredictable. It's a daily struggle to be on two mental train rides traveling parallel through time. In one train, there's happiness and life in the present. The other contains my grief, my broken heart, and the emptiness of missing Lilian Grace.[5] They don't stop, which keeps me in an emotional tug of war. "I Lift My Hands" by Chris Tomlin reminds me, just like a conversation I had today, that God's

---

[5] Note from author: I mentioned this in entry 147 in *The Fall to the Climb*.

love and grace are also unending. The Bible says they are abundant. When I look at my circumstances, milestones, anniversaries, etc., I stand in faith and lift my hands to God. He keeps making my path straight. Every time I hand over my heavy burdens to Him, He fixes things quicker and smoother than I could ever fix them as He moves and provides His grace.

> *It's a daily struggle to be on two mental train rides traveling parallel through time.*

Time after time, I pour my heart out and see His faithfulness and provision in every situation. I love that He has given me a brain and a heart to keep track of everything, even when I'm too busy to consciously notice. When the tears flow, I look to Him and lift my hands, knowing He wants me to process the lessons while He continues to be a refuge through my brokenness! He wants me to actively work on our relationship along the journey.

Returning back to the playlist from this morning, when my phone froze, I figured He was done. I counted out how many titles I had typed—thirteen songs to be exact! How many days are there until Piper's 103 days of life? Exactly thirteen! The last one, which I'll play on Piper's 103rd day, is "The Story of Your Life" by Matthew West. What can I even say to that? His plans are intricate and vast—perfectly orchestrated. I've been blessed to know Him and live my life for Him. Hopefully, I've been honoring more than destroying His people's reputation. I don't even know why I question Him or get in His way. Oh, I do know. It's called being human!

As the twelve days come and go, I will be writing and including a song each day until Piper reaches 103 days, because Lilian Grace lived exactly 103 days before she departed. I'll admit this milestone is more emotional than the others at this point in my grieving journey. I have mixed emotions. I'm going to lift my hands to God and let my faith arise while trusting God in His plans for me.

When all is said and done, I'll remember God is faithful forever. He's given me miracle story after miracle story. He's enriched my life. Today, I shared stories that touched only the surface of His amazingness! I have a gazillion stories filled with His grace, mercy, faithfulness, and heart—even His ultimate sense of humor. I praise Him and giggle with a grateful heart knowing He chose me as His. I'm feeling ever so loved and blessed beyond all measure!

Remember God is faithful! Lift those hands and believe again that He will get you through whatever journey you are on. He will meet you on any mountain high or valley low—wherever you stand this minute. He is with you. Love you all!

JANUARY 18, 2012

194 › Be My Strength

Eleven days to go . . .

What can I say that the song "Please Be My Strength" by Gungor doesn't say? Not much, but it does explain a lot of my grieving journey. When Lilian Grace took her last breath, I held her oh-so-tight and felt like the weakest human being on this earth. I wasn't sure how I'd survive after she was gone. I just wanted to curl up in bed most days and cry my heart out. I didn't want to do anything, yet God decided that wasn't for me. We fought a good fight of faith, even before Lilian Grace was here. I was tired, yet my God is strong and will forever be—He continues to be my strength.

Without Him, I'm the weakest of them all. With Him, His strength supplies energy and active living. Through Him alone, I make it out of bed, achieve the coolest moments, live on, survive the unknowns, and thrive despite my circumstances. I don't ever want to know how it would be without Him. Being without Him scares me more than anything. I'm at least intelligent enough to know He's the answer to my questions—to anyone's questions. He's all I need. That's how we're doing this. I hope those who keep questioning the how will know and see Him in all—the strength, the accomplishments, and everything Michael and I do to survive our broken hearts.

We are approaching a different milestone where Piper is reaching the age we lost her sister. I need His strength more than ever. I get beaten down emotionally from the spiritual warfare raging on, bringing more unknowns, fears, and exhaustion. None of it can match God's strength, but I have to keep living and surviving what comes.

Though physically I've been deteriorating recently, I know He will get me through. I don't have any more strength—not on my own. His love keeps me strong and helps me survive.

I woke up this morning with the biggest headache. I'm not one to get headaches; yet, as of late, I've been dealing with them. I assume it's from the journey and trying to do things on my own—my way.

I keep praying for God to push me aside, like He so kindly does when I ask, so His strength can carry me to the next place. I see the possibilities and projects He has in store for me. I say, "God, Your strength and abilities, not mine—ONLY YOURS! When You are my strength, my successes come abundantly."

---

*God, when You are my strength,
my successes come abundantly.*

Tears keep flowing as I draw closer to the 103-day mark, dealing with whatever else hits me along the way. I keep asking God for strength. Oh, God, please be my strength.

Hope and pray. Ask God to be your strength through your trials and things you encounter on your journey. Don't forget Him. Much love!

JANUARY 19, 2012

195 › Hold My Heart

Ten days to go . . .

Tears flow as I go from one song to the next that God gave me to share in these days leading to Piper's 103-day milestone. I love how precisely He communicates with me to bring even more healing. I've been on my grieving journey for over seventeen months. He never stops taking care of me. I've been on my knees more than I've ever wanted to be. I've cried more times than I can count. I've felt the damage of my broken heart. But I am strongest on my knees. My tears help relieve the ache in my soul. I can still feel my broken heart beating. All because God holds my heart!

Hearing the lyrics of "Hold My Heart" by Tenth Avenue North, over and over, reminds me to look at the different prayers I've prayed before, during, and after Lilian Grace. I wanted God to heal her so she could stay. But God had a different plan for my brokenness. I was so afraid—afraid of our journey; yet when I was on my knees praying for God to heal Lilian, God helped me see His plan was much greater than that. He helped me see early on that everything I'd gone through up to that point was preparation for my daughter's journey to expand His kingdom and strengthen His people's hearts. He was equipping me for the greatest loss I will ever know.

I may not have Lilian here physically, but I see His impact through her life—103 days! It's enough time for a mission to be fulfilled—impacting the world and His kingdom. How do I know? Because He chose 103 days for her to do it. Through her life, I see those He touched conquering and surviving their own broken journeys.

I look at her little sister, Piper, and see His fingerprints all over her. I was lucky to see Lilian's journey early with appreciation of His will for her. For Piper, I will get more time as life plays out in the way He decides. She gives me that same amazing feeling that Lilian Grace gave me—complete godly favor. It's a sense of knowing she is going to do incredible things when she chooses to walk with Him. One day, I will have to step aside as I watch her struggle, learn, and thrive while I make sure I give her the opportunities He encourages me to give her.

Knowing Lilian Grace had a time limit was heartbreaking, but I didn't let it get in the way of helping her finish what He started in her. Being a parent is a tough yet rewarding job. I hope God works out just as many blessings and achievements through Piper as He did through Lilian. It will be a fabulous journey to be on.

Today marks Piper Allegra's three-month birthday. She was all dressed in girly wear. We shopped at the mall, attended a basketball game, and snapped pictures with Armadillo Jim and company. The joys of getting to do anything away from machines is the best gift God can give. On Lilian Grace's three-month birthday, we had her cousins over and dressed her in the Little Mermaid costume with the red wig. We had our own fun despite her limitations. Oh, Lilian would have loved the mall and Mabee Center. Her favorite part would have been gazing at the bright lights during the basketball game.

I was thankful that Piper had to be fed twice at the game, because I was emotional not having Lilian with us. The grieving doesn't prevent me from enjoying every minute with Piper; it just takes my breath away. I have to collect myself if Lilian's path crosses ours while something is happening. I figure this is my current season where enjoyment for one and longing for the other coincide. I'm not upset at it—just sharing the realities of our walk.

If anything, it's a perfect reminder to take nothing for granted. I hold my second baby girl while she cries, but I don't get to hold my first until this life is finished. I wish Lilian Grace could have just gone to camp for the summer and I'd be seeing her soon. Reality bites—she isn't returning.

I ask God to continue to hold my heart along my journey. A broken heart never works how it used to, but I think it works even better—with time and leaning on Him. No one can predict how each of our hearts will function after such sorrow. God's got my heart—a better place than anywhere else it could be or go. I hope this finds you giving Him your heart and journey—tis no sweeter thing than to trust Him and experience His peace. He is the ultimate Comforter, placing the exact things and people we need in our path to carry us through! Lots of love!

Piper's three-month picture

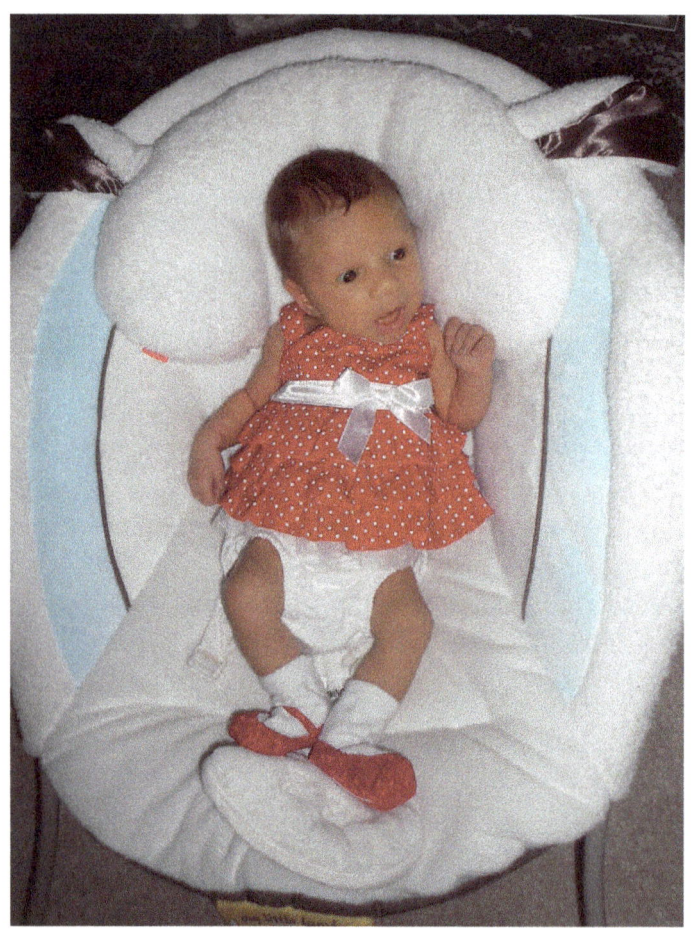

Piper's turn to show off the red dress

JANUARY 20, 2012

196 › Not Alone

Nine days to go . . .

As the days draw closer to 103, God reminds me that I'm never alone with the song "Not Alone" by Jamie Grace. This version includes Jamie lifting her angelic voice while magically stroking the black and white keys on the piano. It's stripped down where I can absorb the lessons of late.

I am eternally grateful for His love. I look at relationships—dysfunctional ones specifically—in my own life and wonder why it's so hard for me to apply His example and lead. Love should always be given without restraint and not based on others' behaviors or actions. Love gives life.

The songs keep my tears flowing. As I work through the playlist, I'm blown away by His perfect timing and the content of the songs. I hope songwriters realize how impactful and important their lyrics are to someone who's going through an emotional ride or losing hope. My song, if ever written, should include two major themes: 1) the devil can keep beating me down, but I will get up; and 2) God is the answer to surviving.

All the hurt I felt before Lilian Grace is nothing compared to the hurt I've felt from her journey alone. I remember the days prior to her passing when I didn't know how much time I had left with her. In each moment with her, the joy laced with pain was a wacky feeling as we tried our hardest to treasure each day gifted to us. I kept the tears in more than I should have done—still do at times.

I'm glad God made sure I was in the moment—

comforted and never alone. He never left me—not for even a second. Thankfully, we have hundreds of pictures documenting our enjoyment while our time with her dwindled down. We couldn't let the limitations of time get in our way. We had to live it loud and live in the now! It's incredible what can happen when we are in the moment.

Many nights since Lilian Grace's celebration of life service, I've tried not to cry while taking each hit—what happened around me, to me, for me, and against me. And again, this song reminds me that I'm truly never alone. I will feel pain, but His name is greater than my pain. His arms are constantly wrapped around me. He sees it all. Sometimes I have to fake my emotions just to get through, yet I try so hard to keep them real. Sometimes you just can't force yourself to be or feel something you don't.

The moments I try to forget are the memories that hit the hardest. I pray I'll always look for the positives in our journey. Sadly, life makes that hard because it does move on—passing quickly and continually. Days multiply as my heart heals and adjusts in its own time. I'm no longer meant to be in everyone's lives that I used to be in nor are they meant to be in mine. But it's still hard to adjust to the change and loss of what used to be.

For any of us on a grieving journey, we need to remain buckled and comforted that we are in this together.

For any of us on a grieving journey, we need to remain buckled and comforted that we are in this together. Our journeys go on until we transition from earth to heaven. Hopefully, we can enjoy what we do have while processing what we've lost.

Today, Piper has been very clingy and emotional. I have a feeling she senses and knows where Michael's and my hearts are right now. I hope it's a wonderful lesson showing her how to be real while moving onward toward health and healing! Praying for all my friends and family who are going through their own journeys. Remember you are not alone!

Lilian—the original red dress wearer

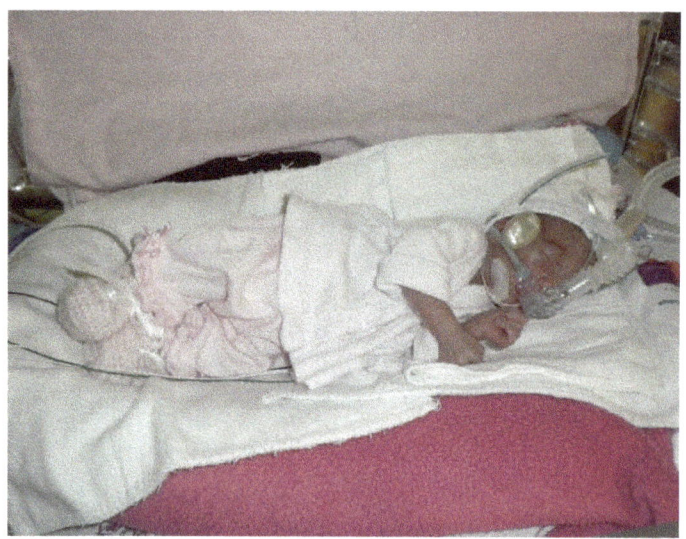

Lilian resting in pink

JANUARY 21, 2012

197 › Fall Apart

Eight days to go . . .

Before I get started on tonight's entry with the song "Fall Apart" by Josh Wilson, I want to remind you to Google each song and play them on YouTube as you read. I listen to each song on a continuous loop while typing and crying through my journal entries. It's an experience worth trying—enjoy!

When I'm at the end of me, God shines brightly. I wish I could always step aside for Him, yet that doesn't often happen. Looking at the chaos and trials of my life over the years, you'd think the devil would just leave me alone. In those moments, I cling to God even tighter when my world is caving in. I don't want anyone else but Him!

Since Lilian Grace, I've been more in tune with things around me. I've set up boundaries. I've learned to live in the present. I look back at my life while smiling big, because the worst times of my life have been some of the best for me. Holding an incredible miracle in my hands when she departed was the worst but also the best. I knew my heavenly Father was calling His child to come home, because she had finished her mission.

I was fortunate to borrow her—even for just 103 days. I remember whispering to her that I was going to be all right because God would take care of me. She could go because she had done very well! I didn't want her to feel like she had to stay because I might fall apart. I see mothers and fathers with their grown children, trying to hold on when they should let them go so they can fly. You never know how

God will use them until you give them a chance to go—even if it means they may never come back.

> *You never know how God will use them until you give them a chance to go—even if it means they may never come back.*

If we always keep our children tied down or guilt them into doing what we want them to do, they will never reach their full potential—what God created them to do. My 103 days with Piper feel shorter than my 103 days with Lilian Grace. Piper's milestone came quicker than I expected. Enduring 103 days while feeling like I was going to fall apart if Lilian Grace didn't get to stay . . . well . . .

Trying to take a breath—a mother's worst fears include having others watch her babies, experiencing them sick, sending them off to school, trying to let them attend camp for the first time, sending them off to college, watching them move far away, marrying them off, or seeing them pass away before their time. I have always thought that a parent should go before their children. It's the perfect timeline, yet either way—parent first or child—it's hard on the ones left behind.

I remember going back and forth between the number on the heart rate monitor screen and Lilian's angelic face before she passed away. Knowing I would get to hold her for the first time without all the wires meant her heart had stopped beating. A knot swells in my throat, and my heart beats faster as tears roll down my cheeks. My worst fear of her dying happened that night. There was no more worrying or trying to hold on to her. I couldn't keep her from living out her dreams or plans because of me and my inability to let go.

Nope! This momma—well—God raised me right! He taught me to let go even when falling apart. He taught me to trust Him by letting her go so she could live out God's plans. When the machines stopped, I frantically wanted to change my mind. I wanted to yell and scream. I wanted to keep her on life support because I—for a minute—wanted to be selfish. I wanted her to stay, even if it meant she'd have a machine breathing for her.

I praise God a million times over for taking my selfishness and replacing it with His peace. The minute I wanted to change my mind was the minute she was already gone. His plans were being completed. I had sung to her and rocked her that evening as she faded from us, and I was proud of that. I was thankful Michael and I were with Lilian when she passed. God was getting the glory as lives were changed forever that night.

Today, I took Piper to the place where her sister breathed her last breath on earth. The nurses were amazing. I was so thankful to share Lilian's little sister, Piper. When those doors opened and Lily's room was staring me in the face, I took a deep breath and walked toward it. I told Piper all about this special place. I kept it together and crumbled afterward. I have to face my grieving head on at times. I have nothing to prove to anyone. I have to keep working through my grief. I pray that my pain in the brokenness keeps me on His path—always knowing God!

Life is full of plans with busyness attached. I pray I can keep slowing down when needed. I'm getting better at spreading things out so I have time to soak it all in. When Piper is crying and needs me, I hold her tight and live in the moment. I want her to know that everything (within my power) will be okay. As I feel her heartbeat, I remember Lilian Grace's. Tears well up, and I smile the biggest smile. Why? Because I hear Lilian's heartbeat like it was today.

Though I fall apart often and realize God needs me to release more, I trust Him to get me headed in a better direction! Just like Lilian Grace, Piper will need me to let go so she can fly and be who God made her to be. I do see His hands working in a lot of lives around me. PRAISE HIS NAME ON HIGH FOR IT! I look at my husband and get chills knowing he has grown into my knight in shining armor—the one God meant for me. I love watching God work! He's everywhere—every day—so wake up and pay attention.

When you are falling apart, look up! God's right here, waiting to put the pieces back together. I promise that the new you will be better than you ever were before. LOVE!

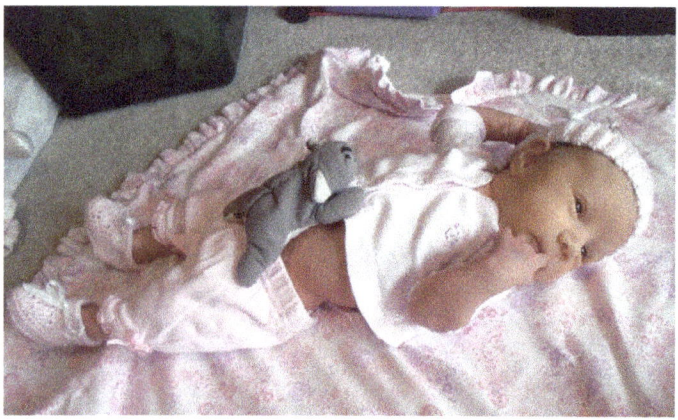

Piper—pretty in pink

JANUARY 22, 2012

198 › Survivors

Seven days to go . . .

Surviving! Yes, that's what I've been doing. I AM A SURVIVOR of many battles! The song "Survivors" by Matthew West is my song for this entry. I am blessed to know other SURVIVORS in my life—some I watch from a distance, and I get to share life with others. I praise God for continuing to battle for us—allowing us to survive the unthinkable. What happens after the war?

I've had an abundance of experiences along my grieving journey. I thought I'd highlight times when God worked in the wings through people in my life.

Women of Faith Conference (August 2010)—When I was there, I thought it was nice, but I had no idea that everything I heard was going to be used over the next two years along my journey—the exact words and tools that were essential for the battlefields!

Jamaica with Michael (2010)—We had to get away after Lilian Grace passed. I am so thankful we did this trip. I wasn't sure we should spend the money, but I look back and smile. We were barely hanging on, but God gave us a paradise to escape the unknowns. It gave us a chance to gather ourselves before trying to jump into our grieving journey. There were numerous challenges and broken relationships—wounds that needed to be healed.

Houston with my father-in-law (2010)—Oh, this was the trip of all trips. We loaded up all my milk, including the freezer, so we could donate it to a wonderful mother and daughter. Thanks to Michelle (Anderson) for making this happen. We are in a documentary called *Donor Milk: The Documentary* that premieres this March or April 2012. I just can't believe how one act has taken me to many places and continues to do so. I'm honored that Denise (Williams) accepted my breast milk for her daughter, Trishtan. I love watching her grow. It has brought a significant amount of healing!

Volunteering at Solace Church (2010)—I was lucky enough to work with our pastors during the fall of 2010. I don't think they know how much I needed to be there. I was just starting my full throttle boundaries during this time. It was the best experience, and I hope to rejoin them at some point.

New York City (NYC) with my brother (2010)—My brother was the best at taking time from his family to go to NYC with me. He was a crazy tour guide, but I loved getting to walk my bum off and experience an incredible city with him. I love him so much! Also, I got to meet some wonderful trisomy 18 families, whom I adore: Hilarczyks, Amatos, Duartes, and Clearfields. Our time together was fun and brought me happy tears. It was a crazy moment getting to experience NYC while sharing a first meeting with people who know what I'm going through. I got a chance to watch two Broadway shows, *West Side Story* and *Lion King*, by myself. It was exactly what my soul needed. Lilian Grace even got featured in the cookbook created by Stefanie Hilarczyk, *Timmy's Tasty Treats II: To Topple Trisomy 18*.

AZ/CA Trip with Marsha and Cristin (2010)—These two girls have known me since elementary school. They were amazing, especially when I broke down emotionally numerous times. They are more than best friends. They are my sisters—part of my rock team! I cherish our long-term friendships! My greatest memory from this trip was going to Pixie Hollow at Disneyland. They were patient with me as I enjoyed an emotional rollercoaster going from one part to the next. At the end, the phrase Fly with You Later appeared. This wasn't an accident. Major healing occurred as I repeated the phrase. Dressing up brought my feelings of sexiness back. I wore a feather headband and felt like a model on one of our picture days!

The Phoenix Experience: New Business Adventure (October 2010 to present)—Oh, the clients are helping me live out a dream come true of owning my own business—priceless. My clients think they need me more, but I would not be as far as I am without them all. I desperately need them more! To live out my passion—especially part time after the birth of Piper—is the best medicine for my soul. I love all my clients—past, current, and future! I've even gained an amazing friendship from this adventure. You know who you are!

Enid Trip to the Hartlings' (2010)—They are a safe place for me. I don't get to talk to them as much, but I could never repay them for what they've done for me through this entire journey. We got to have an early Thanksgiving meal—delicious—because Amy rocks. It was just what I needed as the holidays were approaching back in 2010. I spent many "in the middle of the night" hours on the phone with Amy. Thank you all from the bottom of my heart.

Kansas City for my sister-in-law Leslie and brother-in-law Kyle's move (2010)—It was hard to say goodbye to them, because I loved having them so close. They had a tough job throughout Lilian's life here. Leslie jumped in the car and drove for four hours at a time—multiple times—when we thought it might be the end. I don't know how she made it through all those trips, but I'm thankful she did—and Kyle too. This particular trip to Kansas City gave me peace, thinking about how we felt closer to them. Michael and I experienced the most amazing pink sunsets on this trip—Lily's way of letting us know she was with us. We adopted their fish tank and fish, which sadly led to Flush-a-cur 2010—sad times but helpful along our grieving journey.

Thanksgiving Branson Trip with Tiffanie, Lance, and Waylynn (Barto) (2010)—This trip was a blast. I ate a Thanksgiving meal at the Dixie Stampede with my bare hands. Healing can happen with great-tasting food! The Barto family will never know just how much we needed our first holiday without Lily to be different. They shared their first Thanksgiving with us and their baby boy. It helped tremendously and impacted our hearts forever.

OKC Trip to see Cassandra (Clark) (2010)—She gave me two phenomenal concert experiences. More importantly, she let me stay in her special guest room where her mother prays abundantly. It was the most peaceful room I've ever been in. I felt like nothing bad could get me there. I slept the best I've ever slept in my life. She is an amazing friend who has the kindest heart. I'm so happy she's being blessed, as we speak, with a miracle of her own! I could never repay her, either, for being there for me in a unique and unexpected way.

Christmas Road Trip to see Leslie and Kyle (Hall) in Richland, Washington (2010)—This was incredible. We took Lilian's urn with us. I want to keep the details of this trip private and special to us, but I will say I enjoyed every minute of it. I can never thank them enough for opening their home and letting us join their first Washington Christmas. On the road trip back, we drove through a messy storm, but Michael proved, yet again, that he's a warrior—a road warrior. During this trip, we started reading our grief book.

All Access Women of Faith Conference in Nashville, Tennessee (February 2011)—What can I say about this trip? Not enough! I met some of the most unique and spiritual ladies. I attended multiple concerts with learning opportunities for myself and praise for God. Thank God I was able to reach my selling goal. I ended up having to stay by myself on this trip, but it was meant to be since I bawled more on this trip than most of the others.

Supper Club—My girls from my career at Oklahoma State University (OSU) Extension—oh, they make me laugh and feel like the best ever. We had so much fun with themed dinners, which I'm hoping we can start again. I needed to see them once a month—the laughter through the tears. May God's blessing be on each of them. We, as the she-wolves pack, seem to be battling many a battle lately. I'm praying we all keep surviving and thriving!

Finishing the Lily Quilt (March 2011)—More than ever, I needed to finish the Lily quilt. We finally finished it in March 2011. Thanks to my Whitten women—my sister and my mom—we were able to complete this quilt that I started after I miscarried in 2006. To see the stories behind each quilt square being pieced together made my heart heal even more.

Warrior Princess Trail Run (April 2011)—My heart wept and rejoiced. My RunnersWorld and TATURS connections over the past five years helped make this an amazing moment for us and all our friends and family. This was Lilian Grace's first birthday anniversary! We would have been completely lost without the 130-plus individuals who joined us in celebrating her life and cause. This made her birthday enjoyable, instead of devastating.

Branson Trip with Monty and Janese (Whitten) (2011)—This trip was another healing moment for me. We relaxed and enjoyed family time. Our parents watched everything we went through and could not do anything to fix it. If it were up to them, they would have slept right on the hospital floor with us. I thank God we've been able to share memories with them.

OAE4-HA State Conference in Ardmore, Oklahoma (May 2011)—Even though I had been away from my peeps/coworkers, I was able to rejoin them for a conference, bringing more healing. I love my OSU Extension family and miss them immensely. Even though I don't get to be with them on a daily basis, they will always be here for me. I am so glad I got to go to this conference—even with a major tornado storm. I remember sitting in the hotel bathroom and realizing that, no matter what happens, I will always be taken care of.

***Cats*—my childhood dream** (2011)—To hear the song

"Memories" live brought many tears. I'm glad I finally saw this musical, which unexpectedly gave me healing I wasn't aware I needed.

Girlfriends' Spa Trip to Eureka, Arkansas, with college girlfriends (2011)—My college girls are always there at the right time, just when I need them. I experienced the greatest massage, manicure/pedicure, the most scrumptious Italian meal, girl talk, the shower, the ghost tour, and shopping. Let's just say relaxation with my girls was worth every penny. I cherish that we got to go on our girls' trip together. Finally, after years of wishing and hoping, we made it happen. I'm grateful I get to share time with them and their kids monthly!

Kansas City Getaway to see the Martin family and their new arrival (2011)—I thought that Michael holding a baby for the first time since Lilian Grace was going to be hard on him. I didn't realize that it was going to be the hardest on me. The Martin family was wonderful as I held their baby boy, only three or four days old, as my tears flowed. They sat there with me and let the healing moment be beautiful and wonderful. I just love them.

Florida Road Trip with my sister (July 2011)—This is something my sister and I have never gotten to do—a road trip. I can't express to my sister how much she means to me. This trip was magnificent and healing. We were able to visit the Miller family. Ale is one of my best friends, and I just needed to hug her. She makes things easier, more peaceful, and better!

Roaring River with family (2011)—Healing! I wish I could come up with another word, but healing will have to do. I connected with my mom on a different level after this trip. She has always been here for me, but I just felt like things were even better than before. I'm so glad Michael and I went.

Scrapbooking Project (2011)—Oh, I owe a ton of everything to Sandra Burton for helping me complete ten scrapbooks from my birth to now. I am forever grateful that she gave of her time and resources. She is a warrior like no other. This project helped me see my life for what it really was. We all have our view of what happened until we really look at it closer and embrace the truth. This was a project suggested by a grief counselor. It worked! I healed several broken relationships after completing this project.

Lilian's Shutterfly Project (2011)—Oh, my heart—my healing—the hours spent crying, enjoying, and laughing mixed with sadness. An emotional rollercoaster that gave me an abundance of healing. I now have book after book of Lilian's pictures with us, friends, family, supporters, and important people. Oh, my heart is happy to have this documented. Oh yes, there are thousands of pictures. It's the only thing I have left where I can see her at any given moment in a tangible way.

Attic Decluttering Project (2011)—I had to go through box after box while cleansing my life. Everyone should clean out their attic. It's a great way to unload emotional baggage too.

Deep Cleaning Project (2011)—My house is mostly clutter-free now. I ended up making ten or so Goodwill donation trips. I was clinging to countless items. I needed this house cleansing. I love having less stuff. It's nice not seeing clutter. It's even sweeter to let go of the emotions attached to those items.

Nursery Project (2011)—Transitioning Lilian Grace's nursery into Piper's was not an easy task. I ended up putting most of Lilian's stuff in containers, which are currently located on top of the closet shelf. Rachel (Foley)—oh, my sister for sure—was the best at helping me take pictures of Lilian's stuff. I needed to get ready for when Piper could have her pictures taken in her big sissy's clothes those first couple of weeks. Rachel could have said I was crazy, but she was right by my side—tears and all. I love her for this and many other things. I will be making a big sis/lil sis book to give to Piper. I just want her to know how special she and her big sister are to the world. Most importantly, I want her to know she got to play dress up while connecting with her big sister through shared clothes.

The Love Dare (2011)—This woke me up for my relationship with my husband along with a few other people. It was challenging, and I didn't like it a lot of the time. Why? Because it helped me see just how lacking I was in my relationships, especially with my husband. I wasn't being alive in our relationship—I was just getting by! Thank God that I did the study, because our relationship is richer for it.

Books Project—I will be writing children's books with Lilian Grace as different characters, using her nicknames in the Warrior Princess series. Hopefully, I'll be adding her sister in this or the next series. I've been gathering verses and getting my act together to make this happen. I love working on it because it keeps me connected to Lilian

Grace. She isn't here, but I can make her come alive on the pages.

Mahogany Steakhouse Meal—We went out for fine dining on Lilian Grace's one-year angelversary, and we are planning on doing this every year. I love the environment and the delicious food. It's indescribable and melts my heart. It's way expensive, but it makes me excited instead of dreading the day. We actually picked Piper's name when we were there. It's a very special place to us, and I thank God for it!

Piper Allegra Whitten—the birth of our second daughter—The days along the journey leading up to her birth were overwhelming yet were more healing than all my adventures combined. Watching and experiencing Piper is a daily healing adventure. I praise God that He knew I needed her. I'm eternally grateful for this new journey, even with the overabundance of tears.

There were others, but I will end here. Just know that each moment—each adventure—has been filled with tears and healing for my soul. I hope I can always listen and spread His love, especially after I've gone through a battle. Looking back at these trips and projects, I thank God for knowing exactly what I needed in my grieving journey—it never stops.

Today, I was emotional while Michael and I took Piper shopping for new developmental and teething toys. I wish I didn't miss Lilian so much when we do these special moments with Piper, but for now I will just have to live it out. The battle wounds from our time with Lilian Grace are deeper than anything I've ever known. Michael was awesome today in telling me that I'm not meant to stop missing her—it's part of the journey. I agree. What have you been doing after your battles?

For me, God has opened doors by giving me opportunities that provide healing and broaden my horizons. The list is limitless. I won't ever give up or give in because He has made me strong. I am thankful for every opportunity that brings healing to wounds, diverse experiences, and more life to enjoy!

One major opportunity God has given me is the Warrior Princess Foundation. I've been working on Lilian Grace's Second Annual Warrior Princess Trail Run for the past few weeks. I'm overjoyed at what this event brings to me and others. I've been super blessed with important, helpful people in making this event happen.

I look forward to celebrating Lilian's life two years later. It doesn't seem like that much time will have come and gone. I can't wait to share information and get us all together on Wednesday, April 25, 2012, so mark your calendars. I'm excited to announce that we will have three races: 1.03 miles, 10.3 miles, and 10.3K—our newest—which is 6.44 miles. Spread the word and join us!

Check out the Warrior Princess Foundation website for sponsorship and miscellaneous information:
http://web.me.com/c2mist8/Site/Warrior_Princess_Foundation.html[6]

I get chills thinking about what I get to do because my daughter lived 103 days. I love getting to keep her mission, memory, and purpose alive. May we each realize there's opportunity and purpose as we heal after our battles. Love you all!

---

[6] Note from author: This link is no longer active.

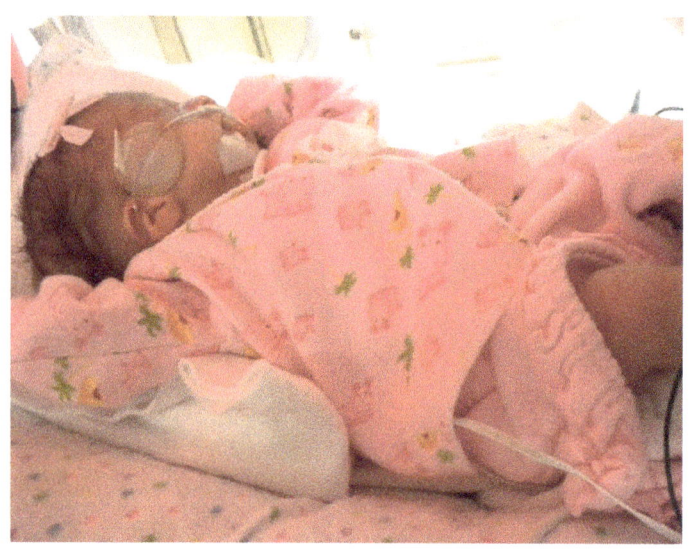

Lilian in her cute hippo outfit

JANUARY 23, 2012

199 › Strong Enough

Six days to go . . .

Strong enough—not on my own—only through Christ will I ever be strong enough to make it through each day. "Strong Enough" by Matthew West exemplifies this truth. We survive the grieving journey—any journey—because God is with us. I will repetitively say for the rest of my life that I am weak and He is strong—nothing can separate us. I trust Him through my wisdom that I am not strong enough without Him.

I'm not sure why each of us tries to do this journey without Him. I watch what happens when we don't have Him in our lives, and I thank God I don't have to experience life without Him. Depending on Him daily is necessary for the battles. I know firsthand when I give my struggles over to Him, He works them out. It's not necessarily on my timeline, yet He does work it out with purpose and perfect timing.

Lilian Grace could have lived or not lived, but He chose exactly 103 days. That's roughly 2.57 forty-day cycles when comparing her time to most biblical experiences. Also, her days lived ended with three—the Father, the Son, and the Holy Ghost. I'm sure there are a multitude of comparisons in the Bible. He always has a purpose in everything He does or allows. I appreciate that He chose for her to live longer than her first breath.

As I looked up Psalm 103, reading it over and over with goosebumps rising and tears flowing heavily, I wanted you to read the words written in the chapter:

Memory Verse 2

🗡️ *"Praise the LORD, my soul; all my inmost being, praise his holy name. Praise the LORD, my soul, and forget not all his benefits—who forgives all your sins and heals all your diseases, who redeems your life from the pit and crowns you with love and compassion, who satisfies your desires with good things so that your youth is renewed like the eagle's. The LORD works righteousness and justice for all the oppressed. He made known his ways to Moses, his deeds to the people of Israel: The LORD is compassionate and gracious, slow to anger, abounding in love. He will not always accuse, nor will he harbor his anger forever; he does not treat us as our sins deserve or repay us according to our iniquities. For as high as the heavens are above the earth, so great is his love for those who fear him; as far as the east is from the west, so far has he removed our transgressions from us. As a father has compassion on his children, so the LORD has compassion on those who fear him; for he knows how we are formed, he remembers that we are dust. The life of mortals is like grass, they flourish like a flower of the field; the wind blows over it and it is gone, and its place remembers it no more. But from everlasting to everlasting the LORD's love is with those who fear him, and his righteousness with their children's children—with those who keep his covenant and remember to obey his precepts. The LORD has established his throne in heaven, and his kingdom rules over all. Praise the LORD, you his angels, you mighty ones who do his bidding, who obey his word. Praise the LORD, all his heavenly hosts, you his servants who do his will. Praise the LORD, all his works everywhere in his dominion. Praise the LORD, my soul"* (Psalm 103).

Nothing more has to be said, but I'm blown away as always. I love my heavenly Father! I love the intricate details for every journey that He provides—His God winks. He continuously takes my breath away. I'm not even sure how much more I have to learn. All I know is that Michael and I are able to be strong enough because He steps in with His mercy and grace.

He is making a gorgeous symphony with the seconds to hours to days to months to years with our story. He places the right people, words, Scriptures, and moments at the exact time we need them. I am forever grateful for it all. No matter what you are going through, He makes it all gather into purpose—molding, shaping, and creating. I hope you see the good in any situation—the past, the present, and the future ones.

Many keep wondering how we can stay positive in such a horrible situation—the death of a child. I point to God—it's His strength, not mine. Reading the above Scripture because of the number 103—103 days she lived—tells it all. Without Him giving us the right perspective and golden nuggets through Scripture, we wouldn't be in a good place. I'm better, and so are others, for knowing Lilian Grace—more importantly, for knowing God and being saved!

My life, though not perfect, is better than it could ever be. I have no clue what or how it will go. I'm living in each moment, whether big or small, complicated or simple, dynamic or average. I'm present and accounted for. I'm leaning and trusting Him the entire way to home base—heaven!

May you all wake up to see the intricate details He wants you to discover in your situations through your journey. He wants you to know Him. He is vast and complex, yet simple when translating His love for us in unique, mind-blowing ways. I pray for clarity, vision, and openness to see Him daily so you can experience the Alpha and Omega!

I say to six more days to go that I'm buckled up and ready to experience what this ride has to offer. My God is Big!

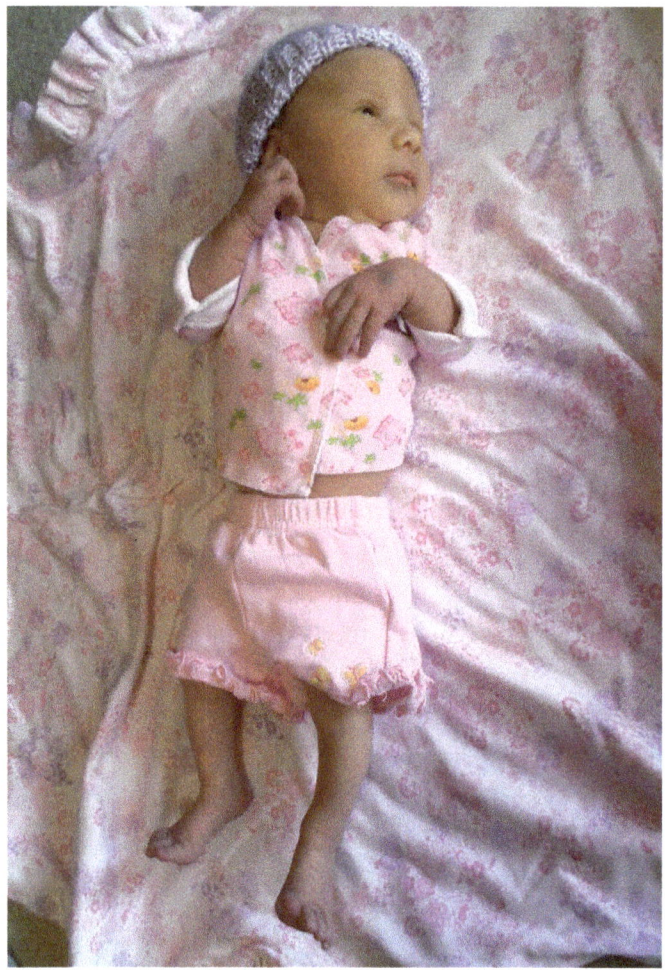

Sweet Piper in her sister's hippo outfit

JANUARY 24, 2012

200 › Change This Heart

Five days to go . . . God change my heart again and again . . . as many times as needed!

There have been countless days along my journey when I haven't been happy with my attitude, words, and actions—throughout my whole life. Some moments I can be proud of, and others I'd bury in a deep hole never to relive again. We all have moments we wouldn't want to spotlight. I give God praise for His unconditional love while He changes our hearts countless times.

Even when we feel unworthy of His love, He never stops loving us. When we push Him away, He stands right there waiting for us to return to Him. HALLELUJAH for His unconditional love and patience during our brokenness and sinful ways!

I wish we all could be more like Him in our relationships with others. Sadly, I have broken relationships—some before Lilian Grace and many after her life. Listening to "Change This Heart" by Sidewalk Prophets brings a comforting perspective. God changed my heart when He made me Lilian Grace's mommy. He was able to break my heart so I could get out of His way for the puzzle pieces to come together—a picture worth viewing. My life continues to never be the same—constantly changing.

After Lilian Grace, I haven't been able to return to who I was before her. He changed my outlook, perspective, and heart. I was a people pleaser before her. I wanted everyone to like me. I would let them run over me emotionally by allowing them to use and abuse my giving heart—eventually, they would leave me. I would completely drain myself and get sick. It only meant that what I did was never enough. How many of you can relate? Unfortunately, too many!

I'm forever trying to find common ground with people. The word "balance" comes up too often, triggering the need for boundaries. It's never easy transitioning after a broken heart, yet I'm glad I'm changing so that I can do God's work. What I witness through His work is enough, and at times even more!

Some of my relationships have ended during my grieving journey. I hope those people remember the good times. May they realize—just like I have painfully grasped—that we aren't meant to keep traveling together at this time. Michael always jokes with me about those I keep in my life. He says that, in general, a person should carry over just a small amount to the next chapter, but I try to carry hundreds—I would bring everybody if I had the choice.

I will admit that with my current priorities changing, it's harder to keep everyone active in my life—it's humanly impossible. Have you ever been there? I love people. I see how God never leaves us, and I don't want to leave anyone. I'm starting to acknowledge the purposes for people's seasons—some for the long haul and others for a short assignment.

If you find yourself trying to run away from change, stop running and pushing. God needs to adjust your life so He can help you live out your mission. We all struggle time and again by doing the same things and expecting different results. We aren't meant to go through the same motions. We are meant to produce spiritual fruits in our lives. We are meant to experience new things.

I pray God heals your brokenness and gives you strength while He changes your heart. He will give you new directions, passions, and desires—enabling Him to help others more through your healing. When I allow God to change my heart, I see how Big He is and what He can do.

When I tried to do things myself—not knowing I was wrong—I didn't get much done in my life or for His kingdom. I pray He changes your heart! I pray you won't hide from life. You have so much living to do.

Lilian Grace taught me to live a full life. I'm continuing to do so with her little sister, Piper—however long He decides to give us. We have five days until the 103-day milestone that must be worked through and passed. God is reminding me of lessons learned, even the ones I forget often. He's changed my heart for the better. I pray He keeps going until mine is in His image.

The tears keep rolling. Michael and I both have not felt well. Perhaps we are trying to wear a mask to cover up our true emotions. We know it's hard for people to help us when we usually don't let them. I can happily say that I've been getting better at letting others help. I still have a long way to go, but I do lean on others more than I used to. Sometimes, life has to be processed in private and, at certain points, with others.

I appreciate everyone who has been patient with us. For those who still can't understand our choices and changes, I pray one day you will understand. There are some relationships that need healing, but I have forgiven myself and them. I have to keep forgiving them on a weekly basis, which makes it hard to stay in a relationship with them. I pray your relationships in life are healed, happy, enriched, and blessed.

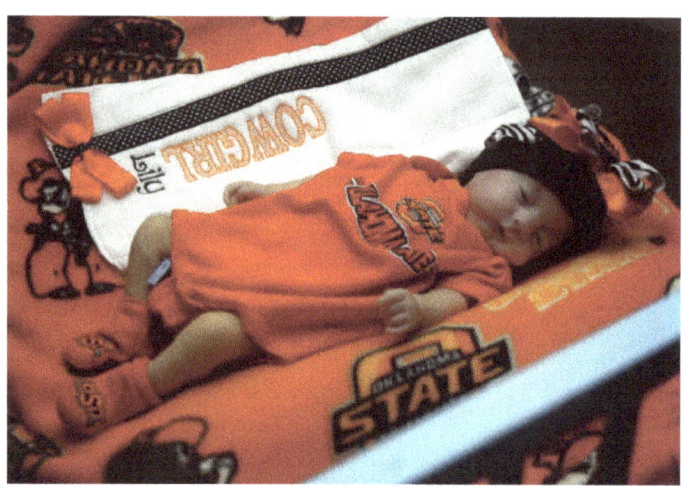

Cowgirl Lily

JANUARY 25, 2012

201 › Angel by Your Side

Four days to go . . .

I find myself stopping in the hallway . . . in a room . . . at the mall . . . in a dressing room—really anywhere—trying not to cry most of the time. Just tonight, I went to check on Piper. On the way back to the living room, I stopped to collect myself as tears welled up. I took a deep breath before rejoining Michael. I catch myself doing this more times than I'd like.

Today, Wednesday, January 25, 2012, marks twenty-one months since Lilian Grace was born. I didn't get to hold her that day. I had to wait days—even weeks. I would stare through her incubator, waiting nervously, yet feeling so blessed that I got to meet her alive, fragile, little, and wonderfully made. I was told my chances of being a mother were only limited by God's miraculous ways. The day she was born, I became a mom and witnessed a miracle. I've never stopped being hers since.

When I spoke to my mom for a couple of hours today, the question of where has the time gone came up. In three months, I can't believe Lilian would have been two years old. My days have been filled with wonderful moments, and the time has flown, but I've learned how to live with the hole she left. It's never easy when you are connected deeply with another human being and your time with them comes to an end. My relationship with Lilian will never disconnect with time, distance, or her status in heaven.

I don't want people to worry about me. I only share my

heart and thoughts so you can learn. We can learn from one another. We all have holes in our hearts that we live with, whether small or ginormous. We have to learn how to live and carry on while the heart and its connections stay alive, even though we grieve.

> *Dear Angel Baby, Lilian Grace:*
>
> *It's been some time since I wrote a letter to you. I talk to you all the time, but I need to type this out tonight. Today, twenty-one months ago, my life changed, and my heart deepened; my life board lit up; my faith was tested; and my spirit was strengthened. I love to picture you partying it up every birthday and angelversary with all your angel buddies. I often think about the themes you might pick, and it makes me smile.*
>
> *Your little sister keeps finding ways to remind me of you. She has your fighting spirit. Even in her sleep, she's a warrior—it runs in the family! I hope you are getting to be an angel by her side in life. I pray she gets to live out God's plan that He has for her just like you, her big sissy, did.*
>
> *After grieving for almost eighteen months, there's not a day that goes by that I'm not thinking about you. I picture us doing normal things that are abnormal for the rest of the world. I see you in your sissy's smile, which makes me cry happy tears.*
>
> *The connection I have with your sister is similar to our connection together. Alive or in heaven, I feel like you are right here. I wish I didn't feel sad at times, but a mother's heart hurts for her baby. I'm not sure where this journey will take me, but I smile, knowing that I won't have to forget you—ever.*
>
> *I love you to the moon and back and for all eternity. I look forward to the day we reunite as much as I look forward to watching your little sissy grow. It's a parallel kind of living, but I know I'll live it out until God calls me home.*
>
> *May you dance and sing with all the angels while praising God on high!*
>
> *Love,*
> *Your Mommy for Eternity*

I have four days until Piper is 103 days old. A lifetime of trying to enjoy her life while I walk with the ginormous hole Lilian Grace left is before me. I don't ever want Piper to miss out because I'm not strong enough to keep it together. I will continue to walk my grief journey, knowing it will not end until the day I leave this life. I will continue to do my best at living in the moment so we can build beautiful memories as a family. I will continue to stop when needed so I can be stronger when I feel weak. I will continue to trust God even when I don't want to.

The bottom line, after hearing many stories of parents losing children, is that you never forget the birth and death dates each month when it's a baby. From one month to the next, things seem off. I feel more run down. I get grumpy. I eat more sweets than I should. All these are due to my heart remembering the twenty-fifth to the fifth. I've heard that scars from painful lessons and loss never go away. They're rigid and hurtful. Somehow a smoothness settles, but the hole remains. We acquire strength from these lessons that we need to survive.

I've been blessed to have angels by my side—always. God knows and picks who needs to be my angel—ranging in all ages. I praise Him for each one. Many have been called home; others are on a break; and some are presently by me. We can't do this life alone. I hope I can be an angel by someone's side. We all need angels by our sides. May we be blessed to have them around to get us through anything. Take time to listen to the song "Angel by Your Side" by Francesca Battistelli and know we all have angels by our side—just look around.

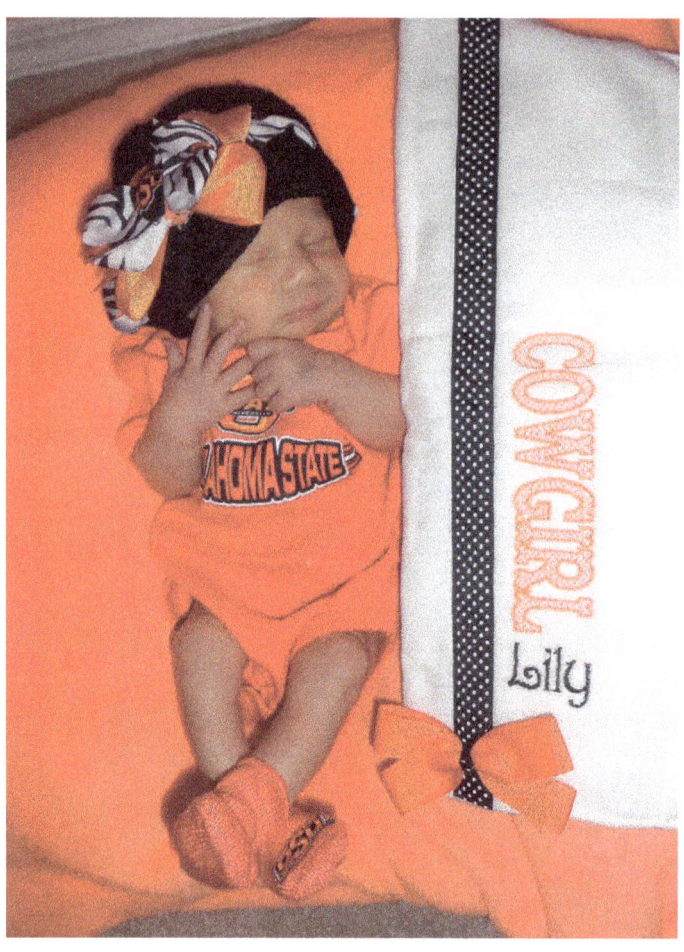

Cowgirl Piper

JANUARY 26, 2012

202 › Break Through

"Love Is Gonna Break Through" . . . *Three days to go* . . .

When it comes to this life, change doesn't come easily, but it always comes. Life can take many twists and turns. We have so many surprises and unexplainable journeys. Love can break through anything and everything. It will always remain through any change we must go through. Love is the greatest thing—surpassing all.

Piper has had a rough day. She tends to feed off our energy. I've been worn out emotionally these days. This part of the grieving journey has been rougher than expected. I let Piper rest on my chest for over two hours—her breathing and heartbeat took me back to the night before Lilian Grace started going downhill.

I've written about that night many times. Holding Piper tonight like I held Lilian Grace is almost like a time machine ride to that hospital room. I remember holding on tight to Lilian—never wanting to let go. I prayed and prayed and prayed for complete healing. I wanted it all to last forever. Losing Lilian was something I didn't know I could survive.

I never thought in a million years that I would continue to see it all as a blessing. I'm thankful God awakened me during our time with her. I needed to be in the moment. I needed love to break through then, now, and always. God's love breaks through on my darkest days. He reminds me just how much love there is around me. He's given me so many examples, and I hope to continue living them out. The sun always rises. Even on my roughest days, the song "Love

Is Gonna Break Through" by Chris Rice reminds me that God will win!

Many of you are going through your own journey. I pray God keeps feeding your soul and strengthening your abilities to keep living and persevering through the survival stage. No matter the circumstances, love has to keep fighting. We have choices to make. We are free. We have freewill. I hope we choose the right path at the fork of each road. Each of us must make choices in life that can affect others at some point.

So many things in life coordinate to shine brightly! The world seems very small when we pay attention. I love thinking of all the people in my life who, while battling their own journeys, are reflecting God's love brighter than ever. I applaud you! I praise God for giving you the right perspectives! I hope you continue to let love shine through, especially when you are tired.

Remember that love is gonna break through! God is gonna get you through! We all row in a boat, so why not let Him be our Captain? When we are tired, it's because we are trying too hard to do it all on our own. I'm doing my best to rest in His arms. I'm praying I keep letting Him be my Captain! Only three days to go, and I'm letting love break through! Love you all.

JANUARY 27, 2012

203 › Broken

Two days to . . .

God keeps walking with me as I listen to "Broken for Love's Sake" by Tricia Brock. Love—the love I have for my children is a love I don't ever want to lose. I totally get God's love for me since becoming a mother. I can relate to His desire to connect with me—with each of us. We are His children—miracles formed in our own mothers' wombs. He wants us to succeed and be with Him for eternity.

His love magnified after He made me a mother. I understand how He can love me no matter what, how, or who I am. I didn't know just how deep my love could go until my girls were born. I praise Him for choosing me. I appreciate the details He's included in my journey. I trust and obey Him, knowing His plans are good.

I will bear my brokenness for love's sake. God goes before me, walks beside me, and gets behind me. The unfolding of the journey gets harder. The tears are abundant as my heart yearns for relief from all the pain, yet I know all of it is for a greater purpose. He will always mend my broken heart to make it stronger than before. On a daily basis, my heart feels like it is breaking and mending on different sides. I hold Piper knowing He has blessed me with a rainbow baby. She is meant for healing, while Lilian is on the broken side, meant for love's sake—to provide a balance for strength to grow.

As this week gets closer to Sunday, I have unraveled. I look in the mirror and see a woman who is run-down. But tonight—thank God—I got to do a gooey dance. That's what Cristin (Handlin) and I are calling it. I got so excited about some gooey brownies with mint chocolate chip ice cream that it gave me a goofy, chilling, wonderful feeling inside. My body reacted with a hilarious little dance in the kitchen with a huge smile on my face. We laughed and laughed as tears flowed. I felt like a kid again, standing back in my mother's kitchen with no worries or brokenness.

---

*I will bear my brokenness
for love's sake.*

God was helping me see—through the cracks of brokenness, with the joy of another child shining through—that I'm still here. I may have emotions that cover the whole spectrum, from utter happiness to complete bitterness, but God stands in any position and direction, guiding me toward where I need to go.

I accept whatever mission I must go on. Being on one of His missions gives me the biggest blessings among the pain. Lilian, Piper, Michael, family, friends, and people in general—for love's sake—you are worth it to Him; therefore, you are important to me. May we all be broken of our negative ways and attitudes—even stubbornness—so we can heal in love and get to our destinations. With two days to go, my heart knows that it has been worth it all—especially for love's sake!

JANUARY 28, 2012

204 › Weeps for You

In less than twenty-four hours, we will celebrate 103 days with Piper as we reflect on the loss of her big sissy in the same amount of life. We have gotten to do a million times more with Piper than we did with Lilian Grace when it comes to everyday living and experiencing life outside the hospital walls minus the wires and assisted breathing.

I remember the 103 days with Lilian Grace like it was today. We were blessed with a very different view and journey with her. There was no going to the grocery store to push her around, looking at fish at the Oklahoma Aquarium, strolling with her at the OSU Walkaround, posing for professional pictures at the photographer's house, traveling on a business trip with her daddy, or even holding her without the wires and machines. When it came to Lilian, there were a lot of nos, yet there were many alternating yeses.

We had the opportunity to respect and praise God for the hospital staff. We learned to dance with wires and machines. We got to take tons of pictures and play dress up with Build-A-Bear clothes. Monthly birthdays were the greatest celebrations, along with quality time with people. We praised God at the highest of highs and lowest of lows. We got to experience a life that we were told would not happen. We never cried alone—He wept with us!

My girls each have many things that are different in their 103 days of living, yet the biggest link that connects them is God. He's always here with us. He knows our story better than we could ever tell it. I remember the heavens crying on Lilian Grace's celebration day. The rain was the hardest rain I'd ever experienced. We are a tighter family because of both journeys with our girls.

As I held Piper tonight at the Oklahoma Aquarium, I thought of the vast differences in the 102 days for my daughters. Lilian Grace was on life support while Piper was getting to experience life. We were with Lilian Grace in her PICU room with a glass wall/door. People watched us through the glass as we tried to finish the journey. Tonight, we were with Piper on the other side of the glass—watching the fish swim around in the tanks.

I weep—God weeps—we all weep! I prefer being on this side of the glass indefinitely. I couldn't have planned a night where a parallel observation of 102 days of life for my girls would occur. As I realized this moment, I held back the tears until I could type this entry.

Remember that we can be on either side of the glass at any moment. The small things are small, and the big ones are big. You never know where each person is in their life. One side is pure happiness and worry-free living, while the other, dreaded side contains sadness, pain, and unknowns.

I pray for each of us as we stop to appreciate how God weeps for us in our storms. The song "Weeps for You" by Johny Diaz sheds light on this topic. I love that God went before us so we could be prepared as we lean on His wisdom. On either side of the glass I've lived, I still need to know God's there. I need Him every minute of every day.

I love how God gave me 103 days with Lilian Grace! Would I have loved to have more? You better believe it, yet you have to understand that I was told I'd get no time with her. One second to 103 days felt like forever—icing on the cake. I don't ever want to forget those hard, glorious 103 days. May we all get to be on the side of the glass where there's true happiness and living no matter what life throws at us.

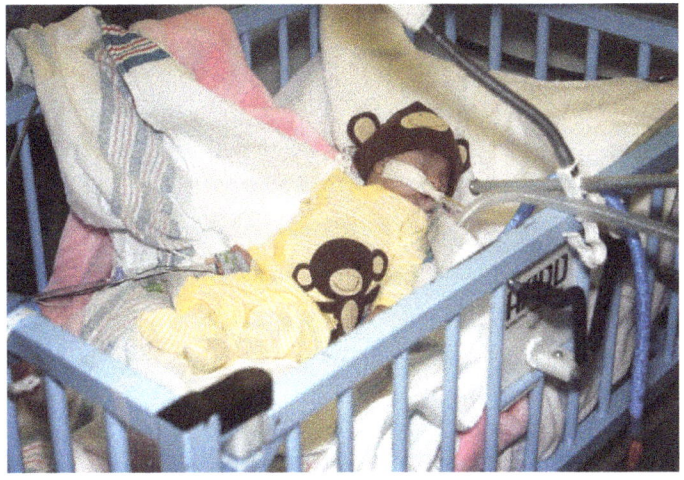

Lilian's 103rd day

Piper's 103rd day

JANUARY 29, 2012

205 › Piper's 103-Day Milestone

Today has been filled with many tears and breaking moments. Piper could tell I didn't have it together. She wanted to nurse a lot and just snuggle with me, which I needed. I broke down the story of her sister's last day. The tears would roll, but I'd continue on, telling the story.

Through all the tears I shed, I know my story—our story—is worth telling. It's a chapter that I shall never forget. Looking through pictures in Lilian Grace's Shutterfly books, I witnessed through a different lens—a camera lens—how our lives looked to the outside world. It wasn't perfect, but it was beautiful. The pictures are a blessing as I look back and remember all the emotions, feelings, thoughts, tears, and moments—just perfect! "The Story of Your Life" by Matthew West is my anthem.

We each have our own story to tell. If you find your life unsatisfying or you are far from your destination, perhaps this is just the beginning. We all have choices in life. We can choose to let our battles be endings or new beginnings. I'm glad God has taught me to see our story as magnificently woven and just the beginning of another chapter in life. I may never be able to stop the tears, but I can make sure they are happy ones filled with love and fond memories of a life well-lived. I won't ever forget Lilian nor will any of you. God was able to show us that life can continue while being broken.

Today, I found myself waking up at 4:32 a.m.—only one hour and thirty-two minutes after I woke up on Lilian's

103rd day. Lilian was coding on her day, and Piper was snoozing like a princess on hers. Lilian coded two more times that morning, and Piper was snug in her bed with no worries. Lilian was taken off life support because we were doing stuff to her instead of for her. Piper was all smiles and needed me to get her from one activity station to the next. I got to hold both my girls on their 103rd days of life. Lilian was held as she transitioned from this life to the next. Piper was held because she just needed me to hold her till the next activity.

At church, the sermon was all about open and closed doors. In my life, the door to being with Lilian is closed, but her purpose continues to be an open door. For Piper, many doors will open and close. God graciously provides soul food in my sorrow to get me through it. I love that God opens and closes doors, even if it takes me some time to adjust. We also sang a song that was sung at Lilian's celebration service called "God of This City" by Chris Tomlin. I couldn't stop the tears—happy ones. God's kingdom is richer because of Lilian's work. I pray it will be even richer as Piper lives out her mission. There are greater things to come. I see God every day, working in everyone's life. I rejoice when others get to see that as well. I pray for those who don't, that their eyes and spirits will one day see His greatness.

My 103 days with both my girls have been unique, purposeful rides. With Lilian, I had never been on my knees so much. I was tired because I hardly ever slept. Her alarms went off all the time. I was scared out of my mind while hoping and praying for more time yet praising God we'd gotten as far as we did. I lived hard because any second she could have been gone. We made mundane things be big things every day.

RAINBOWS AND BRAINSTORMS

With Piper, I've prayed many prayers to get me through the grieving process while rejoicing in our wins. I've been tired from having a healthy baby while my heart tries to heal from the loss of the other. I've wondered more times than I should if we were going to get more time with Piper. I have no idea how long we will get, but I hope it's a very long time. I've been fearful, yet God has reminded me to trust Him always. We've been able to go, explore, and do whatever we wanted with Piper without chains. We've appreciated the mundane yet been able to travel all over.

One hundred three days! I thought it was forever when it came to Lilian Grace. I thought when she left that day, I might not make it—life would stop. I dove into busyness to get myself through. Piper's 103 days have been filled with many firsts—pure happiness and health. I wish Lilian Grace could have been healthy. I wish she could have experienced all the firsts. I wish we could have taken her places and watched her discover them all beyond a hospital or living room.

I'm glad we got what we got. Lilian's 103 days changed me for forever. She gave me a completely new identity, which God has used in wonderful ways. Piper's 103 days have given me hope with more healing and love—lots of love. I love both of my girls. I've loved having them in my life. I will watch Piper grow and wonder what Lilian Grace would have been like at each stage. Tomorrow marks unknown territory for me. I've made it through miscarriages, the death of my baby, and a baby living. I look forward to the rest of the story. There will be many highs and lows, yet God will be wherever I go.

I pray your life is not at the end. I pray you get to where God needs you to be. I pray you'll live through each chapter gracefully, with God's love and mercy. I pray you live, but more importantly, that you live with purpose. Living out God's will is the most breathtaking ride you will ever experience. A magnitude of emotions will always exist, yet God will be there with you as you go from one emotion to the next. He will shape and reshape your heart to become more like His.

I want to thank you for taking the time to read this mother's story—my story. I can't promise I will always have it together. I am human, hopping through all the obstacle courses. I promise you that I will keep trusting God through all of life—always living life with Him. My tears roll freely so my heart can get relief. The soul needs a break—we all need a break. I'm going to let each day come and live it to my best. I'm going to pray that God pushes me aside so He can do His best. I love you all. I hope whatever your story becomes that you are in it by living life out loud!

The Child Who Was Never Born by Martin Hudáčeka

FEBRUARY 2, 2012

206 › Race Details

I have been working hard at getting the Second Annual Warrior Princess Trail Run details finalized. I am happy to post this year's T-shirt color and logo. Our theme goes with Lilian's two-month birthday, where she dressed up as *Tinker Bell*. The door on the shirt is a fairy door representing her preemie status and how God opens and closes doors.

I love how things have come together. Visit our Warrior Princess Foundation website for foundation, race, and sponsorship opportunities and details at: http://web.me.com/c2mist8/Site/Warrior_Princess_Foundation.html[7]

For online race registrations, visit http://warriorprincesstrailrun.eventbrite.com.[8]

We have four race opportunities:
- 10.3 Miles
- 6.4 Miles (10K)
- 1.03 Mile Fun Run/Walk
- Shadow Runner—for those who can't be here but can run/walk from anywhere.

This race has been the best therapy for us. We don't have to dread Lilian Grace's birthday. We have a positive

---

[7] Note from author: This link is no longer active.
[8] Note from author: This link is no longer active.

anticipation that comes from organizing a race while spending time with others for a great cause. We had over 103 runners last year. I'm hoping we have more participation this year, in order to raise more funds and provide much-needed money to T18/T13 families.

The shirts and medals are a great token. I love seeing people wearing Lilian Grace's God Be Big T-shirts and the 2011 red race shirts. Just today, I caught a glimpse of a girl wearing her God Be Big T-shirt at Walmart. It made my heart happy.

Volunteer opportunities will be posted soon. Please pray for this event, including the participants, organizers, and the families touched by trisomy 18/13. Love you all.

Race logo

MARCH 20, 2012

207 › So Small

Absent. Disconnected. Tired. Exhausted. Silent. Screaming in my head. Heart aching. Constantly missing. Wishing my girls could be together and play here on earth. Crying. Bawling. Breathing. Dreaming. Wishing for a different outcome. Wanting everything and more. Believing. Desiring to fix it all yet knowing I can't.

Oh, I just wish the holes in my heart weren't so big. I wish I could make the pain go away. I hope that each day gives me relief from the last. Don't get me wrong; I make the best of it all, but it wears me out trying. I do trust God with all my heart. But even with Him carrying me, I'm still exhausted.

For my second sweet baby girl, I constantly try to put on a smiling face. She sees right through me, especially on the bad days when my emotions take over and more tears fall. I wish Piper could have me without the brokenness, yet I know this brokenness has been good. I just need the holes to shrink.

I share my heart because I'm supposed to share it with you. You are meant to read this right now. Words seem to be lacking in lessening my grief at this point. I don't wish to leave this world anytime soon, but there was a time I would have been fine with God taking me from this journey at any moment.

People have asked me lately how it's going. To be perfectly transparent, there is so much that I don't understand about my grief. I'm having a rough go even among all the fantastic moments with Piper and others. I've continued traveling and living, yet I have this other part of me that is destroyed. The brokenness lingers, and I push it down so that I can walk, talk, and enjoy life and blessings from God.

I picture myself as Cinderella, cleaning up broken pieces of my heart instead of glass. The brokenness—the season of grief—can catch up to you if you aren't working on yourself daily. I recently learned that taking twenty-four hours at a time is the best way to survive. Reminders and realizations that I've been trying too hard on my own again are appreciated. Here's me saying, "God, please take back over. You get the job done right. Amen."

> *Taking twenty-four hours at a time is the best way to survive.*

The above was written almost a week ago but not posted. I'm picking up where I last typed.

Energy. Motivation. A race. A mission. The roller coaster of emotions. A journey continues.

Today, I'm more energized and motivated as I accomplish one item after another. It goes to show you that there are many faces, emotions, strengths, and difficulties on this journey. You may know because you have your own journey you are walking. The only difference between you and me is that I am typing and displaying it for all the world to see. I feel rawness, tenderness, emotional weight, and bipolar reactions when it comes to my walk. Since I typed my little message to God, life is easier as things fall into place smoothly.

It's been seventy months since I held what was left of

my first miscarriage; twenty-two months and twenty-four days since Lilian Grace's birth; nineteen months and fifteen days since I last held her; twelve months and seventeen days since learning I'd be a mommy again; and five months since Piper Allegra's birth. I type this out to remind myself that time rolls on as God works through the mountain highs and valley lows.

Putting a date into an age calculator shows how long it's been since a particular event changed our lives or broke us. I've felt very distant lately, but I think I needed a break more than I thought. The time and distance from my babies made me uncomfortable but allowed me to think more clearly and turn to my energy source—God. I may not love all my days, emotions, attitudes, and energy levels. I may be totally in love with it all on another day, but one thing that remains is that God is next to me as I go through every detail, teardrop, and smile.

In a little over a month, Lilian Grace would have been two. What has God done for me? He's given this mommy a day to look forward to, as well as supporters, trisomy families, and even new people joining our journey. I couldn't have planned this any better. God is way bigger than any idea I could come up with.

The Second Annual Warrior Princess Trail Run is set for Lilian Grace's two-year birthday anniversary, Wednesday, April 25, 2012. To guarantee a race shirt and medal, please register by the extended deadline, Tuesday, March 27, 2012. You can register at RunnersWorld Tulsa on Brookside. You can also email Chrissy to request a paper entry at warriorprincessfoundation@hotmail.com or go to http://warriorprincesstrailrun.eventbrite.com. We are still looking for more race sponsors. If you are interested, go to http://web.me.com/c2mist8/Site/WP_Trail_Road_Fun_

Run.html for a copy of the sponsorship level form.[9]

This race will be here before we know it. I love how this race is a great reference for our grieving journey. We know we have a path to run, but we don't always know how our minds, bodies, and souls will handle that day. Each day is unique. A race is an adventure, ready to be unraveled as each footprint is made on the running path.

I know many who may not be able to make it to the race, but you can always register as a shadow runner and do your own race—even walking it—wherever you are and whenever you can by Thursday, April 26, 2012. I love that anyone can do this at any time. I wish all races would adopt this concept, especially when the proceeds go to a good cause. Even if you can't participate at all, you can pray for the race from pre-organization to the last car that leaves the lot post-race.

I love you all so very much. It means the world to me that you keep reading my thoughts and emotions. I think I may need you more than you will ever need me. I'm looking forward to all the crazy, busy 2012 jam-packed adventures. "So Small" by Carrie Underwood is a wonderful song reminding me that love is all we need at the end of the day, because God is love! Enjoy!

---

[9] Note from author: The email and links in this paragraph are no longer active.

MARCH 26, 2012

208 › Footprints & New Days

Today calls for two songs, "Footprints in the Sand" by Leona Lewis and "A New Day Has Come" by Celine Dion, while I process and type. Have you ever wished that you could be Snow White? Well, I seem to have wished this a few too many times in the last couple of years, especially as of late. I'd love to be her—inside a glass casket, asleep but not dead. A sleep chamber with a piece of glass would separate me from seeing or hearing about more children dying; others diagnosed with disease, illness, or defects; some having to go through more than they should ever have to in a lifetime; and more parents and families fighting the battles before and after. My heart breaks into more pieces. It fills me with sadness to see so much suffering.

I see all of us suffering yet smiling through the struggles and trials. The energy it takes to smile and make each moment positive that we go through before, during, and after—no matter the results—is tremendous. Just go on YouTube and see all the beautiful faces with big eyes who face too much, too young. Actually, I wouldn't recommend that because you'll need a hundred Kleenexes to make it through a few of them.

I've had a couple of pity parties tonight—one for myself and one for others. If you really think about everyone suffering in some way, it can overwhelm your heart and soul. My heart throbs and pours out for everyone. All this suffering will disappear in the end when we begin life in eternity! I just hope I can keep jumping up in His arms to be carried by Him. At times, I wish I could chain myself to Him so I wouldn't ever have to get out of His comforting arms, but I know He wants me to walk beside Him as well.

Many of you have shared your stories with me. My heart hurts for you. I wish I could wipe it all away—the tears, the situation, and the turmoil. I wish I could make it exactly how you need it to be. In exactly a month, two years later, I will be with loved ones and strangers to celebrate a life while honoring others who are walking a trisomy journey and memorializing those whose journey has started on the other side. Watching others celebrate with their babies, I feel happiness, but—for some reason—my heart has needed to cry and cry and cry. Reality has set in more than ever. I'm feeling more emotions than I've ever wanted to feel.

I wish Lilian Grace were Snow White and that I could find a way to break the spell to wake her up. Poof—she'd be back. I'd be able to watch her grow, be a two-year-old, and interact with her little sister. I imagine her running up to me to give me sweet kisses and hugs—making the past two years fade. I know I can't do anything to change it. I just needed to share my thought process, even if I sound like a broken record or whiny mommy.

My husband is amazing in so many areas, but today when I needed him to listen and hold my hand while I cried, he sadly wanted me to quit talking. I was mad at first, but then I thought about his own healing journey. Perhaps talking isn't his way of working it out. I'm not mad anymore at him. I understand that talking about it may make it harder for him. I wish men and women could be more alike, but the reality is that we are vastly different in the way we grieve and handle things in our lives.

If I have ever made you feel horrible or not taken care of, please forgive me. I have not been the best at being there for people like I used to be, especially for some of my dearest friends. I do have to take my time, but I want you to know that I am here. I just may not be right by your side at this moment or all the time. I used to think I could do it all. Humbly, I am finding out that I don't have it in me. None of us can do everything all the time for everyone. I'm struggling to figure out how to be okay with this truth.

Looking back at Snow White, she probably felt pretty distant from everyone since she had to flee from the huntsmen in the woods to save her life. After watching myself on *Donor Milk: The Documentary*, I thought about the Chrissy I was during that moment—not even a month after Lilian Grace passed away. I wanted so desperately to help everyone in the world. I wanted to do and do and do so I didn't have to feel. The woman on the big screen hadn't even given herself a chance to let reality hit her or set in, for that matter.

She saw something that needed to be done and went after it passionately with gratitude, so she didn't have to face her own huntsman. As I watched myself talking and trying to hold all the emotions in, I found myself holding back even more until now. Lilian Grace's journey caught up to me. Though I had many wonderfully blessed moments, the reality is that she's gone. It is devastating! It takes everything I've got, plus God, to make each day a good one! She is never coming back, and the pain from her last breath is never going away.

There is hope! One day, I will be strong enough to face the day without it taking so much energy. I will wake up and not have to fight so hard. I will learn how to walk with it all and not feel so numb, distant, or broken. The sting of her death will always be here—my love for her and my suffering from the loss of her. God will get me to a place where I will be prepared and armed without effort. It will become second nature. I will feel like I've slept, like Snow White. I will wake up and not be exhausted. I will get to experience and enjoy motherhood without guilt or loss of energy.

I know many of you can relate. I'm praying for you in all your brokenness—no matter who, what, or where it comes from. The important factor is to let God teach, grow, shape, and mend us so the effort takes less and we get to live more—struggling less. I say that I might be depressed, but I'm not. I know why Lilian Grace was here and why she had to go. Getting stronger than the brokenness is going to take time. I don't have to have it all together, nor do you. We can cry without feeling guilty or weak. We don't have to be around everyone all the time. We don't have to be at every event either. Sometimes bad days come when the brokenness is stronger, and that's okay. We are entitled to just be like every human being in the world.

I pray we each get through the lessons God has prepared to make us stronger. I pray we keep looking up and trusting Him even when we are so tired and fed up. I pray we always remember that each day is meant to be lived to its fullest, even if it means sitting on the couch to regain energy. I love you all. I already feel better by just typing this out and sharing—my therapy. I know my day will come! I see God working daily, even if my days don't go how I want. I'm glad He loves me enough to humble me with His continuous and abundant grace and mercy wrapped with love.

APRIL 17, 2012

209 › Reality

I walked out to the mailbox thinking there would be junk mail—perhaps a magazine. I never expected a letter about a kit that is coming in a few days with surveys, requesting updates on my daughter, Lilian, as a toddler. When I opened the letter and started to read, I saw Lilian's name. I couldn't comprehend how this department repeatedly has failed to update Lilian's status to deceased. Needless to say, it's been a rough day.

I desperately needed today to go differently, but I got hit in the stomach again. I've already struggled with toddler birthday parties as of late, but this made those situations seem like child's play. I wish I had wise words to say, but I don't. The only thing keeping me together is God! He continues to be who gets me off the floor when I get knocked down.

In a week, Lilian Grace would have been two years old. Truthfully, it's harder than her first birthday. I guess the further out I get from her existence, the more reality sinks in. The before, during, and after of Lilian Grace must be seen through a stronger lens called truth—a reality stripped of overcompensation to avoid negative thoughts and feelings.

I've learned more lessons, facts, and truths as of late than I really care to learn. I have discovered that no matter what is going on, how hard we try to paint a perfect picture, how deep we try to bury it, or what we end up doing or saying—the truth always reveals itself in due time. Perhaps in our situation, we can't hide behind a themed anything, continue to bury emotions further down because there's no more room, or paint a different picture since we know and see the outcome. Moving forward is complicated, especially when certain departments contact me for updates that don't exist, and other people want to continue living in another reality.

I want to be real! I want to see the truth about what it truly means. I want to keep processing so I can keep living. I want to keep being vital for what God has in store. I'm tired of the nonsense! I'm worn out from the manipulators. I'm disgusted with the selfishness. I'm exhausted from it all. Though it's a scary prayer, I pray God keeps me in the real while continuing to unveil the wolves in sheep's clothing. I'm asking Him to guide me toward recovery after experiencing each moment.

To those who are on the right path—trusting God while being selfless, secure, and content—I pray I can be like you. For those who are off the path—stop trusting in yourself, being selfish and discontent, and living insecurely—I pray I'll never be like you.

Michael and I have a new favorite song, "Somebody That I Used to Know" by Gotye. I'm not sure if it's a healthy one, but it says a lot. We've got our own song lyrics in progress for personalization. I wish certain things and people were something or somebody that I used to know. I am being real again—not wanting to be negative. I am just tired of the games. At the end of a day or season with such a person, I feel crappy, used, manipulated, unheard, and forgotten. It makes me want to scream so they can hear what I've been trying to say the whole time. I've been more transparent than in any season in my life. Breathe, Chrissy, breathe!

I do hope we can all find ourselves in good places as we process and live a life full of unconditional love with no games or secret agendas. Today's letter made me face this past year where people have continued to forget, ignore, or accept reality. I don't want to deal with any of it right now. God's been good, as always, helping me cry it out on a car ride date with my hubby and baby girl this time. It was exactly what I needed.

Other favorite songs for grieving during a car ride (or whenever) were "Powerful Stuff" by Sean Hayes and "When It Rains" by Eli Young Band. I don't want to give up the power of knowledge and wisdom gained through my circumstances. I am evolving and growing. I want to rise like the Son! Being open and present is beautiful and strong. I want to learn to sing on my darkest days of grief. When it rains and circumstances alter my life, I want to be real and face each day head on. I don't want to be afraid of crying and processing. I can't change the world, but I can work on myself and move in a powerful direction that impacts my world for the better.

> *I don't want to give up the power of knowledge and wisdom gained through my circumstances.*

I find myself getting stronger and breathing without the weight of the hidden, unprocessed realities of grief. I don't want to get rid of everyone, but I do wish I could stop the unwanted parts of confrontations or misunderstood words and actions. I need us all to use more compassion and empathy—keeping in mind that we don't know what's weighing someone down.

The final song we listened to, "When I Get Where I'm

Going" by Brad Paisley and Dolly Parton, made me cry it out the most, yet gave me hope for the day I get to meet my Maker and see His amazing face. Plus, my sweet Lilian Grace can jump into my arms and give me the biggest hug of all time. I'll give her a million kisses on her cheeks—and never have to say goodbye again.

JULY 25, 2012

210 › Time

Some things take time . . .

I'm listening to a wonderful new song, "The Hurt and the Healer" by Mercy Me, that's fitting for this time as I write. To no one's surprise or even mine, some things take time. Yesterday, Piper and I were watching the fish tank. Out of sheer excitement, I gave a loud shriek, spotting Herbie—our smallest pleco—on the palm tree chilling away. The significance of this moment is that he had stayed hidden for almost two years. His one act inspired me to write another journal entry after being silent and putting it off for months. Stubbornness runs deeper in my veins than I would like, but this huge act of a little fish made it impossible for me not to share.

I related to Herbie—a fish—more than I wanted. I've been struggling lately, trying to keep up a brave face and a strong attitude, so I'll be bearable around others. I've hidden my deeper emotions, reactions, and attitudes toward the past and now current decisions people around us are making. It's hard to watch everyone while I work through my brokenness. I'm searching to figure out how to keep moving while a part of me has died.

As I emerge from my hiding place, I allow more emotions and parts of myself to open up after almost two years of trying to keep things hidden. I'm trying to stay above the water—to keep from drowning, suffocating, feeling the pain, crumbling, being paralyzed, and avoiding my fears and anger. Today marks the day Lilian Grace celebrated her last monthly birthday with us two years ago. The past few weeks have brought more struggle than usual—I've been pulling pieces out from under my own rock. For some reason, Herbie and I must have had breakthroughs. I bawled and processed those hidden pieces. No matter how long Lilian Grace has been in heaven, my heart yearns to see her and my arms long to hold her. I feel lost without her here.

To add to the grieving process, I've witnessed several people destroy their lives and others by their decisions. It's crazy how someone's decisions and actions can cause so much pain and sorrow. People never stop to think about the consequences of their selfish acts affecting not only themselves but others—we all suffer.

After Lilian entered my life, my eyes were opened to the truths of endless struggles and stubbornness—their motivations behind decisions and life. I have shut down a majority of people in my life. One truth—my relationships were due to me doing all the work, so I stopped. I stopped calling many people. I stopped trying to get with them. I stopped talking to them—some on purpose and others because I hid under a rock, struggling to figure out how to be from that point on. *A quick note: I am thankful for my equal partnerships and those who took on more of the load than usual. Many of you have hung in there with me while I try to figure out how I need and want to be.*

My trust issues with people are lacking due to their actions and the hurtful aftermath. Once Lilian left, I hid most of what was left of me under a rock to protect myself. I've stayed busy to avoid giving people a chance to prove that I can or can't trust them.

Luckily, God wants all of me healed. Sadly, there is more work to be done. Last night, I realized that the depth of my brokenness is greater than I could imagine. It goes beyond trust issues. It's about me—struggling to figure out myself and how to keep breathing while I live with a part of me gone. Sure, I can put on a happy smile. I can listen to life and other people's joys, sorrows, and pains. I can sing, pray, and dance. But through it all, I have to own that I'm exhausted, rundown, and emptied. I'm struggling to accept that part of me will never be and that I have high expectations—trying to force myself to be the Chrissy everyone wants me to be.

At this point, I know that I have a piece of me in heaven. Lilian is gorgeous. She is missed and loved. Lilian is my angelic daughter. I have another piece of myself whom I get to watch grow here on earth. Piper is gorgeous. She is here and loved. Piper is my earthly daughter.

I am loved by God. He makes me be better than I am. I am imperfect. I say too much. I dream big. I love big. I am limited by myself. I care about others. I can't fix everything. I can't make people want to be around me and vice versa. I am only one, but God does big things when I step aside.

Some things take time. That's why I'm trying to pull pieces from under the rock. I have broken relationships that need to be mended. I have a heart that needs continuous repair. I have a mouth that could speak differently and more positively. I have anger that I need to let go. I have disappointment in others that needs forgiveness or to be forgotten. I need to give myself a break.

I am still hurt but love it when that hurt collides with my Healer. I am at a place of helplessness in fixing my broken relationships, torn heart, hurt, confusion, partial death, everyday living, paralysis, judgment, inability to look past people's poor decisions, and the past meeting the present. The list goes on and on. My answer to myself and others is God. He can fix it all!

My answer to myself and others is God. He can fix it all!

Here I am, God! Take my fears I've tried so desperately to hide. Take all of everything in my life and heart! Please have your way of fixing and healing it all. I'm exhausted! Forgive me for trying for the millionth time to do it on my own. I don't want to be angry! I don't want to be broken! I am tired of disappointing others and making them mad because I can't be who they need me to be or do things the way they want me to do it. I want to be free, happy, and whole—and most importantly, who God wants me to be.

Death strips you while changing everything. I must remember to keep moving forward in my grieving journey, as I have learned time and again. Some things do take time. I'm hoping to keep handing it over to God as it seeps through the scars and ventures out through my tears.

Praying for all of us as we try to work through what life throws at us. Life doesn't stop whether we want it to or feel it will. I hope we can all trust God to continue to pull us through. Michael, Piper, and I will be celebrating Lilian's second angelversary on Sunday, August 5, 2012. Please remember us in your prayers. This time of year is our biggest struggle. Many tears are shed as more healing comes. Having another child after losing one is bittersweet—a constant reminder of what we are missing with Lilian Grace. We love the fact that we get to watch Piper meet each milestone—that needs to be said—but many tears of joy and sorrow are shed as we cheer for Piper and grieve for Lilian. This is a path that will forever contain mixed emotions and levels of cheering.

For Lilian, on what would have been her twenty-seven-month birthday—

> Dear Sweet Angel of Mine,
>
> As I hold your baby sister, tears often flow down my cheeks, knowing that holding you is in the past and missing you. Often, I talk to your sister about you without overwhelming her. I watch her play while daydreaming about you playing together. More tears flow because it can't happen. It's been twenty-seven months since you blessed us with your fighting spirit. I see that same spirit in your little sister on a daily basis. She does so many things that you did. You both have similar smiles, ornery ways, cries, and gorgeous eyes that are filled with wisdom. It gives me hope, knowing that there is a piece of you in her.
>
> As time rolls on, I find myself behind—trying desperately to catch up. I do hope you are getting to look down on us to see the small things we are doing in memory and honor of you. I hope you smile big from ear to ear as it warms your heart. You are loved—just as much as I love your little sister. No distance could ever change my love for you.
>
> It's not long until we celebrate your second angelversary. I can only imagine that you are healed and loving heaven. We miss you with aching hearts that are filled with love, joy, and peace. No loving parent ever stops missing their children—no matter where they are now.
>
> I love you to the moon and back and for all eternity. You are forever ignited in my heart. I long for the day I get to come home to you.
>
> Love,
>
> Your Mommy Who Is Trying to Keep It Together

SEPTEMBER 28, 2012

211 › Reopen

And He opens me up again . . .

When you give it all to God, He never leaves you to yourself—even when you think He's checked out. Guess what? He never checks out on us. He is always here, but we may not be. He never leaves us—PRAISE GOD!

Lately, I thought I had been traveling down a good road. Yes, I've been tired. Yes, life has been turned upside down with this or that. Yes, I have no control over anything around me. Yes, I feel like running into my Father's arms and never leaving. Yet I really thought I was in a good place on my grieving path and life compared to others' lives.

Well—thanks to last night's *Grey's Anatomy* episode, I am not okay. Deep down, I am in shambles. I do not even come close to having it together. I am exhausted beyond words. I feel like a fake, pretending to stay above the water. I thought I'd lose my ability to breathe as I watched the hospital staff take Mark (Dr. McSteamy) off life support. God knows I needed to wake up to continue His works. Feeling the raw emotions brings change, growth, and health to heal.

I flashed back to the moment when the doctors sat us down to tell us we were doing stuff to Lilian instead of for her (something I had asked them to do from the very beginning so we could be in check). After making the final decision to take her off the vent, the drive with Michael to our home that day was—well . . .

. . .

. . .
. . .
. . . Sorry, I'm having a hard time typing this through my tears. I was numb. I knew that with everything in me and beyond, removing her life support later that day was the only choice. She had coded three times earlier, so there was no "should we" or "shouldn't we." Watching hospital staff revive her multiple times was excruciating.

We gave ourselves enough time to go home and gather some of her pretty things. We got ready to walk back down the long hallway, ride the elevator up, and walk to her PICU room to say our final goodbyes for now. I remember scurrying through the house like a crazy momma. I remember shouting, "Where's this?" "Where's that?" "Why can't I find this?" "Is this or that back at the hospital?" I knew that day would come, but I wasn't prepared. I should have had a box of all the stuff organized, but I had dragged my feet—dreading its arrival. I wanted our final pictures with her to be perfect. I wanted it to be everything.

I—I—I—I—I—

. . .
. . .
. . .
. . .

—just needed those final moments to be everything for so many of us. I tried to gather things that meant something to as many people as I could. I wish I could have taken everything to meet everyone's needs. I knew how important it was to everyone because they didn't get to be there like I did. So for some, I tried to make up for their loss by finding special pieces that could be part of the pictures with Now I Lay Me Down to Sleep (NILMDTS).

The car ride from our house back to the hospital—well—

I remember looking through items, double checking, and making sure I had grabbed the best of what I could. It was unfair that all her clothes hanging in the closet would never be worn by her. It was surreal. I wanted this to be another trip home to swap out my hospital bag. I didn't want this to be the last time I'd be driving from the hospital to home to the hospital. Though that time was hard, it was exactly how it was supposed to be. I couldn't change it even if I wanted to. It was our baby girl's journey—the earthly part was wrapping up.

I prayed with my husband before we let the nurses take her off the vent. It was a hard prayer, full of love, tears, and the unknown. No book could prepare us fully for that moment. I could feel God's presence there. He was holding me and getting me ready to hold my daughter as she left this earth to go to heaven—from my arms to His.

I look at pictures of myself, my husband, all three of us, and us with doctors and nurses—all of them. Looking at her before the vent came out, I remember wanting so desperately for her to come back, cry loudly, and be alive. I needed her to live, but I knew (and know) God needed her more. That realization before they removed the vent was comforting. Yet I hurt so deeply, knowing I would forever long for her to be here—to watch her grow, learn, and challenge us all.

As the *Grey's Anatomy* episode continued, more memories flooded my thoughts. I am forever thankful that a nurse turned off the monitor once the numbers started to decline beyond a brady status. I'm not sure I could have stayed here if I had heard her flatline. I surely would have lost my mind completely. I had Lilian in my arms, feeling her breathing one second and then nothing the next—lifeless. Have you ever felt lifeless or held someone lifeless—no exchange of oxygen? How did it feel to hold someone that is no longer here? It's scary! It's unexpected! It's unexplainable.

I remember trying to make her transition easier and more beautiful by singing. I thank God for a great memory to remember all the words during such a climactic experience of sorrow. It was all planned out. God knew how to turn it into a gorgeous clip. We got to dress her, fix her up, and hold her. Through this special moment, I felt like a little girl with her baby doll that Mommy and Daddy just bought. Somehow, getting to dress my little girl like she was alive felt like make believe after she passed away. It didn't feel real. Even after the last picture was snapped, I looked at her and knew she was no longer here—all was gone, no returning, no changing—it was done.

I see myself in those pictures and wonder what it'd be like to jump into that scene again, watching through another person's eyes. I've seen pictures of what other families experience when losing their baby boy or girl, but I've not been present to watch. I give props again to all those who have anything and everything to do at the hospital. God definitely made you special in order to handle it. I pray to God that He continuously gives you strength and peace.

The staff were wonderful to us. They shed tears along with us. They loved on us. They were patient and kind. I wish we all could be like this to each other, no matter the situations we find ourselves in.

In typing this entry—I hope you can understand that God's working around us, no matter what we are going through—even when we don't know how to put words to our feelings, emotions, or reactions. He meets us where we are and uses the things we need to help guide, direct, and heal us! He used *Grey's Anatomy* last night to open Michael and me back up so the flood gates could pour more out—helping us through this journey. He reminded me of why I started the Warrior Princess Foundation—because I went through the T18 journey and can help lighten the load for as many as I can.

We all are on a journey. For some of us, there's so much happening that we don't have a clue where to begin. For others, it's so unbelievable that we just shut down. For the rest of us, we are so consumed that we can't move. I am reminded through my own stuff that God is good. He takes care of our every need. He will allow things to happen so that we can make progress. We can be too stubborn, too content, too earnest, or too anything. He steps aside to allow mountains to build up, teach, and strengthen us for the next chapter of the journey. He continuously reminds me of the verses He gave me one day at the hospital in the beginning for the why:

Memory Verse 3

"So that Christ may dwell in your hearts through faith. And I pray that you, being rooted and established in love, may have power, together with all the Lord's holy people, to grasp how wide and long and high and deep is the love of Christ, and to know this love that surpasses knowledge—that you may be filled to the measure of all the fullness of God" (Ephesians 3:17–19).

On a positive note—He is everything! He has given me another event to keep Lilian Grace's memory and mission alive and well. Tomorrow, I am opening my home up for the Warrior Princess Holiday Showcase from 1:00–5:00 p.m. Visit http://www.warriorprincessfoundation.com/special-events.html[10] for more details. I have been blessed with so many wonderful people stepping up and wanting to be a part of our mission. We are raising money to help increase the Warrior Princess Foundation scholarship fund.

I am happy that we have a new website for the foundation (www.warriorprincessfoundation.com/)[11] that will keep you updated on special events, available scholarships, the Warrior Princess Trail Run details, and miscellaneous information. I wasn't happy when the previous website program closed down, but the new site is the exact direction we need to go. I still have things to add and update, but it's a wonderful start.

For those who will not be available to come to my house tomorrow, you can still participate by donating or buying at the following websites:

Warrior Princess Foundation
http://www.warriorprincessfoundation.com/opportunities-to-give.html

Avon
http://mgonzaga-johnson.avonrepresentative.com/online_event/view.php?rep_spnsr_evnt_id=351074[12]

Mary Kay
http://www.marykay.com/cheer4osu
Note: Type Warrior Princess in the memo section.

Stella & Dot
http://www.stelladot.com/ts/g1oj5[13]

---
[10] Note from author: This link is no longer active.
[11] Note from author: This website is no longer active.
[12] Note from author: This link is no longer active.
[13] Note from author: This link is no longer active.

Thirty-One Bags
http://www.mythirtyone.com/shop/catalog.aspx?eventId=E2266802&from=DIRECTLINK[14]

Jamberry
http://www.mereshine.jamberrynails.net/home/default.aspx[15]

Scentsy
https://brookecroberts.scentsy.us/Scentsy/Home[16]

I'm glad God keeps my journey alive and well. Remember that wherever you are on your journey, God always has your back. He needs you to hand it all over to Him. You may have a tight hold, but let it go! He will make all the bad into the good. Looking back at letting go of Lilian Grace on her last day forever changed me. I'm still working through it all, but God has transformed the bad into good. Keep dropping to your knees and lift your eyes to Him. The greatest strength is found in Him! He's got this! He's got you!

Love you all! May God always bless you in your journey. May you know, even if you think you don't, that He is everywhere. He is for you! He will turn it around!

---

[14] Note from author: This link is no longer active.
[15] Note from author: This link is no longer active.
[16] Note from author: This link is no longer active.

Piper—smashingly adorable turning one

OCTOBER 12, 2012

212 › Feet over Heart

The saying "head over heels" means showing you are overly excited about something. I've decided that I'm "feet over heart" because my heart hurts so much that I am upside down—flat on my back. I'm not sure I can walk or be normal.

We have eight days until Piper turns the Big One. This should be a wonderful milestone, yet the closer we get—my behaviors have me all over the place in a chaotic spinning motion. I'm spending too much; eating all the time; crying at the drop of anything; feeling depressed, mixed with happiness; and dealing with allergy attacks—the list carries on.

This past week, I made a trip to St. Francis Hospital just to eat a comforting meal by myself. I sat in the cafeteria with Piper and watched everyone. Of course, like all of Tulsa, it's under construction—like you and me!

Sadly, I wished we were there to spend time with Lilian. Being in that dang cafeteria brings me comfort I can't get elsewhere. I know many of you try to comfort me. Thank you for your efforts! I'm blessed you care so much. It seems I don't know what I need most of the time. Somehow, sitting in the place where Lilian died gives me comfort that not even a hug can give me. (If you know me, I think hugs are amazing.)

I built up my strength to see our hospital family. As I rode the elevator to the fifth floor, I got super emotional. Seeing my ladies is not the problem—I love them all. I owe them my life for what they did for my Lilian! It's hard sitting on this side of the doors, knowing I won't get to make ump trips inside to spend precious moments with my baby girl, Lilian Grace. I couldn't even go to the other floors to visit other family members. The fifth floor was all I had in me. I praise God that the ladies remember and come out to spend a few minutes with me.

I'm still not sure why two years, two months, and some weeks plus days hits so hard, but it really does after the birthday anniversaries and angelversaries. I know Michael and I both struggle more. Right at her two-year birthday anniversary, we made the drastic decision to move out of the house Lilian lived in. It was time. Though moving was a whirlwind, I feel like we made the right choice.

Two months after trying to work through Lilian's two-year angelversary, Michael quit his job and will start a new one in a week. I'm not sure how I feel about it. Perhaps scared, yet I know God has our backs. This has been our year to make major elective life changes—voluntary on each of our parts. Right now, it feels like we are trying to run away from it all. Yet—somehow, as I reread this post, I know we're moving toward our next chapter.

The funny thing about grief is that you can't outrun it. You can try, but you will lose. Just looking at my credit card statements, my weight on the scale, the amount of toilet paper used (it's cheaper than Kleenex), the amount of time it's taking me to get out of bed each day, how long I procrastinate to go to sleep, and my increase in allergy attacks (careless about eating bad foods)—I know I'm worse off than I can put into words.

If I talked to you right now, we both would think I'm not bad. Actually—if we looked at the food in my pantry or fridge, house I live in, car I drive, and activities I participate in—you would think it's all going great. If we both took a deeper look, we could see a girl with her feet above her heart—flat on her back—just hoping she makes each day matter through her aching heart and sadness. This is something that can't be fixed on earth. The day God calls me home is when the pain will be removed. He gives me hope like no other! Living with it all drains my energy tank quickly, but I praise Him for filling it back up each and every day. It's those days—yet again—where I try to be a solo pilot that's gotten me really worn out.

I will love the day that I don't need maintenance, emptied and filled up, or repaired! I look forward to total healing when I leave this place. For now, I have to keep dropping to my knees for strength. I have to know He has plans for me—for my family. This time in my grief journey is a small piece of the path. Just because I can't explain it all doesn't mean God isn't working it out. I was reminded today that He can still be working while being silent. I just needed to type all this in Lily's journal. I needed to see it on paper. God wouldn't let me stay in this bed all morning. I had a huge desire to write again.

I am head over heels for my baby girl, Piper, turning one. I'm also feet over heart for my baby girl, Lilian, not getting to be here and for not having the ability to change circumstances with individuals or things.

Watching Piper leap into our hospital family members' arms brought a ton of emotions the other day. A couple of the ladies commented that it's like she knows them. As crazy as it may sound, I sometimes feel one of two things: Lilian came back healed, or Lilian has let her little sister, Piper, know about everyone. Who knows!

I know many of you are at this feet-over-heart stage right now. It seems like there's never going to be an end to the chaos. Today, I can say that God is bringing us peace in the midst of our journeys. He never promised life would be problem free or struggle free. He did promise that He'd be here with us through it all. Here's a prayer I need to type and say out loud:

🕯 *Dear heavenly Father, I love You more than I ever thought I could. I praise You for never letting me go. I come to You right now in a state of being feet over heart. My days seem full of chaos—full of mixed emotions, untimely events, possibly depression, and more. I am at a place where I'm weary, and I need rest that only You can provide.*

My relationships with many are wonderful, yet with others, I struggle to want to be around them. I just can't get past certain things because they keep making poor decisions and expect everyone else to act like it's no big deal. What each of us does in life affects everyone.

I cannot change people or the past. I can't change circumstances. I can't make people be who they are not. I ask that You take them, me, and us. I pray You give us each what we need, whether in knowledge, direction, or guidance, and that You heal/mend where needed. I pray for peace, strength, and ability for each of us in our own unique journey You have created. I pray that our learning through lessons is short and quick. Please continue to put Your hedge of protection around each of us.

You, O God, know each of our hearts, minds, bodies, and souls. Search each of us and let Your work be done. May we all feel serenity during the sunny and the stormy days of our lives! We all have our own struggles we live out and battles we fight daily. May You fill us up so we can have the energy to make the best of whatever our journey looks like. In Your precious, glorified name. Amen.

DECEMBER 10, 2012

213 › Never Easier

Memory Verse 4

⚔ *"When you pass through the waters, I will be with you; and when you pass through the rivers, they will not sweep over you. When you walk through the fire, you will not be burned; the flames will not set you ablaze" (Isaiah 43:2).*

It never gets easier when a child gets called home too early, earning his or her heavenly angel wings—no matter the age or whether born sleeping or living hours, months, or years. Each of God's children has a purpose. At times, it can be hard to understand the reason behind their short stay. I am closer to some who have lost a child than to others, but I still feel the pain of the mother as she forever misses that child—never fully relieving the pain or satisfying the longing.

She always misses—always wishes—always longs—always hopes. Her heart aches every day—as does mine. I've gotten good at setting my grief to the side when it is too much in order to live and—more importantly—breathe. I wish I could design a gimmick that would make it all easier, but there isn't one.

November was my month to reflect as I took a break from all the chaos—like the ashes had finally settled since losing Lilian Grace. I've taken many looks back. I now see different friendships, living spaces, jobs, and lives changed. I wish I could have some of these things back, yet it may never happen again.

Friendships: I sadly discontinued some friendships because I didn't have it in me to keep fighting the good fight with them. I miss them often, but I know I couldn't be who they needed me to be. What did I do? I cut them off. It was easier that way—no explanations—nothing. I just didn't have it in me. The energy was gone.

Living spaces: We moved out of the house where Lilian lived. This has been hard but essential in our journey. I couldn't be there anymore with all the reminders of harder times. I took the good with me and reflect often with happiness. It's never easy letting go, but leaving that house was easier than letting go of her for the last time.

Jobs: I left my job before Lilian Grace passed away, and I never went back. I miss it more and more every day. I miss the people there. Now that the aftermath is settling in, I have more time to get myself into a working form. Perhaps, someday, I can rejoin that career or another. Michael left his job mid-October, and we are still adjusting to that change. It's crazy how some things need to change so we can breathe. In time, it will be exactly what we needed for our family—for Michael.

Lives: I know we have changed. We continue to adjust when our journey gets rocky. Sometimes we still feel like we are drowning. Sometimes we try to step outside our comfort zones to feel when numbness consumes us. We go back and forth on so many things in our lives because of that very point—numbness. We watch people feeling and acting out, but we feel nothing on many occasions. But tonight—

After hearing about another child earning their wings, the numbness broke as the floodgates opened—pinned up feelings came pouring out. All the emotions overwhelmed me, but I praised God that I could still feel. I praise Him that I'm not numb for once. I unveiled all the tucked-away feelings and realized for the millionth time that I'm not dead! I'm not numb! I'm alive!

Too often—every day—the mundane things can make me numb, but I appreciate everything from the mundane to the insane, the sad to the happy, and the lighthearted to the intense. If there's any advice I can give you, it's to take life as it comes. It can surprise us, even if we are numb.

I'm continuing to lift all the trisomy families up in prayers to be protected, guided, and comforted—whatever else they need. As of late, I've wanted to give up on the Warrior Princess Foundation. I praise God that He refuels me. I don't want to stop or quit. I may do only a penny's worth in the millions of dollars of life, but this foundation gives us all a way to help babies on earth and honor those in heaven.

To go further, it's a reminder that life is meant to be challenged, enriched, and lived. I'm going to do my best to keep it going for as long as God intends.

Visit Stinky's (Annabel Leigh Villadiego) website at http://sweet-annabel-leigh.blogspot.com/ to witness a life lived out loud. She lit up the world!

Stinky: You and your family have given my family so much. You gave us hope when all was dim. You gave us an example of living life out loud. You made our family thrive and burn bright in the midst of chaos. We are forever grateful to you all. May God be with you all through this transition to the grieving journey. It's possible to live through it and thrive. Stinky, give my sweet Lilian Grace a big hug and kiss from her mommy. I miss her more and more every day. I know she loved watching you on your videos—dancing to the music you had on your website. I can see her precious little smile—excited to hug your sweet neck—finally! You girls rock it out in heaven until we can join you.

No matter how many days I want to quit, I'm going to keep going. I needed the reminder that there's a purpose! Love to everyone. Hug your babies tight—no matter their age—and cherish every minute you can. We are not guaranteed any amount of time here on earth. Live out your purpose no matter what. Life can drag us down and keep us from living out God's purpose. Step out of the haze—the numbness—and get back to it! I can't seem to stop crying with more to feel, release, and heal. It never stops! Praise Him for taking care of us!

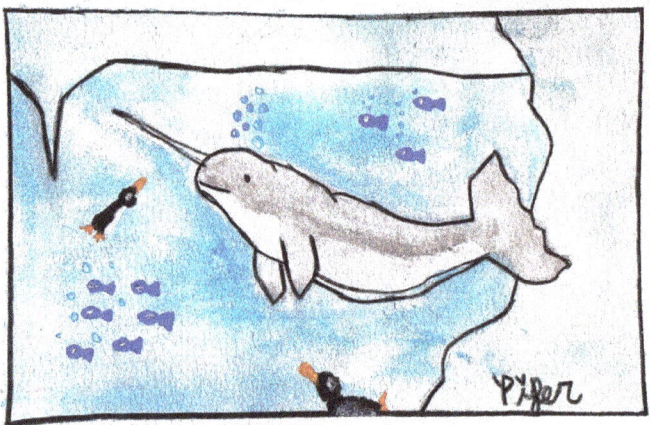

MARCH 13, 2013

214 › Wander with Focus

Can you be wandering while focused? I'm not sure if you can, but that best explains my life at the moment. I feel like I wander while getting distracted and off track, yet somehow there is focus and purpose happening as well. Maybe there's another terminology to define my life right now, but I've not made the time and don't have the energy to find it.

Months have turned into years. We are approaching my sweet Lilian's three-year-birthday anniversary in forty-two days. I'm wide awake yet feel like I'm sleeping. Half of my life feels real, and with the other half, I'm not sure if I'm dreaming or not. Perhaps it's my coping mechanism I've created to survive all that comes on this journey.

I've been having so many pity parties lately. I've questioned my decisions, motivations, emotions—off and on. I struggle because I'm trying to measure it all with someone else's standards. I go back and forth on whether I should put on the next race or keep the foundation and personal business going. God continues to be a God of clarity, love, and direction. All this chaos, questioning, and more is not from Him.

My heart breaks as I see one mother after another join a road that I would wish on no one—grief from the loss of a child. My life goes on even after hearing their stories, but mine stays with me. Every day, I don't wake up with their grief, just my own. I hurt because I know their grief will last until their final breath. There's hope knowing that this pain will dissolve when I get to physically jump into my heavenly Father's arms. I hold on to that image and feeling.

Last night, I couldn't stop thinking about finding a journal I had started called *My Road to Forty*. I had a huge desire to read it to refresh my memory about what my top ten things to get done by forty were. What was I supposed to see? I had checked off the first item on the list and wrote about it. Bear with me because I'm adding the excerpt to this entry. These are the words I wrote almost five years ago on April 13, 2009. This entry was exactly what God needed me to read at this exact time. May it help you with your battles.

Journal Entry from April 13, 2009—LASIK Eye Surgery

Wow is the first word I read when the doctor asked me again to read the blue sign on the wall. Wondering what was the first thing on my list that I did for this round of my road to forty? Well, I got bladeless LASIK eye surgery. I'm saying farewell to contacts and glasses and hello to new eyesight—PRAISE GOD! It is amazing! GOD makes so many miracles happen!

I've waited for a long time to have this procedure done. I remember when I first got my glasses from Dr. White in Cushing, Oklahoma. I was in the third or fourth grade. He told me to look outside at the street sign before I put on my glasses. I told him I couldn't read it. He placed my new pair of glasses on my face and ta-da—I could read the street sign. It was an amazing day!

In fifth grade, I got my first pair of contacts. Oh, that was tough. I remember being in the girls' bathroom next to the fifth-grade classroom, trying to put my contact back in after it had been bothering me. It was tough because my first pair was semi-hard.

In sixth grade, I remember when Dr. White gave me my first pair of gel contacts. I was going to be able to wear them 24/7—I was very excited! I got to stay at Jana Woods's house that night. I'll never forget waking up and being able to see. It was fantastic—nothing like I ever thought it could be!

The years went by, but I do remember losing a contact at the Cushing High School football field. My mom was not happy. She made me look until we found it. Impossible, right? Nope, we found it. Believe it or not—we did. My mom taught me a valuable lesson in not stopping until it was done—on anything! Zoom forward— twenty years of wearing contacts—when I first checked in to LASIK, they told me I needed to wait until after I had my kids. Well, it's been almost five-and-a-half years of trying and no kids yet. I needed a distraction—but more than anything—I needed something to happen.

Six weeks ago, I started wearing my glasses daily. This was not fun. Since I've been running, it makes for a pain in the butt! I decided to get it over with and made an appointment at TLC LASIK Eye Center over the phone. My nerves were twisted—what if they told me I couldn't have it done, because I wasn't a candidate for the procedure? That would have surely sucked since I had waited ten years to get to this point.

I went to TLC LASIK Eye Center on Monday, March 23, 2009, at 2:30 p.m. Cristin Handlin, best friend for twenty years, was with me. The people were great. They told me that my eyes couldn't get any worse. I was lucky they didn't say that I was ineligible. I owe that to God! Thank You, Lord!

Since I wore contacts for four hours the Saturday before—yes, at the Snake Run—I had to wait one more week before they'd make a final decision. On Monday, March 30, for three whole hours, I got tested and did my pre-op testing for the bladeless LASIK. Yippee, I was on my way!

For the next week and a half, my nerves—lots of nerves—built up for the actual surgery day. I thought I was going to vomit, but I survived by the grace of God. Surgery day was on Thursday, April 9, 2009. With my mom driving, I showed up at two thirty in the afternoon. The time did not zoom or go by quickly! I sure am glad my mom and hubby were there with me! Time is never easy for me. I don't ever have enough of it!

Anyway, I looked out of Liz Schad's office, thinking back to my early moments with my eyesight. It's hard to believe it's been twenty-two years since my journey started. Joy overcame me, knowing that this, too, would be a moment that I'd never forget. As the young lady gave me the lowdown on eye drops and prevention, my pulse beat pretty fast! Beat after beat—I questioned my decision and thought to myself that I was Krazy with a capital K!

Finally, it was my turn. When Dr. Anthony Economou told me to get on the table and relax, he stopped and said, "Wait, what does that sign on the wall say?" I said, "It's blue!" He said, "No, what does it say?" I said, "Blue, because all I can see is a blue sign!" We all laughed.

Now let me tell you—having LASIK is nuts! It is the most bizarre thing I have ever done in my life. First, I was under one machine where my flap was created on both sides—probably the weirdest feeling ever. Next, I got moved to another machine—daring, I would say. I thought I was going to freak out and not make it through. I had to keep looking at this orange fuzzy light, which at some point came into focus—oh yes! Finally, they had this little tool to smooth the flap back to normal. The thought of this really does make me squeamish.

The time came for the same question he had asked at the start: "What does the sign say?" At that point I said, "Wow!" He responded, "No, really, what does it say?" It really did say, "WOW!" It was funny. I could see it! It was nuts! It's been four days since the surgery and post-twenty-four-hour appointment on Friday. I was already a week ahead of schedule. My vision is in and out. It will take three to six months to even out, but it truly is a miracle from God. I go back for my one-week checkup on Friday, April 17. Praying God will keep the recovery going in full, complete mode!

Highlighting some truths:
- *Faith in God is the way!*
- *Hope that He will always have my back through anything!*
- *Peace in knowing He takes care of me no matter what!*
- *Time heals all things when given to Him!*
- *Quiet time with the Lord brings great healing!*
- *"Wow" is what I say when I see God's hand at work!*
- *Happy to believe!*
- *Dedicating my miracle to God above!*

> - *Timing is everything!*
> - *Quietly resting in Him!*
> - *Understanding comes from God when you listen!*
> - *My family and friends—Mom, hubby, Jodie, Cristin, Jennifer Tresslar, Ale, Aunt Tracy—who were here for me!*
> - *Prayer came from many people, and I'm grateful!*
> - *Ultimate trust in God above that nothing can come between Him and me!*
> - *Value what God has given you because it is valuable!*
> - *I'm in God's hands!*
>
> *XOXO,*
> *Chrissy*

Tears are still streaming as I reread and typed this for you. Last night, I bawled and let the tears pour out. This is something I forgot I wrote before we stopped fertility treatments and the pregnancies with Lilian Grace and Piper Allegra. God has always been here for me while truly placing me in crazy but beautifully unique places—always choosing with purpose.

My pity parties are signs that I'm just overwhelmed with my current load. God is working in and hopefully through me. I have more processing to do on this side of someone else's grief journey, which has really highlighted many moments from our past and current journeys. I can only do what I feel God has led me to do to the best of my ability, especially remembering to step aside so He can do what is needed on a daily basis. The pity parties and confusion reveal I've tried to control it all. I'm scooting over to the passenger side once again so He can take back the wheel. I may have to jump into the back seat to avoid taking over again!

I want to always be where He needs me to be. I don't

want to be rundown because I was selfish and self-dependent. God has so graciously blessed me with an amazing life. My common problem is getting in the way. He links me with some very powerful journeys with godly people who could relate to Job in the Bible.

Life is not guaranteed here on earth, but eternity is a promise to those who believe! So many of us right now are walking a journey where the desires of our heart overwhelm us daily! We feel like there is no progress or forward movement into success. God has got you! He has His comforting arms wrapped around you! He's got this! He is the Almighty! Step aside and let Him bless you and further His kingdom!

I may not know what my future holds when someone asks about the Warrior Princess Foundation, Warrior Princess Trail Run, The Phoenix Experience, book deals, etc. But my God holds my future! He's always done a tremendous, miraculous job when I let Him lead! I know He will open and close doors that lead me to continuing or adjusting my direction to current or new purposes. Praying for clarity and peace in all our journeys!

MARCH 20, 2013

215 › Beam Me Up

Traveling and processing—a change in the journey . . .

And God answers . . . He always answers—especially in His timing. I struggle with His timing every day, yet I see the beauty of His timing when I get refocused.

Morgan Haynes, daughter of my dear friends Rick and Robin Haynes, became part of a select group over a week ago. She became a mother and now has an angel baby in heaven. Little Zoey Nicole lived four days, yet she helped this mommy see from a whole other perspective—someone on the outside looking in.

This past week and a half has been really hard, especially seeing little Zoey carried down to her cradle at her celebration of life service. See, I only have my grief, my daily battles, and my daily successes. Morgan has to do her own walk at eighteen years old—remembering Zoey while processing daily for the rest of her life.

Being the outsider on someone else's journey is hard in its own right. I recognize the urge to fix it or make everything go away. I understand the desire to do anything and everything for that person. I see the needs yet feel helpless. I acknowledge what each of you had to witness in my journey and wanted to do but couldn't. Some people are not always meant to do, be a part of, or are given the opportunity.

Even though I was on the inside, I didn't know what I needed. I typed and shared everything. I tried my best to communicate, but at the end of the day, I really didn't know.

I'm speechless a lot of the time (I know that's hard for some to grasp since I'm a talker). I have a vast array of emotions I go through daily. I ride a rollercoaster daily with no clue what that ride will be like on any given day. I have a good life—a very blessed one despite all that I go through on this grieving journey. It's all part of life!

Since I have been trying to stay afloat, I've missed many boats to help me get to the next destination. I've swum and been successful with some opportunities, but I've missed many more. Perhaps the fog is finally lifting. My numbness has almost worn completely off. I'm waking up and realizing that life has moved on. It's natural! It's okay! It's a good thing.

On the outside, I get what it's like when you are not solely connected to the main source of grief. We get a pass! We each have our own stuff to live out. I've missed a ton of life cycles—mommies being pregnant, babies being born, lives expiring (deaths), beginnings with new jobs, and families uprooting and moving to new homes. It's natural to not be able to keep up, but I've also been wrapped up in my own little world. Little Zoey will be remembered by me once in a while. Her mother will miss her baby girl every single day—not forgetting, even when life gets busy.

On the inside of my life, I wake up every day and make the decision to stay as positive as I can—trying not to miss Lilian, where it completely consumes me so I can keep doing life. I admit that I've not had it together. I've been negative. I wish I could have been more present and completely rid myself earlier of dwelling and griping. We truly are all human—especially me!

I wish some people could have been more patient with me. Others were too patient. I've been reading through my "need to read" email folder that originally held almost a thousand messages. I'm finally down to a few hundred. To those who sent me the most beautiful, encouraging words, I thank you a million times for taking the time to type them out. I wish I could have read them back then, but I was overwhelmed, tired, exhausted, and not ready to read what might be there. On one hand, I may have needed to string it out this long because I was afraid of what I'd do when I had read everything. Perhaps I thought it would be over—done—finished. On the other hand, I hope you didn't think I was ignoring you.

I believe God gives us His perfect timing, even if we can't appreciate it at the moment. He knows exactly what we need when we need it. There are people I don't even know who sent me love and encouragement. There are others I completely missed who were so involved in messaging. Know that if you haven't heard from me, you have touched my heart and helped make this grieving mother cry happy tears of joy, peace, grace, and love. I thank you from the bottom of my heart.

Sometimes our goodness is met with silence. We will never know how our good deeds have blessed someone. Know this: you have given me life, fuel, hope, and strength. More importantly, you've helped me keep walking this blessed journey God has given me. The only way I can repay you is to keep doing what God needs me to do!

Sometimes our goodness is met with silence.

I hope to get back to each of you, yet I may not ever get to everyone. Thank you for being here for me without needing anything in return. I'm sorry to those who felt neglected. I do appreciate all past and present help, even if I haven't personally ever gotten to tell you. I pray God blesses each of you—no matter how big or small your part in our lives.

April 25, 2013, marks Lilian's three-year birthday anniversary. Three—three—yes, it's already been three years since I caught a glance of Lilian Grace from afar while the doctors worked on both of us, one of the greatest adventures of my life. What has time taught me? With an abundance of wonderful skills and strengths, I've gotten a swift, heavy dose of "it's not all about me."

And you know what? It really isn't about me. I want to remember what God taught us through Lilian Grace's life. It's not about you, me, or us. It's about Him and His kingdom—a bigger purpose—while forgetting about what doesn't feel right and remembering what is right! All is a miracle! Each of us has a purpose to live out with the exact amount of time it should take to complete—some short, some long.

Little Zoey has warped me at full speed to climb out of the mud—pride, skewed perception, bitterness, anger, etc.—I've been stuck in. Her family's journey is helping me forgive so many that never needed or deserved my anger. Her journey is helping me get out of the way for the millionth time so God can make things happen. Watching from afar has given me a space for peace that I should have let God give me a long time ago. I just didn't want to see it through someone else's eyes.

I don't want to take away from those who think about Lilian Grace often while shedding tears and always loving her. I want you to know that being her mother and watching another mother with her baby girl has helped me lower my expectations for others. I had let bitterness and anger exist in places where it never should have existed.

I'll be as honest as I can be—as you know too often that I am—I have been mad at many (people) for so many reasons, like not participating in events that involve Lilian Grace. I at least expected that they'd call and say, "Sorry, we can't be a part of this or that." Guess what though? I was mad. I kept hearing how everyone knew what I was going through, yet they happily continued their lives so easily. I, on the other hand, had no choice.

For me, missing Lilian Grace will always be a daily challenge because God made our connection extra special through shared blood, nursing, and life. I was constantly in charge of healthy choices to help her grow in my womb. I was her direct line. She was a part of me. I look at Piper, our second baby girl, and that connection is just as strong as I watch her grow. When I'm away from Piper for an hour, I want her right here with me. I feel the same with Lilian Grace—a natural feeling for a mother. It's what we do. I know I can't get the relief I need until I'm reunited with her. God provided what I needed to survive the separation anxiety from her. I praise Him for His constant support.

I've lifted many prayers up about the Warrior Princess Foundation, the Warrior Princess Trail Run, and my life in general. God answered many prayers, concerns, and directions by communication through other people. I absolutely love all of you who are loving God and loving people. Your connection with God is important and helps me daily in my walk with Him. He has blessed me with you and your obedient hearts. I found it fitting to make some announcements here first:

Today is the last day to guarantee a shirt and medal for the Third Annual Warrior Princess Trail Run. The price goes up by five dollars. We can't guarantee a shirt or size that will fit you after today. Make sure to complete your registration. Can't be there? Sign up as a shadow runner and support us from a distance. We completely understand if you can't be a part of this. Just lift us, runners, volunteers, businesses, and T18/13 families up in your prayers! We've got November Lily blessing us with live music and also a photo opportunity with the Little Mermaid on race day. The theme is Lilian's last monthly birthday with us—Under the Sea! She was the most precious, gorgeous, red-wig-wearing Little Mermaid I've ever seen. Oh, how I cherish remembering that last monthly birthday with her!

EXTRA SPECIAL ANNOUNCEMENT: This will be your last chance to run the trail race at Keystone State Park Bike & Hike Trail for Lilian's birthday anniversary on April 25. Since we followed Lilian's life from months and years (each race represented a month she lived), we will transition the Warrior Princess Trail Run to the Warrior Princess Angel Run set for Saturday, August 3, 2013, for our Three-and-a-Half Annual Run (this will be the race from now on, set for the first Saturday of August every year). Chandler Park is tentatively the new home of our race to help raise money for T18/T13 families while getting to bless all families who have lost loved ones.

There will be the traditional 1.03-mile fun run/walk with an added 103-minute race where you run a loop (two to three miles) and see how many times you can run the loop (miles) in the allotted time (103-minute run is created by Ken Childress and inspired by his Three- and Six-Hour Snake Run). We will have an option for people to honor their loved ones, who are now angels, no matter the age or how long they lived—each life has a purpose!

We appreciate all of you who keep walking, running, and

supporting us along our journey. This is a perfect transition from Lilian living to her angelic journey. She lived three-and-a-half glorious months (103 fun-filled days). I love that we get to do two races in one year to make this transition extra special for all of us. More information will be at the race and updated on our website as soon as we can. Since her angelversary is August 5, we chose this time of year—the heat is a perfect bonus to represent one's journey through T18/13. It will be a morning race due to the time of the year! Here are the proposed dates for the new race until our Tenth Annual Race:

Saturday, August 3, 2013—Three-and-a-Half Annual
Saturday, August 2, 2014—Fourth Annual
Saturday, August 1, 2015—Fifth Annual
Saturday, August 6, 2016—Sixth Annual
Saturday, August 5, 2017—Seventh Annual (Seventh Heaven, so cool)
Saturday, August 4, 2018—Eighth Annual
Saturday, August 3, 2019—Ninth Annual
Saturday, August 1, 2020—Tenth Annual

This year's theme for our August Warrior Princess Angel Run will be Sleeping Beauty in memory of the last time we held Lilian before saying goodbye. The races after this will be focused on angels. So far, everyone has been very enthusiastic, which gives me a different kind of energy that I need. I feel a great peace about it all. I'm glad to feel like I'm headed in a good direction.

Again, thank you for everything, especially for the continued participation in my crazy journey. I know I say it often, but I really am far from perfect—I'm human. I do wish I could be beamed up and see Lilian now and then, but

I understand this is how it's supposed to be. God truly does know what's best. God is Big and continues to show how big, every day! God puts up with me. Talk to Michael—he definitely understands how big a job that is every day! I'm glad God is Big enough!

I leave you with the beautiful song "Beam Me Up" by P!nk that says everything and gave me a good cry today. Thanks to multiple people who posted and talked about it. Someday I will live it up with all the family I've lost. Being able to see Lilian Grace and her siblings, whom I never got to see or meet, will be awesome, but seeing God will be even cooler.

I picture Lilian Grace as an almost-three-year-old—running into my arms with a huge smile on her face. She kisses me all over my face as I hug her so tightly—never wanting to let go. I'm glad He's made our brains so complex and complicated because that image is everything to me, as well as the other images I think up every day when it comes to her.

God, beam me up! I'd love a minute to check in. I know it would never be enough though. I'd want to be beamed up on a regular basis. If I knew it could happen often, I'd be satisfied. I'd hold her and give her as many kisses as I could in that minute. I'd say, "I love you to the moon and back and for all eternity." What would you do or say if you could be beamed up? Who would you want to see?

JULY 11, 2013

216 › Ticktock

When my birthday approaches, my grieving picks up speed. Ticktock—ticktock—the ticktock sounds can't even be heard because life keeps going and moving at a steady pace, with me feeling left behind here and there. Besides getting to experience a second birthday without Lilian Grace, I've decided to start running and training again to counter that feeling. For the past few weeks, it's made for lots of time to think, cry, and process while beginning new healing in my journey. Praise God that I'm back!

Perhaps, someday, I will get to run 103 miles for my sweet Lilian Grace and honor the number of days she lived here on earth, as well as conquer a major accomplishment for myself. Training has been good for my soul, yet it's hard to tackle such a ginormous-sized goal. Many baby steps are required, with dedication, hope, mercy, and grace. Life will always include interruptions, but I trust God to keep me going through each of the distractions!

As I put more mileage on my legs, I know running is my one stress reliever where I can process and deal with my journey—one press of the foot at a time into the dirt or pavement as sweat forms and helps remove the processed by-products from my system. It all gets me closer to another part of being mended and healed. One thing at a time in life is just as important as each step at a time on a trail or road in training—one mile at a time!

Many of you who are going through your own loss—death, divorce, or disappointment—can relate to the fact that there's never an end here on earth. Though I'm stronger than I used to be, I can't sit here and say that my grieving journey is done or close to over. Not talking about my grief doesn't make it go away. I still have to wake up each day knowing I can't change the situation or what happened. I can't hide what was revealed of people and life. I can't fix people or relationships. I can't have Lilian here to make millions of memories like I do with Piper. Lilian gets to be loved and missed from afar. There's no remedy for missing her until the day I die when I joyfully join her. I can't change the past, but I can face, process, and move forward from it. When it comes to Lilian Grace, I accepted that she's not coming back on the day she left. It was her destiny and purpose, and I am so proud of her fight and spirit. She gave me new sight and purpose.

What my grieving journey involves, more now than anything, is dealing with the aftermath—seeing and dealing with people's core character, discovering what life really involves, and becoming very disappointed in many realities of life. I saw people who weren't ready for our journey and who still aren't. I experienced simultaneously how ugly and beautiful life can be. I discovered the realities of my relationships and experiences—the real-world version. I fought while losing so much energy in stupid, petty circumstances. Still, fighting and dealing with them has prevented us from being better people and making the most of our present situation.

Since my eyes were opened three years ago, I've discovered that we as humans can wallow in the past—even letting it become chains that prevent us from being ready to climb our next mountain. Those chains wear on us as we waste energy not dealing and letting go. I don't want to miss out on being prepared for the next mountain. I want to be at full strength. I want to embody the full armor of God. I was on my biggest mountain with Lilian Grace, and I praised God that I was prepared like He wanted me to be. I want to be at that level again.

Right now, I'm in a holding tank, perhaps in limbo between Lilian's mountain and my next one. Ever feel like you have a thousand options to move beyond your circumstances but have no clue which way to go? Ever feel like you keep trying one thing after another, yet you aren't getting anywhere? This sums me up at this point. I'm sure I'm exhausting to those who hear one crazy idea after another from my mouth. I can only imagine what goes on in their minds when I come up with yet another idea that I could be doing. Maybe they see me in a circus—my life—where I'm several acts in one show! I'm sure it's entertaining.

I've been paying more attention to my thoughts, words, and directions lately. As I reflect, it scares me because I see a broken woman—loving God but lost and stuck—all over the place with her ideas and direction on what to do next. I'm that kid who gets to be in a room with a hundred toys and somehow finds ways to play with about 90 percent of them at once. It's tiring! It leaves me stuck in the room with all the toys, not able to escape and share them all. I know God is not a God of confusion. I have plans—dozens of them.

The ticktock of the clock seems louder—it freaks me out. I put pressure on myself for a handful of commitments, yet I feel distanced from most of them. Don't get me wrong—I have been living life and making beautiful memories when it comes to family and friends. I just know that, when it comes to my purpose in life, I'm all over the playing field and spreading myself thin.

Looking at the bigger picture of the journey I'm traveling, I've decided it's time to start choosing the fork in the road that bears multitudes of fruit, not just surviving with some fruit. Yesterday, I was mapping out the fun run/walk at Chandler Park for the upcoming race on August 3. I did about a dozen loops and started to crack up. For many things, I've been on the same loop for so many years. You can still be moving and using energy when looping, but at the end, you are still where you started. You miss out on what's beyond the loop!

I don't want to loop! I want to be the pioneer God designed me to be. I want what God has in store for me. I don't want to waste His time. It's time for me to buckle down, get focused, eliminate the distractions, and start living out what God has in store for me. I need to pray, meditate, and listen for Him to reveal what is next. I need to let Him guide me through each fork in the road so I can go down the right road He has created for me. So far, I've been moving yet looping on my journey.

> *I need to pray, meditate, and listen for Him to reveal what is next.*

I don't know about you, but I'm exhausted from holding on, looping, and bearing small harvests. I do want my "God be Big" moments, because God is Big through all parts of my life. Living out His purpose and owning His timing is the greatest feeling. It's a high that can't be taught, only lived out. Perhaps the feeling of limbo or the holding tank is because I checked out. I let life get in the way of attending church, spending quiet time with Him, and being more

RAINBOWS AND BRAINSTORMS 153

consistent with praying—just talking to Him.

I prayed, but not like in the past. I tried to do a Bible study but didn't complete it. I attended church but took a seven-week sabbatical. You can live a life for God and still not be where you could be. You can check out easily! Enough is enough! I'm checking back in. I'm done wallowing. I'm done not being as committed. I want to jump off the loops and see what the next road has to offer. I want to bear an abundant harvest for Him. I am done being stuck!

Hang on, because the ticktock of the clock can keep doing its thing while I create my own ticktock in pioneering His plans for me with His guidance all the way. Ticktock, here I go! How about you? Praying God guides each of us in His plans for us. May we each face our pasts to break the chains that hold us back! Hoping we can all bear fruit for Him—AMEN!

Never let go! Don't ever stop looking at Him. He truly will turn our storms into magnificent rainbows to change and make a difference in other lives. If it were easy, we'd just be sitting on a couch, getting nowhere. Who wants that? Not me! Love you all!

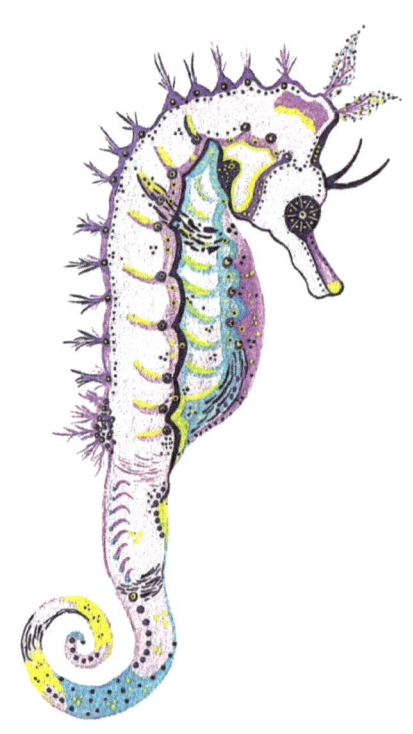

AUGUST 14, 2013

217 › Three-Year Angelversary

Most of this entry was typed earlier in August (*the part in italics*), yet I forgot to post it. I think it's time that I posted and added some commentary (in regular type). Updates were made to this entry on August 21, 2013, and September 27, 2013. Hoping it's not too confusing. Sorry for the length!

August 5, 2013, marked three years since Lilian Grace earned her wings. Two days before, we had the honor of hosting the Three-and-a-Half Annual Warrior Princess Angel Run. I am always amazed at how God pulls it all together, even amid my stress and life. I'd like to type many wonderful reviews and give all the beautiful details, but it's not what's on my mind and in my heart.

To tell the rest of the story, I must go back to May 3, 2013, when I found myself in a magnetic resonance imaging (MRI) machine, listening to some rockin' Christian music mixed with scary, loud noises. Since November 2012, I've been experiencing a multitude of symptoms that led me to a neurologist and heart doctor. (The heart, thank God, has been ruled out.) I can't remember the song that was on, but I do remember part of my daydream while in the machine.

I saw myself in the full armor of God, which brought tears to my eyes. I wasn't sure if it meant to buckle up and put on the armor to battle again or if it was just to remind me to always fight. Life, thus far, has proven to me that no matter the situation or circumstance, God's armor has been a big part in my conquering and survival wins. God has not ever left me. He has been merciful and faithful.

I prayed after that daydream. I told God, through my tirelessness and brokenness, that I'll do whatever it takes to further His kingdom by living out whatever comes my way. I just need Him to push me aside daily. Also, I need Him to keep being Big and give me what and who I need throughout this or any other battle I face. I hope it doesn't wear out my husband, baby girl, family, and friends.

I am truly blessed by so many believers in my life. I have amazing fellow prayer warriors who battle right next to me. Though I'm not in some of their lives currently, they are here for me whether we talk or not. It brings me comfort. I am fortunate that God has surprised me with phenomenal friends that I never would have expected to be right here at this time, battling alongside me—even better than I can.

To continue—I did find out before leaving on our summer trip at the end of May that they discovered a pineal gland cyst in my brain. I just had a cousin, who at the time was fighting brain cancer, come back into my life after years of not being in contact. Then there's Stevie Patrick, who has fought brain cancer for over three years. Come to find out, there are many added to the list dealing with cysts or tumors this summer.

I'm not sure what it all means, but I know that everything happens for a reason. My cousin passed away this summer. Currently, Stevie is still fighting. There is much prayer needed—a miracle even—for so many still fighting. All this has made me more nervous and scared than I like to admit to the world. I try so hard to do things on my own, but I am trying to change that. Update: Stevie was called to her heavenly home last night (9-26-13).

My symptoms have worsened in the past month (July). I had my three-month MRI on August 1, 2013. A deeper look was taken, yet I've had to wait to talk to the doctor to break down the reports. This afternoon, on August 21, 2013, I will find out how my journey changes. I've researched and compared my two reports with online data and such. At that appointment, I felt more confused and frustrated. I know the cyst grew a tiny bit and that the measurements make it a large cyst. Thankfully, God is taking care of me, and I will see a neurosurgeon on October 9, 2013. I'm at peace knowing I'll be in different hands, and hopefully, he can give me peace and more choices.

I've pretty much had myself completely scared out of my mind. My close friends and sisters have been wonderful in listening to my fears through tears. I apologize to everyone for not sharing this until now. This summer has been full of sickness for my loved ones, relationship changes, deaths, new discoveries, and stresses. I'm not sure if some of my symptoms are related to the stress, but regardless, I know something is wrong. I've been right seven other times when dealing with sickness and surgeries. I really hope I'm wrong this go around. September hasn't lessened my stress much, but it has been a month of making peace.

I decided after my last appointment that I would finally face some of my wounds and let God start to heal them. These have been postponed because I let pride and bitterness get in the way. Those two things can really make a person stagnant. I praise God for giving me these past three years to learn and change—God willing, to change into who He needs me to be. I'm thankful for listening ears and forgiving hearts.

I've let myself go to the best- and worst-case scenarios in order to ready myself for the good, bad, or ugly of what news the doctors will give me at any point in this new journey. Right now, I'm not as afraid. God has been gracious in reminding me of some powerful things—He will never fail me.

Michael and I had a date last night (8-20-13). I like to think of it as the calm before the storm either finishes or another one begins. It felt good to know we had a plan for many scenarios. He has been here with me the entire time. I feel like he's gotten a lemon when it comes to my health, but he stays right by my side. I'm glad God gave me him. He is a fighter and a survivor. He's willing to uproot our lives and get me to the best of the best if that is where the journey leads us—now that is dedication and true love.

We laughed about me having nine lives. Sadly, if it were true—I've used up seven lives thus far when dealing with major medical issues and surgeries. I do know that God has wanted me here because I could have easily been called "home" seven times already! Thinking about it all, I'm not as scared—either way, I'm blessed beyond measure. After watching two Warriors earn their wings this week, I want more than anything to be where God needs me. Wyatt Griffith and Stevie Crowder lived out their mission and purpose here on earth. They graciously earned their wings.

PRAISE GOD for healing! PRAISE HIM for showing us that when we live our lives for Him—though it is not without pain and suffering—the ultimate reward is spending eternity with Him instead of fire and eternal heartbreak. God does have a purpose for each of us, no matter how small or big the role we play in life.

If this cyst is (fill in the blank), I'm going to be good. God's got my back. For three years, my heart has been torn between heaven and earth. For almost two years, I've experienced what it's like to long to be with one daughter in heaven and another here on earth. It's never easy, but God comforts me. He has healed me of many things. I'm not saying I want to die. I'm just saying I'm not afraid of living out God's plan for my life so He can call me home.

I've cried many tears for Stevie, my cousin, and others. The major one on my mind right now is Stevie Patrick, who is a wonderful example of the Proverbs 31 woman. She has fought a good fight for over three years now. I know that whether God heals her on earth or in heaven, she has proved God is Big and provides. She has let His light shine bright through all that she does. God decided to call her home last night (9-26-13). She got to be with her family. She is healed and showing off her gorgeous smile at the pearly gates. I'm excited that Lilian will get to meet such a beautiful soul and get lots of time with her.

Also this past week, our lil buddy, Superman, a.k.a. Wyatt Griffith, earned his wings. My heart breaks for the beginning of a new grieving journey for many, but it rejoices knowing that Wyatt is getting to be his amazing self with heavenly superpowers. I picture him walking and running around with his super long hair, laughing and playing with my sweet baby girl—cape and all.

The night Lilian Grace earned her wings, I accepted that her purpose had been completed. I've always had peace about that. I've just had to deal with the aftermath of relationships, adjusting to a different me, and missing her like crazy. I thank God for answering my prayers. I wanted her to live out her purpose and to be healed. The how and length weren't what I thought they would be, but the what and why were answered.

In all of this, I've done my share of reflecting. I've made phone calls that should have been done long before now. I want peace with everyone and peace flowing through them as well. I know I've scared some by my calls, but I needed to do it before I found out how my journey will change. I needed some of it completed just in case I found out everything was going to be okay—minor with hardly any treatment.

Sadly, we wait until it's really bad to change our paths with some of those in our lives. It's easy to let pride and judgment get in the way. We all make choices. We all sin. We all try to live out our lives each day in the best way we know how. I want to do more than just try and get by. I really want to be where God needs me to be.

I'm glad I never posted this earlier in August, because it was meant for exactly today. I know that my cyst has grown just a tiny bit. My symptoms make life interesting, but I'm not letting it stop me—Stevie and her family taught me this. Stevie's and Wyatt's families taught me a courage that I never knew I could have above the time with Lilian. They have given me new hope!

I'm at a place in my grieving journey where I can look back and see the things I should have done differently. I've made peace with those times, because I know where I was at the time and why I originally made the choices I did. I do know I've learned from my childishness, selfishness, and controlling ways (I'm still a work in progress). When I'm faced with the negative and sad, I stop to think a lot more before reacting than I used to. PRAISE GOD!

Wyatt Griffith and Stevie Patrick have been a major link in my life with Lilian Grace—with and without her. This week has been rough, because I'm having to let go of more things I wish I could hold on to. One thing is for sure—I can hold on to what God has in store. He's moving some major mountains. He's everywhere, and I'm seeing Him even on major networks, on TV shows. It's really cool to watch.

I hope that, wherever you are or wherever you go, you remember to step aside and let God. I've watched these families show the greatest courage and obedience. I know for me, there are days I'm tired, frustrated, and negative, but God only asks that I give it all to Him to do the rest. He gets us through battles that never stop coming.

Piper and I had a rough day on Wednesday for different

reasons. She got up at three thirty in the morning and never went back to sleep. I was dealing with food poisoning, and Michael took care of her. She struggled the whole day. When it was my turn while Michael went to church, she did not want to sleep. Actually, she didn't want to do anything but cry. I thought I might lose it.

I held her in the rocking chair and started laughing through my tears. I was trying to take care of her by myself. I started praying out loud and just let everything pour out that needed to be said at the time. Piper and I both calmed down. She even went back to sleep. PRAISE GOD! It sometimes is that simple, yet other times it's not.

"Overcomer" by Mandisa is a strong song that reminds us we can overcome when we trust Him. The hits will keep coming, but He will make you stronger so you can keep getting back up—staying in the fight! His promises are true! He sees and does it all. He wants us to make it to the final round—our winnings will be heaven!

Thanks to everyone who has called, texted, and messaged me this week—knowing that losing Wyatt and Stevie is a bigger deal than I let myself realize. I'm blessed to have you all in my life. May God continue to be with each of us on the journey we are walking. Don't quit! Don't give in! You are an overcomer because God has you!

DECEMBER 9, 2013

218 › Worn Yet Calling Me Higher

> *Journal Entry from October 8, 2013*
>
> *Come daydream with me for a few minutes... I see myself sitting on a fabulous swing hanging from an enormous old oak tree. The sun beams down on me, keeping me warm and safe. I look out into a golden field and see a three-and-a-half-year-old sweet little girl with golden, wheat-colored curls flowing in the wind and a gorgeous smile highlighting her tanned face. She runs up to me and stops to stare. I want to get up, but I can't. I stare back in amazement. I take in all her beauty and grace. I place my arms out in front of me, hoping she will move forward. She can't. I can't. We are stuck just looking at each other, wanting it all to be different.*

Two months ago, I typed the paragraph above. I've sat down at this computer multiple times and typed out rather lengthy entries, yet all of them somehow were wiped clean except for the above daydream. I'm cracking up at this moment, because I can now see that all the time spent on those entries was a painstaking representation of my life at this point.

Each time, the words typed had their own agenda and were full of wisdom. Each made me feel like I was on a roll that left me right back at the beginning. How true is this in our lives? At least in mine, it rings true. I find myself going in every direction, yet somehow find myself at a standstill or back at the beginning. I'm exhausted and worn out from all the busywork I'm doing. "Worn" by Tenth Avenue North has played on my radio and computer a lot lately. It has given me the chance to let go of some of that weariness and tiredness.

No matter how worn I am, God is letting me do really cool things despite my ability to get in the way—thankfully, only in small increments. I know I'm meeting wonderful people on every adventure, yet there are many more I could be meeting. I have seen God's amazing plans. He graciously has produced fruit during it all, yet I know I'm not harvesting the abundant fruit that He has planned for my life. I'm so worn out from trying to be a million things while going in a dozen directions. I feel like my percentages are out of whack and I'm misguided on my path.

My newest busyness and craziness started in August when I decided to start working outside of my personal training business to catch up on unpaid bills since my clientele had diminished. It led me to take on a handful of jobs that were three to five hours here and there, because I was scared that I wasn't capable of doing full-time work in this season of my life. I wouldn't recommend it to anyone, unless you are a college student earning your degree. A full-time job would have been easier.

There it is—that's what I feel like right now. I feel like I've been thrown back to my beginnings after high school. I had a ton of little jobs to make ends meet back then. I didn't mind because I was earning my degree. It's hard when you've had a career and loved it with all your heart and then find yourself after major brokenness to not be there. I know that leaving my amazing career when Lilian came was meant to be, but it doesn't make three-and-a-half years later any easier when trying to get to where I need to be.

I have to admit that each job has actually been a wonderful tool for God to sharpen me and heal more of my broken heart. I've gotten tougher. I've learned I have some hidden skills. I've realized I miss my full-time career and the people I've worked with. I know right now it seems that the door is closed, yet I get tired of trying to bust that door open. It's meant for me to trust God and let Him reveal the next steps I should take.

DECEMBER 13, 2013

The above was last typed and saved on December 9, 2013 (with a few words added to complete the thought process). It's interesting to note that, less than a week later, my life has warped light speed ahead. The door to my next mountain swung wide open. I'm still in shock about what the last five days have been like for me and my family. Many of you have been updated on my health, but most of you have not. I am at the point where I need to start my own CaringBridge journal. I apologize to many of you whom I have not personally gotten to call to give you the updates and changes in my health and life. Know that I love you, but there's just not enough hours or energy to call everyone, or I would.

I must stop writing in Lilian Grace's journal today. This makes me sad knowing that this is possibly my last entry in her journal. I say this here and now—I owe God, Lilian, and her God-filled life with getting me equipped for my new journey. Without God and her help—along with a multitude of others—I wouldn't be in a good place. Of course, I find it fitting to end this entry with the song "Called Me Higher" by All Sons and Daughters that I heard Shad and Rachel (Foley), my fabulous, God-loving friends, sing at our church (Solace Church) recently. I sat among my fellow brothers and sisters in Christ and cried like a baby. I knew at that point my journey was getting ready to alter drastically, and I needed to focus on God because things were going to be far from easy!

The song is a perfect reminder that God has always called me higher in my life. I've been through many mountains, and He has always provided for my every need! During this past year, I have felt as if I were on a hamster wheel—not getting anywhere yet working my tail off. I now see how He graciously has been molding, shaping, and preparing me for what this mountain was going to hit me with next.

This one is a doozy, and I know you are ready for me to share. Please visit http://www.caringbridge.org/visit/chrissywhitten to get filled in on my next mountain. Brace yourself, yet know that God is all over this. He knows what He is doing! I was born for this! I am better on the extreme, stressful mountains than I am at the normal, daily ones. God doesn't make bad things happen. I believe the devil really doesn't like me, so here I am to climb, fight, and lean more on God—once again!

I love you all and want you to know that I am so blessed to have you on this journey!

CHRISSY'S CARINGBRIDGE

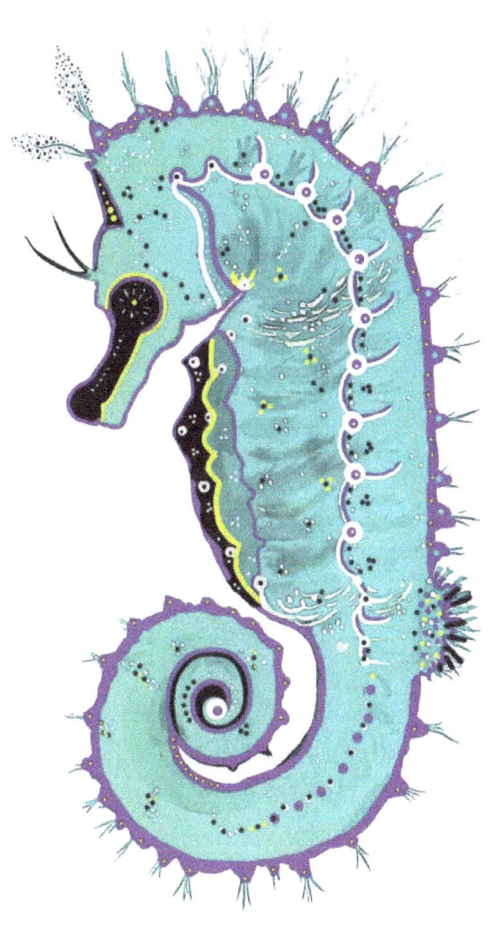

DECEMBER 15, 2013

1 › The Journey Changes

First off, God is Big! His fingerprints are all over my journey. He has given me grace and mercy in all. I love that He has me in His hands. He meets me where I am. I feel total peace and know He's going to be victorious in this, no matter the outcome. I am so blessed to be part of His will and family. He loves me unconditionally, and I am forgiven with a promise of everlasting life with Him!

Bear with me. This first entry in my personal CaringBridge account is lengthy because I need to get everyone on the same page. I will have other relatives and friends giving updates about my progress when I cannot do it myself. Please know that informational updates may be posted multiple times per day or may not be posted every day. Please note that this will be the only place we update people. I wish we could call everyone individually, but it's just not possible or feasible. I'd like to encourage you to sign up for text or email updates that will automatically let you know when a new journal entry is posted here.

Please stop and say a prayer before reading this. Ask God to give you comfort and understanding while remembering that He will keep providing in all that consumes this journey. I know those who already have heard the story got intimate details, which shook many. This is a summary of my journey to this point. I need all my prayer warriors and beyond on this new mountain. It's going to be my second hardest mountain (the first being the loss of my baby girl) that I've had to face thus far in my life. My journey to the present started a year ago in November 2012, when I started having the following symptoms:

- Passing out or going to sleep without being able to wake up: I would know that I was getting ready to go out, but there was nothing I could do to stop it. I'd be out anywhere from twenty minutes to almost two hours.
- Blurred and double vision: I went to several checkups to make sure that my LASIK surgery from 2009 wasn't failing all of a sudden.
- Constant nausea: I thought I was pregnant often, but I'd take a pregnancy test and it would be negative every time.
- Super tired from lack of sleep: I would be in bed for eight hours, but my wristband sleep tracker would only register three hours at times.

I went to Dr. Nickels, my allergist (who has saved my life twice), thinking my allergies were all out of whack again. All my blood work and prick tests showed I had no food allergies. Yet I'm still having allergic reactions to seven foods. He decided I needed to go to a neurologist and heart doctor. I saw Dr. Karathanos, my neurologist, in early 2013. He decided we would do an electroencephalogram (EEG) and do the wait-and-see technique. I saw Dr. Tulloch, my heart doctor, and wore a heart monitor for a month with nothing wrong as far as the heart goes (June and July). The conclusion was a high possibility for hypoglycemia, so we changed my eating habits and diet to see if this reduced my symptoms—no such luck.

I had my first MRI on May 3, 2013. As I waited for the loud noises to begin, God gave me a vision. There was a very bright light as I emerged with a sword drawn and dressed in the full armor of God. I remember weeping and saying to

God that I was ready to do whatever He needed me to do. I wanted Him to be glorified! I didn't know if we would find anything out, but I knew something was wrong. My symptoms had increased, and I didn't feel right.

I remember being at my neurology appointment when my doctor finally got the report from the MRI, and he was not happy. It was the end of the day, and he didn't like what he saw. They discovered a pineal gland cyst. He later calmed down and stated that usually this is an accidental find and it's no big deal for the majority of people. He told me we would wait and do a three-month follow-up MRI in August to check for any growth.

The summer brought many challenges for me and more symptoms. I felt a huge desire to try to get back into the working world. This didn't happen until the fall though. Moving forward to August 1, 2013, I had my second MRI. Twenty days later, I got to meet with my neurologist along with his three interns to review. This appointment left me more confused and frustrated. I gave them this list of all my current symptoms:

- Nausea
- Pain in front of head
- Pain in back of head
- Swelling of face and head at various times (also eyes)
- Right arm and hand go limp (dead and can't move at times)
- Tingling sensation in hands, arms, and legs (a handful of times)
- Blurred and double vision
- Psychedelic vision (a few times where multiple color blobs would be everywhere, lasting thirty minutes)
- Sleep problems

- Weight up and down drastically
- Dizziness
- Passing out or going to sleep without being able to awaken. I would know that I was getting ready to go out, but there was nothing I could do. I'd be out anywhere from twenty minutes to almost two hours.
- Forgetful
- Feeling worn out no matter how much sleep I got

He decided we needed another EEG, and I needed to find a neurosurgeon. After giving him a very detailed list of my symptoms (listed above) and concerns, he didn't want to wait any longer. The EEG showed nothing. On October 9, 2013, I met with Dr. Han, my neurosurgeon, in Tulsa. On my way there, God was wonderful in giving me music and peace. I knew He was going to give my doctors the wisdom they needed to help me. God was all over this. He made it all clearer and gave me the peace I needed. My doctor decided I needed a third MRI (six-month follow-up from the first) and time to get to know me and my cyst.

Michael and I, at that time, were going to take part in a Daniel fast with our Solace Church family starting November 1, 2013. We decided our personal focus would be my cyst. With my symptoms getting worse, we knew something else was happening. We wanted to make sure that God revealed it all to my doctor(s), because we were getting scared about the intensity of my symptoms. I was lucky that Dr. Han was already having a second doctor in Arizona on my case for a second opinion.

On November 4, 2013 (four days into the Daniel fast), I remember praying a different way in the MRI machine. I knew my neurosurgeon had requested a deeper look, and I needed God to give him answers. My original MRI review appointment was moved from November 21 to December 5. I really wasn't excited about having to wait longer, but God needed me to go through some growing pains to better prepare me for what I'm about to tell you.

That appointment on December 5 did not happen due to the snowstorm. My symptoms magnified and, at that point, made me come to terms with the fact that something was very wrong. Due to some personal scheduling problems and continued bad weather, I asked the doctor's office if my husband could take my films to the office so the doctor could call me during our scheduled time the next day, Wednesday, December 11, 2013, to discuss the findings.

On Tuesday, December 10, 2013, Michael took my film to the doctor's office. I got a personal call from my neurosurgeon within an hour or so. I wish I could remember all that was said to me in the phone conversation, but I can't. I can only try to recall the important pieces. The bottom line is that we weren't dealing with a normal cyst. I had three options, which all led to surgery. This was serious, and he wasn't the one meant to do the surgery. His number one recommendation was full removal. He was going to get me to the best for my case, which led me to Dr. Sughrue, my neurosurgeon in Oklahoma City, who at the time was giving me a second opinion on surgery. I'd be getting an appointment with him either that week or the next.

Forgive me, because I feel like I'm throwing out a ton of words yet not getting it all out. I got a call the very next day from Dr. Sughrue, picked up my films, and headed to a scheduled appointment on the morning of Thursday, December 12, 2013, in Oklahoma City. I felt like my snail's pace had warped into light speed. I was shocked yet at peace—knowing this could only be God taking care of me. I read the email from my patient navigator the night before my appointment. I had a team of doctors already getting recruited and ready for me. I knew that we weren't dealing with just a cyst at this point. I gave my newest doctor (that I met two days ago) all that I had, and I trust him completely with it all. I can only explain that it's all God.

When he walked into my appointment, we immediately dove headfirst into all the information. He put my films up, then proceeded with an anatomy review. The whole time I stared at the tumor. It was a beautiful picture of such a horrible, ugly mass. He was amazing at explaining everything to me and why we needed to be rapid and aggressive. My "cyst" was now a tumor. It's not the biggest he has seen, but it's an ugly one. It has a tail. The outer layer is bright and scary-looking. It screams cancer, but it could still be a cyst trying to be a poser. My percentages are higher for cancer, but we won't know for sure until they get to it and perform a biopsy.

I could go into all the scientific words used and how high the percentages are, but all you need to know is that this is serious. It's really happening. I remember asking my cousin, who passed away this summer due to brain cancer, if she could change anything, what would it be? She said that she wished she had listened when they said they needed to remove her cyst/tumor when they first found it. I decided that was divine advice, and I will be having brain surgery this Wednesday, December 18, 2013. Yes, that is in three days! I'm trusting God completely in this. He has got me in His hands, as always. After the year I've had, I'm beginning to see the why behind each part of my life. Everything has been essential—training and preparing me for such a time as this.

For the first time on this journey, I'm completely at peace knowing and seeing the risks—either way, there is life! I will have two places in my brain operated on. Their goal is to remove the tumor. I will be in surgery for up to five hours. We are hoping it can be completely removed and that it hasn't entangled itself to the point it can't come out. I know you are in some sort of shock, as my family and friends who already know still are.

I've already had many questions, such as how can this be happening to me? Or haven't I been through enough in this life? My answer to these and other questions that will come up is that I signed up for a life that lives out God's will. I'm choosing to see all my battles and scars as a sign that the devil really doesn't want me to be here, yet my heavenly Father does. My goal in life has been to help further God's kingdom. I knew that making this decision meant that my life wasn't going to be easy, yet it would always be blessed beyond measure.

I know that God has never left me nor forsaken me. He has been shaping and molding me my whole life in preparation for each mountain I have had to face and will face. No matter what happens from here on out, I know that God will provide as He always does, for me and others in my life. I need God's prayer warriors to suit up once again on another mountain in my life. We are going to be victorious whether I get to stay on earth or go to heaven. I have fought the good fight like so many of my fellow Christian brothers and sisters, who are living here on earth and in heaven above.

I have shed many tears with my family and friends. God gives us tears to relieve our hearts and souls. I have my prayer cards ready. I have my Christian music blaring. I have my constant prayer conversations with my heavenly Father continuously open. I already have a team of prayer warriors dropping to their knees in prayer.

God gives us tears to relieve our hearts and souls.

I've had people stop me in conversation and bust out a prayer right there. A lady in Enid bought my husband a cross for encouragement while in line at a Christian bookstore and proceeded to pray with me and the worker there. One of my customers who is battling cancer came in on my last day at work Friday, and now I have her information for support. The stories go on and on. GOD IS SO COOL! HE IS SO BIG!

I bought Mandisa's newest album *What Scars Are For* while in Enid today. I had been listening to the songs on YouTube and decided I needed the whole CD. It's like she witnessed my life and wrote about it through each song. It's just blowing me away. I listened to her live back in February 2011 before I knew I was pregnant with my second daughter, Piper. I needed to hear her angelically powerful voice then and definitely now. The song I've been listening to, "What Scars Are For," over and over while typing this entry perfectly fits my life. I've been through so many valleys and storms filled with pain, suffering, and sorrow. God has never left me. He's been purposeful in using the bad for goodness and richness. My scars are a story that reveals His faithfulness and promises. What was meant to harm and destroy me God has turned into a beautiful inspiration for me and others. This journey is worth it.

I have my share of scars from most of my major mountains due to surgeries. I even have unseen scars from within. God has been graciously working with me to heal these wounds mentally, emotionally, and physically. My scars prove that I have fought in numerous battles and lived to tell about each of them. My journal entries are my testimonies about how Big my God is!

I'm so blessed that I'm on this journey with Him. I'm in the place where I found myself during my first daughter's, Lilian Grace's, celebration of life. I felt like I was stepping on the devil's face. I'm pumped because I'm not using my strength and abilities—I'm using His! He makes the weak strong and courageous. I love you all, and I'm glad you decided to either stay with me or join in.

Soli Deo Gloria,
Chrissy

DECEMBER 16, 2013

2 › My Cup

I'm blown away by God's grace! God is doing so many cool things for all of us at such a time as this. Thank you from the bottom of my heart for the kind words, sweet descriptions, and powerful soul food you've been sending. I'm shedding happy tears knowing that God has an army fighting with me during this battle and giving me the exact soul food I need for this fight. The devil messed with the wrong woman and fellow warriors of God!

I've spent the last two days trying to get caught up as best I can. I know I've driven my husband crazy with my ridiculous task list. To him, it didn't matter. To me, it means I don't have unfinished business crowding my thoughts. I know we can try to plan and organize as much as we want, but sometimes there's just not enough time to get our agenda completed. I do still try though. I'm praying that God's will be done! I'm ready for whatever!

I looked in the mirror earlier today and saw a very tired woman with the face of a teenager—pizza face in parts. I guess staying up till four in the morning two nights in a row at thirty-five years old will cause acne, red eyes, and bad hair. I wanted to tie up some loose ends though. I hate having a to-do list running through my mind. I will be headed to Oklahoma City in about six hours, so pray for safe travels as I get to the OU Medical Center to check in and get my tests and pre-op completed.

I've been very blessed by all the calls, texts, Facebook comments and messages, and CaringBridge comments. It has been overwhelming, and my cup runneth over. Keep lifting those prayers up and sending soul food my way. I love you all and feel your love all around me. I'm putting on my armor of God and remembering my vision from May! God is Big! Let's do this!

Memory Verse 5

"Finally, be strong in the Lord and in his mighty power. Put on the full armor of God, so that you can take your stand against the devil's schemes. For our struggle is not against flesh and blood, but against the rulers, against the authorities, against the powers of this dark world and against the spiritual forces of evil in the heavenly realms. Therefore put on the full armor of God, so that when the day of evil comes, you may be able to stand your ground, and after you have done everything, to stand. Stand firm then, with the belt of truth buckled around your waist, with the breastplate of righteousness in place, and with your feet fitted with the readiness that comes from the gospel of peace. In addition to all this, take up the shield of faith, with which you can extinguish all the flaming arrows of the evil one. Take the helmet of salvation and the sword of the Spirit, which is the word of God. And pray in the Spirit on all occasions with all kinds of prayers and requests. With this in mind, be alert and always keep on praying for all the Lord's people" (Ephesians 6:10–18).

DECEMBER 18, 2013

3 › Going into Brain Surgery

I made it through yesterday's tests and beyond. Many hilarious things have already helped entertain me and those around me. Two minutes after being in my room, I got my gown drenched in the toilet. It made me giggle. I was like, "Wow, here we go. I know how to really get things started."

The hardest part was not getting to eat the whole day. If you have ever spent time with me in person, you know I need my food. God was good at keeping hangry Chrissy at bay! I had an electrocardiogram (EKG), echocardiogram (echo), blood work, bubble test, and MRI. All looks good—a green light for my one o'clock brain surgery today.

I've already met incredible people here at OU Medical Center. There's even a transporter who wears a Texas lanyard—he has got some balls! I love how many of my caretakers are from all over the world. It makes God's reach even bigger in how He coordinates our lives. Everyone has gone above and beyond, which keeps my heart at peace. I really love all the encouragement and prayers from you all—such blessings to me.

I have gotten to speak to several of you—sharing God's grace, mercy, and purpose that He has placed in my heart to say. I wish there was enough time to call each of you. God will always provide for you and me, no matter where our journey takes us. Know that I love you all so much! I need to make sure I say this—no matter how today goes, God has me in His loving hands. I trust Him completely. Life or death, I'm at peace with His will. I've learned to appreciate the good, the bad, and the ugly. I'm in *God's armor*—ready to battle with Him as my strength. I was born for this!

I know many of you may find yourselves angry and confused, which is not of God. Be mad at the devil. Praise God for His preparations for such a time as this. Esther and I are soul sisters. Her story inspires me to be brave and show up—God will do the rest. I hope each of you yearns to live out God's will to further His kingdom. We have a choice every day. How are you choosing to live? I hope by God's grace, mercy, and will. I love you all. Here's to seeing you either on this side of heaven or there with my heavenly Father!

What a blessed ride I have been a part of. Yes, it has been filled with lots of trials. More importantly, it's been filled with God's unconditional love and forgiveness for me. He has blessed me beyond what I deserve. I have been very human in my life. I wish I could have done many things differently, but I'm glad God has made it right while providing forgiveness!

Love *en Theos,*
Chrissy

DECEMBER 18, 2013

4 › Surgery Update

Hello, everyone! The surgery is going well. They've been able to complete the first stage and have the port drilled. They're currently moving Chrissy to a position to attack the removal process. According to nurse Beth, she is handling the surgery great. I will update again in a couple of hours. Thanks again for all your prayers.

Michael (Whitten)
(Chrissy's husband)

DECEMBER 18, 2013

5 › Recovery Update

All,

I just spoke with the surgeon, and all went well. They were able to remove the tumor completely. Chrissy is in recovery now. I will have an update later, but everything looks to be in the clear.

Michael (Whitten)
(Chrissy's Husband)

Chrissy—glad to be here

DECEMBER 18, 2013

6 › His Warrior Princess

From the mouth of His Warrior Princess . . .

🎥 Note: This is a transcription of my first video post-brain surgery that my sister, Kaylee Cooper, recorded using my phone the night of my surgery. To see the video, visit https://youtu.be/T_txmDNeluE.

Dear heavenly Father, we just thank you so much. We praise your name on high. I'm here! I'm not going to lie—I went into surgery going, "This is my last mission, so let's do this! I'm at peace! I know what I'm leaving behind, but I want to fight whatever you have and whichever way this is going."

Then I woke up, and I'm not going to lie—I was like, "Oh man—crap!" It meant I've got more to do, and that's a good thing. It's just—I'm letting you know how human I really am. That I'm going to have to keep doing this, and that is all good.

It's all good, all the time. Because He set it up. He knew. God doesn't cause bad things—the devil does. But here's what's cool—God knows the whole picture. He knew before He ever formed me what I was going to have to go through. He's been putting people in place to get me ready for each walk that I have to take, and I think that is the coolest gift ever.

I just love God, and I love you people! I love His people! And know that there is still more to be done—at least for today—so who knows where this journey is taking me. But it is amazing, and I'm in a good place. Keep those prayers coming up. Bye.

DECEMBER 19, 2013

7 › Update from Leslie

Give thanks to Him and praise His name!

Memory Verse 6

"Shout for joy to the LORD, all the earth. Worship the LORD with gladness; come before him with joyful songs. Know that the LORD is God. It is he who made us, and we are his; we are his people, the sheep of his pasture. Enter his gates with thanksgiving and his courts with praise; give thanks to him and praise his name. For the LORD is good and his love endures forever; his faithfulness continues through all generations" (Psalm 100).

Hello, friends and family! I am writing this entry this morning on behalf of our recovering patient. My name is Leslie Hall, and I'm Michael's sister. I spoke with Chrissy this morning and wanted to share with all the faithful followers and dear friends all over the world who have been following this CaringBridge story. As I sat down to type this, it just hit me what an amazing title for what this simple website is providing to everyone who loves and cares for Chrissy, Michael, and their family. A wonderful bridge full of caring and faithful hearts who have been on their knees before God this past week praying for exactly what we saw happen yesterday. Thank you for praying and caring for this amazing woman and for setting your hearts on God by putting your faith in His hearing all our prayers for her.

As I spoke with Chrissy this morning, I got a good update concerning the pain she is dealing with now and how she would appreciate continued prayers during this time of recovery. She woke up this morning with the continued pain in her head from surgery that is pounding and pretty severe. Much prayer is needed for the pain medicine (morphine) to give her relief so that she can rest and start to heal. She is experiencing a lot of nausea. They are treating her with Zophran to work on that; however, she has been extremely nauseous despite it, and the sickness has increased much of the head pain. Please pray that God will help relieve that pain and nausea.

She missed the doctor's visit this morning as she was pretty out of it. But she has had good reports that things are progressing as they should. She is a star patient as her progress is really great so far. She was up for a short walk this morning and able to talk—might even have done a little singing! Isn't it crazy, wonderful, and amazing how our God interferes in our lives and blesses us beyond measure, even in the midst of something as daunting as brain surgery? My faith is renewed daily!

Chrissy has also been blessed with a great staff at the hospital who are taking great care of her. She is making friends and touching lives even while in the hospital bed. Today, she will be moved out of the intensive care unit (ICU) and into a regular room as soon as the space is found to make the move. They will do another MRI today to confirm that everything necessary was removed yesterday during the surgery, which the surgeon seems very confident in at this point. She did have an arterial line taken out of her wrist this morning, which I believe was from the anesthesia during the surgery—causing her quite a bit of pain this morning. She still has a central line in her throat that is very uncomfortable. Please pray that she will be able to have that removed soon.

One more prayer request before I close this note: please pray for Chrissy as she is missing her baby girl, Piper. She doesn't want Piper to see her in the hospital with all the machines and bandages, so she is really hurting for the comfort of holding her little girl. Please pray for comfort for her mommy's heart and that she will feel well enough soon to go home and hug her tight. Please also pray for little Piper, who is missing her momma very much. She is such a little trooper and so very sweet, but we know she is missing Mommy. Please send some prayers up to comfort her little heart as well.

Chrissy told me that a friend (Rachel Foley) sang "Amazing Grace" to her last night. I think that sums up what we are all feeling today and the day after surgery. All the glory goes to God for the swiftness of the surgery, the able hands of the doctors and nurses who are caring for her in the hospital, and His amazing grace as we can see and talk to her today. Tears of joy are falling today that she is still with us and fighting now for a recovery that will have her back to normal soon.

Please continue sending prayers and love her way—just praising our Lord God and heavenly Father for answered prayers and amazing grace.

DECEMBER 19, 2013

8 › Amazing Grace

And grace my fears relieved . . .

Hello, all! Leslie here again with another update this evening on Chrissy's recovery after just speaking with her. She is in good spirits, sharing with me so that I can update all of you on what is happening with her as she is healing post-surgery. The nurses and staff caring for her are continually expressing their amazement at the speed of the recovery she is making. She has been up again, walking and able to eat twice today while keeping it down. So grateful for the strength God is already giving her—barely twenty-four hours out of this type of surgery! She has been blessed repeatedly by one nurse in particular, nurse Bart, who has told her how surprised he is to see how great she is doing—walking, talking, joking, and laughing while even having the ability to speak to family on the phone. His caring has been a great part of her recovery experience.

I have a little more information today about the cyst that I want to share with you. The correct scientific name of what the surgeon removed was a quarter-sized pineal so ma with absolutely no complications. Although it was originally projected to be a five-hour procedure, it was finished in less than three—only adding to the amazement considering what was expected earlier on. The surgeon said that the procedure went perfectly and she could be released as early as tonight. However, Chrissy did request to stay one more day due to intense pain. She will be leaving on Friday (tomorrow) around three or four o'clock. At this time, she has been moved from the ICU to room 320 at OU Medical Center in Oklahoma City.

I'd also like to add that the central line located in her neck was removed today. She is thankful for all the prayers toward that pain and discomfort from earlier today. God really has continued to move in every hour of the day since the beginning of the journey last week. He truly has a BIGGER plan than we do—plans that we can never see or understand until they unfold before us. Her vision is also doing perfectly, which is a big praise God moment because it is a common complication in patients having this type of surgical operation.

Please continue your prayers tonight, as she is dealing with quite a bit of pain. Pray for rest and healing for her body as she sleeps tonight and prepares for the trip home tomorrow. I'd like to leave you with the words to the hymn, "Amazing Grace." It's never been more refreshing and healing to our hearts after going through tough moments in life to read the words of this classic hymn and marvel at the beauty of the grace that He gives to His children.

Amazing grace! How sweet the sound
That saved a wretch like me.
I once was lost, but now am found,
Was blind, but now I see.

'Twas grace that taught my heart to fear,
And grace my fears relieved.
How precious did that grace appear
The hour I first believed.

Through many dangers, toils and snares
I have already come;

*'Tis grace has brought me safe thus far
And grace will lead me home.*

*The Lord has promised good to me
His word my hope secures;
He will my shield and portion be,
As long as life endures.*

*Yea, when this flesh and heart shall fail,
And mortal life shall cease,
I shall possess within the veil,
A life of joy and peace.*

*When we've been there ten thousand years
Bright shining as the sun,
We've no less days to sing God's praise
Than when we've first begun.*

(John Newton, 1725–1807)

Good night, and God bless each of you for your caring and loving hearts, praying for Chrissy today.

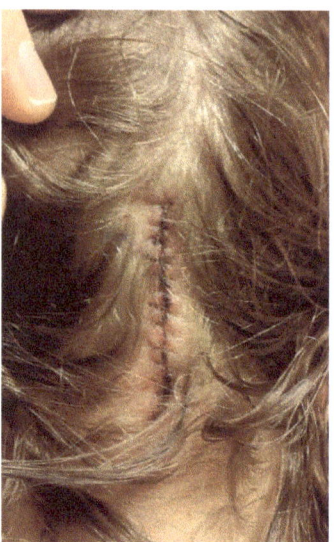

Postural surgery site update

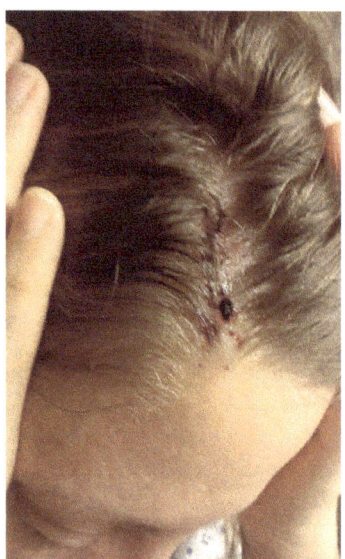

Frontal surgery site update

DECEMBER 19, 2013

9 › Short & Sweet

Thank you for the continued prayers. I am requesting more prayers at this time. I have a low-grade fever of 100 degrees. Please pray for God to heal me where needed and to put a complete hedge of protection around me and my caretakers.

Love you a ton,
Chrissy

DECEMBER 19, 2013

10 › Meal Train

Helping when they come home . . .

This is Karri Howell. I am a friend who is writing this entry to let everyone know of a way that you can provide for the Whittens as they return home to recover. There is a meal planner set up for them on www.carecalendar.org. Calendar ID: 169010 and Security Code: 7196.[17]

This will allow you to see dates that they would like to receive food for dinner and allow us to make sure that their needs are being met. Sarah Fernau and I will be facilitating the food calendar. When you sign up to provide a meal, we ask that you follow the details on the site. It will give you information on food allergies and delivery times. We want to thank everyone in advance for helping care for our dear friends as they walk down the path to full recovery. Chrissy is always there to meet the needs of others with a kind spirit. It is our turn to meet her needs.

Memory Verse 7

⚔ *"Carry each other's burdens, and in this way you will fulfill the law of Christ" (Galatians 6:2).*

Thanks, everyone!
Karri

---

[17] Note from author: This care calendar is no longer active.

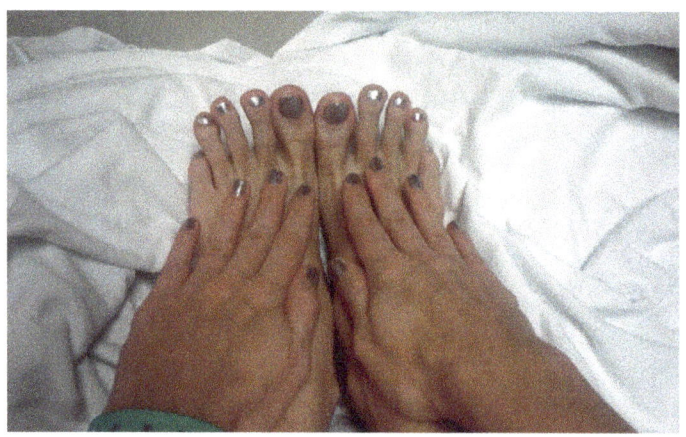

Great Aunt Sharon's beautiful masterpiece

DECEMBER 20, 2013

11 › Scripture for Healing & Hope

God took away the fever—praise God! My two main line sites got cleaned. I completed my MRI earlier—praise God! They can't officially say that the tumor has been completely removed, but there is less than 5 percent left behind at this time. The doctor came in a little earlier and said that it looked like there was nothing ever there—praise God!

The staff continues to be a blessing—praise God! I got to wash my hair—praise God! It feels so good to do this. I have to air dry my hair—darn—giggle, giggle. Not gonna lie, I'm loving this. My great-aunt Sharon (Sloan) painted my toes and fingernails silver just a bit ago—praise God! I get to go home after four o'clock today—praise God! There are lots of praises!

I do need prayer to transition from the hospital to home. I am really tired. Pray for energy and the ability to slow down. God has been so good to me throughout all of this. I know I'm way ahead of schedule for normal brain surgery. I owe this to all your prayers and obedience. God has been in this before I was even created in the womb—praise God! He is continuously showing us just how Big He really is—praise God!

I'm so blown away by God's grace and mercy. I do still need a major hedge of protection from the devil/evil because God stomped on the devil's back. This journey is immaculate and breathtaking—completely from God! I praise His name above the highest of names!

I wanted to share the verses I've been reading over and over. I've had many visitors reading them as well, which has been really special! I wrote them out on a hotel notepad after I looked up verses geared toward cancer patients on Yahoo:

Memory Verses 8–39

⚔ *"So do not fear, for I am with you; do not be dismayed, for I am your God. I will strengthen you and help you; I will uphold you with my righteous right hand" (Isaiah 41:10).*

⚔ *"The LORD is my rock, my fortress and my deliverer; my God is my rock, in whom I take refuge, my shield and the horn of my salvation, my stronghold" (Psalm 18:2).*

⚔ *"The LORD is close to the brokenhearted and saves those who are crushed in spirit" (Psalm 34:18).*

⚔ *"Let us not become weary in doing good, for at the proper time we will reap a harvest if we do not give up" (Galatians 6:9).*

⚔ *"The LORD is my shepherd, I lack nothing. He makes me lie down in green pastures, he leads me beside quiet waters, he refreshes my soul. He guides me along the right paths for his name's sake. Even though I walk through the darkest valley, I will fear no evil, for you are with me; your rod and your staff, they comfort me. You prepare a table before me in the presence of my enemies. You anoint my head with oil; my cup overflows. Surely your goodness and love will follow me all the days of my* life, and I will dwell in the house of the LORD forever" (Psalm 23).

🗡 "Wait for the LORD; be strong and take heart and wait for the LORD" (Psalm 27:14).

🗡 "For I know the plans I have for you," declares the LORD, "plans to prosper you and not to harm you, plans to give you hope and a future. Then you will call on me and come and pray to me, and I will listen to you" (Jeremiah 29:11–12).

🗡 "Peace I leave with you; my peace I give you. I do not give to you as the world gives. Do not let your hearts be troubled and do not be afraid" (John 14:27).

🗡 "He will wipe every tear from their eyes. There will be no more death or mourning or crying or pain, for the old order of things has passed away" (Revelation 21:4).

🗡 "Blessed is the one who perseveres under trial because, having stood the test, that person will receive the crown of life that the Lord has promised to those who love him" (James 1:12).

🗡 "Be strong and courageous. Do not be afraid or terrified because of them, for the LORD your God goes with you; he will never leave you nor forsake you" (Deuteronomy 31:6).

🗡 "When I called, you answered me; you greatly emboldened me" (Psalm 138:3).

⚔ "Trust in the LORD with all your heart and lean not on your own understanding; in all your ways submit to him, and he will make your paths straight" (Proverbs 3:5–6).

⚔ "Come to me, all you who are weary and burdened, and I will give you rest. Take my yoke upon you and learn from me, for I am gentle and humble in heart, and you will find rest for your souls" (Matthew 11:28–29).

⚔ "Blessed be the God and Father of our Lord Jesus Christ, the Father of compassion and the God of all comfort, who comforts us in all our troubles, so that we can comfort those who are in any trouble with the comfort we ourselves receive from God" (2 Corinthians 1:3–4).

⚔ "In my distress I called to the LORD; I cried to my God for help. From his temple he heard my voice; my cry came before him, into his ears" (Psalm 18:6).

⚔ "We wait in hope for the LORD; he is our help and our shield. In him our hearts rejoice, for we trust in his holy name. May your unfailing love be with us, LORD, even as we put our hope in you" (Psalm 33:20–22).

⚔ "Being confident of this, that he who began a good work in you will carry it on to completion until the day of Christ Jesus" (Philippians 1:6).

⚔ "Do not be anxious about anything, but in every situation, by prayer and petition, with thanksgiving, present your requests to God. And the peace of God, which transcends all *understanding, will guard your hearts and your minds in Christ Jesus" (Philippians 4:6–7).*

⚔ *"Humble yourselves, therefore, under God's mighty hand, that he may lift you up in due time. Cast all your anxiety on him because he cares for you" (1 Peter 5:6–7).*

⚔ *"There is a time for everything, and a season for every activity under the heavens" (Ecclesiastes 3:1).*

⚔ *"Do not let your hearts be troubled. You believe in God; believe also in me. My Father's house has many rooms; if that were not so, would I have told you that I am going there to prepare a place for you? And if I go and prepare a place for you, I will come back and take you to be with me that you also may be where I am" (John 14:1–3).*

⚔ *"The Spirit himself testifies with our spirit that we are God's children. Now if we are children, then we are heirs—heirs of God and co-heirs with Christ, if indeed we share in his sufferings in order that we may also share in his glory" (Romans 8:16–17).*

⚔ *"For in this hope we were saved. But hope that is seen is no hope at all. Who hopes for what they already have? But if we hope for what we do not yet have, we wait for it patiently" (Romans 8:24–25).*

⚔ *"For I am convinced that neither death nor life, neither angels nor demons, neither the present nor the future, nor any powers, neither height nor depth, nor anything else in all* creation, will be able to separate us from the love of God that is in Christ Jesus our Lord" (Romans 8:38–39).

⚔ "Praise be to the God and Father of our Lord Jesus Christ! In his great mercy he has given us new birth into a living hope through the resurrection of Jesus Christ from the dead" (1 Peter 1:3).

⚔ "For we do not have a high priest who is unable to empathize with our weaknesses, but we have one who has been tempted in every way, just as we are—yet he did not sin. Let us then approach God's throne of grace with confidence, so that we may receive mercy and find grace to help us in our time of need" (Hebrews 4:15–16).

⚔ "Review the past for me, let us argue the matter together; state the case for your innocence" (Isaiah 43:26).

⚔ "Praise the LORD, my soul; all my inmost being, praise his holy name. Praise the LORD, my soul, and forget not all his benefits—who forgives all your sins and heals all your diseases" (Psalm 103:1–3).

⚔ "When Jesus landed and saw a large crowd, he had compassion on them and healed their sick" (Matthew 14:14).

⚔ "Jesus Christ is the same yesterday and today and forever" (Hebrews 13:8).

⚔ "The thief comes only to steal and kill and destroy; I have come that they may have life, and have it to the full" (John

10:10).

These verses have been so good for me. I really can't believe I'm getting to go home. The biopsy results will be in ASAP. We shall see what we will be facing. I did find out that I have a titanium plate where my hole was created. It reminds me of Cousin Eddie from the *National Lampoon's Christmas Vacation* movie—pretty funny, if you ask me!

The pet therapy dogs came to visit me. This is a wonderful therapy program! I really enjoyed getting to pet them and sharing my testimonies with the ladies. It was needed. The doctor is blown away by how wonderful I'm doing. He said that I don't look like a patient who needs to be here. He wanted me to go home yesterday, but I wasn't ready.

I will post again when we get settled at home. Thank you for all the prayers. You are amazing. Remember to always, always, always trust God. He has the only plan! Get out of His way so big things can happen for you and His kingdom!

Blessed Beyond Measure,
Chrissy

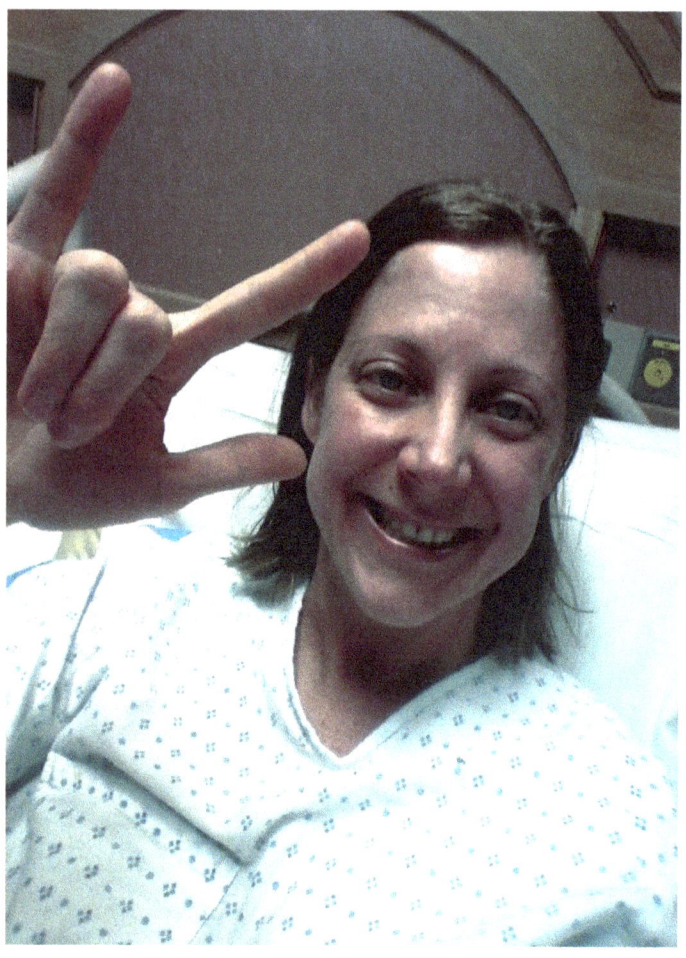
"I love you" in American Sign Language (ASL)

DECEMBER 20, 2013

12 › Home Sweet Home

The ride home from the hospital was rough. They hated to see me go, and I hated to leave. Piper loved seeing her mommy, and I loved seeing her, but she hadn't taken a nap. She was restless the whole way home—unsatisfied. We had to call and beg Reasor's Pharmacy to stay open because I desperately needed pain and nausea medicine. My head was hurting, and we realized we were running out of time. PRAISE GOD that they stayed late for us—totally God's angels! We owe them big time!

We had my sister-in-law over for her last night here and got my mother-in-law over here to open Christmas presents together—we missed our brother-in-law though. I looked hot on the couch, trying to recoup and recover. I miss my morphine from the hospital stay, but we made it a great mini-Christmas with awesome gifts!

I still can't believe I'm already home and alive. GOD really does have His plans! They are way better than ours. I see Him moving and making things better, richer, and more beautiful. Michael said that the doctor told him that I had the walking-talking dead tumor. I could have easily been talking to any of you and just keeled over. Just nuts! God's so gracious in taking care of me and you all. Can you imagine if I had died talking to you? Not cool!

I think back to all the times I lost consciousness, and it could have been my last, yet God had more for me. He wanted to make my story greater and show how Big He really is. My tumor was the size of a quarter and in the smallest place in my brain. He (the doctor) said the tumor might as well have been the size of my brain. It's just so remarkably crazy.

PRAISE GOD for taking care of me and my family. He placed me on the perfect path to line up everyone for this very moment—magnificently planned! Once again, we praise God for putting each of you in our lives. We are truly blessed by each of you. Prayer and obedience matter. Pay attention to God because He wants an intimate relationship with you daily!

God wants an intimate relationship with you daily.

I'm so blessed and lucky. If you'd like to come visit, please let me know ahead of time so we can balance out our schedule with lots of love. I'm home and kicking it. The newest prayer needed is for the pathology to come back benign. If the plan involves a malignant result, pray God will keep taking care of us and giving us what we need. We already have a team ready to take care of me. Of course, God's taking care of us no matter what! I'll keep you posted as information comes in. The current plan is to take it easy—doing things once in a while. I'll be getting back into the full swing of life over the next couple of months, slowly adding things back in.

I appreciate those who have already signed up to feed us. I humbly accept the help—it truly relieves me of feeding my husband, child, and myself. Thank you for the generosity and commitment. Here's to more successful healing and growing. Lots of love, hugs, and kisses on the cheek!

DECEMBER 21, 2013

13 › My Doctor Rocks

Two thumbs up for an amazing surgery—sanctioned by God himself. It really is the greatest feeling to know that you get to be a part of God's agenda and fingerprints. Hoping we all get out of His way to see what He wants and can do! It's huge! He's bigger than we will ever know!

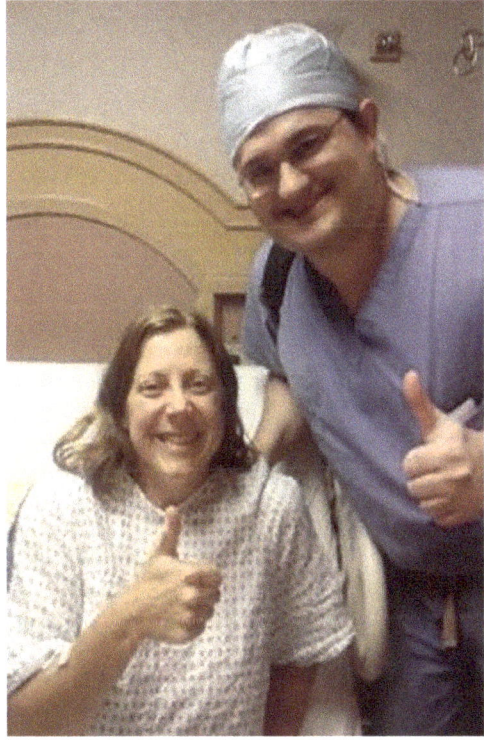

Two thumbs up

Getting to see my doctor and share God with him was priceless. This man who helped save me is incredible. Please lift prayers up for him to be blessed beyond measure and know it's only from God above. He deserves all the riches this life has to offer and beyond in heaven!

Michael has been a wonderful nurse thus far, taking care of me. I'm truly blessed. He told me anyone who would like to come visit should call him. He will be in charge of this as well. We know there are many of you who would like to come, and we would love to see you! We welcome you. Just make sure you or people you have been around have not been sick. We have major precautions for you to take when you arrive. It's to protect me and help me continue down the successful healing road.

If you missed the journal entry on how you can help, Karri Howell and Sarah Fernau have graciously set up a site for feeding us. There is a meal planner set up for us on www.carecalendar.org. Login—Calendar ID: 169010 and Security Code: 7196.[18] We are very appreciative of this. It gives all my helpers one less thing to focus on. We have spread it out for the time being. If the need becomes more, we will have these two blessed ladies update it.

I want to thank Kris Ramsay for making sure Piper never missed a beat this past week. She made sure to do it exactly how I needed her to! Kerri Stark graciously subbed as caretaker for our puppies. She made sure they got playtime and extra love. My mom and sister never left me at the hospital so Michael could drive back and forth to give Piper some consistency. My sister-in-law surprised us by coming and being here—even during her own recovery.

My friends and family who came to come visit—you

---

[18] Note from author: This care calendar is no longer active.

know who you are. There are too many names to type them all out. I'm very blessed I got to see your smiling faces. Your out-loud prayers were precious! We got some awesome goodies, which I have obviously enjoyed! Thanks to all my friends who got late night or early morning calls throughout this. Thanks for answering and blessing my heart! Thanks to everyone from the bottom of my heart for the prayers and continued ones you'll be sending up. It really does matter! He listens to our requests!

I love all my goodies and flowers. It still blows my mind how our journey has come to all this. Thanks to everyone involved in any way, shape, or form! All matters—you matter! I'll be posting more soon. Love you! Be blessed and bless others.

DECEMBER 21, 2013

14 › Calling All Christians

I have been in and out of sleep all day at home. It's been good to relax and let others do things for me—even if that's not part of my nature. Michael has been kicking it into high gear, so pray he is not overdoing it. My sister has been in charge of Piper while she's on Christmas break. I'm asking that you all send me your most powerful verses so I can make more Bible verse cards to get me ready for the next mountain.

I'm not sure when we will find out the results from the pathology, but it's always better to prepare on my end, no matter what. I know the devil wasn't happy when I woke up from surgery. He's already been attacking many people close to me. I need lots of prayers for everyone to be protected, especially those majorly involved in my care. It's always good to be on defense from all angles.

So make sure to post your most powerful verses to get me ready for whatever is around the corner. I'm fully aware that this isn't over yet. God has been so good to me, and I just want to be prepared. Obedience and diligence are key factors in this walk being successful.

I'm hoping each of you is gearing up for life, Christmas, and fun. I still can't believe Christmas is this week. Time flies by so fast. Before we know it, 2014 will be here. May each of you be super blessed this week by spending time with family and friends. I love you all!

I'm so thankful to have you on this journey when you could have easily bailed on me. Here's to many more successes and blessings for us all right now. Love you to the moon and back and for all eternity!

DECEMBER 22, 2013

15 › Born for This

Ashley Patty—close friend and member of November Lily—suggested that the lyrics from Mandisa's "Born for This (Esther)" song were written for me. Ever since, I haven't been able to shake the powerful message these lyrics hold for me. I need to stand on something right now and tell you that I was ready to go and see Jesus. I didn't want to be here anymore. I'm also going to stand and say I'm glad I'm here. I'm glad His plans were different from mine. I am meant to be here with you all.

I've always wondered if I could ever truly get in God's way. He answered this when I thought it was meant for me to be with Him, but it wasn't—I got to stay! My job right now is to be here on earth. He wants me here to share His light. I want to be here. I want to love everyone where they are. I don't want people to think that just because I love everyone that means I accept everything about them. You and I—we will have our differences. What matters most is the connection between you and God! I need everyone to be in a good place with Him and only Him. We all can be way too judgmental. I know—I've been there. I still have things to work out.

I want us to be who God intended each of us to be in order to broaden His kingdom—it's what I've wanted for as long as I can remember. Do I get it all right? No, I'm just like anyone else. I'm human. I make mistakes. I say things when I should and shouldn't. This is no surprise if you know me. I just need you to know that I'm doing the best I can and loving God while doing it. I'm not always going to hold my breath when needed. I'll say things at times I shouldn't. I hope you can understand and know where my heart really is at the time.

I hope that I can be everything He needs me to be and not waste His time and energy. I know I'm a hard pill to swallow at times, but we all can be at points in our lives. I want to trust Him and be where He needs me to be. I definitely got to see people being who, what, and where they needed to be to save my life. I am forever grateful. I wouldn't be here if they weren't where they should have been.

I hope everyone knows where my heart and mind are with my life and God. I want to trust Him; love people where they are; and be who, what, and where God needs me to be. Are you? I was born for this life. I don't want to keep my head down. I want to speak His truth and lean on His strength. God has won! We all were born for a specific reason. We were born for such a time as this. Step into His will—you were made to be a vessel—to be the hands and feet of Jesus.

We were born for such a time as this.

DECEMBER 24, 2013

16 › O Holy Night

"O Holy Night" is my all-time favorite Christmas song. I'm listening to Celine Dion's version. The words of this song have so much power. I'd love for you all to really listen to it and see what comes alive in your soul. As each of you celebrates Christmas and whatever other holiday you like during this season, I want you to know how blessed I am for you to be on this journey with me and hope you feel God's love for us when remembering He sent His Son to die in our place. If today were my last day, I would rejoice knowing I have lived life to the fullest. At times, I was completely worn out due to my inability to say no. I don't know all the answers to life's questions, but I do know that living is the way to go. The darkness will come—oh so often and swiftly. But we must remember we have access to the greatest light source to help us conquer it.

My life has definitely seen more than its share of ridiculous and crazy times, yet it still could have been worse. There is so much bad that could have happened, but thankfully, it has not. I am thankful that God has never left me. I am thankful that for me, He gave us His Son, Jesus, to be born in Bethlehem to save me and anyone else from our sinful ways. I know some of you do not believe this, and it's your right to believe how you do. Please, just let me say what I am grateful for in my own life and what I have decided to believe.

On Christmas Eve this year, I would have loaded my family up and went to my brother's house, where we would have opened presents and built a gingerbread house while eating delicious food. Thankfully, my brother and sister-in-law came up the night before I left for the hospital last week so we could make a gingerbread village together. I didn't get to be with them today, but I do remember our time together, even if I was distracted by my looming brain surgery. It has made me very sad not to be with them today, but I do know I may get many more holidays with them. This just happens to not be one of them.

Tonight, my Cooper family is gathering with all my grandparents, aunts, uncles, cousins, and main family unit to eat some awesome Mexican food and open presents. Again, I will not be there, but I'm hoping they are enjoying some good times and laughter. I can't wait to see my two cousins' faces as they open their gifts via video. I was a crazy woman last week trying to find the perfect gifts, just in case these were my very last. Guess what? They aren't my last.

I wish we could always look at life like every minute could be our last. I want to continue to make as many special moments and memories with people while I am still here. It doesn't take much. It really is the little things that do, in fact, matter. Most things that give an extra sweetness are actually free—a thought, a changeup, or a twist that doesn't take much to happen but is unexpected and impactful.

> *I wish we could always look at life like every minute could be our last.*

Tomorrow morning, my Poteet family will gather and eat an amazing breakfast. It's one of my favorite things in the whole world—my Grandma Poteet's butter, milk, sugar, and rice! I won't be there, but I will be daydreaming of the past holiday gatherings that I hold close to my heart.

Though I'm glad I'm still here, I wish I could be normal. Normal? I'm not really sure what that means anymore. I just want to be healthy again. Healthy was a nice time in my life—a short stint at some points these last couple of years.

Know that wherever you are and whatever you are doing, please make the most of it. The tiniest and simplest details can be the biggest and grandest gestures on earth. Think outside the box. Piper is taking a nap, but I will wake her up and do our own little Christmas festivities tonight. I know how much she loves opening presents. Many times I wish things were different, and other times I wish they could be how they used to be. I know this—I am very blessed to be alive right now, typing this entry for you without major complications from brain surgery. God gave me a Christmas miracle—life!

On another note: Prayers that I need right now are for my brain not to swell, incisions to heal properly, pain to lighten, pain meds to be refilled on Friday, and peace about the biopsy report when it comes. I have been super blessed with people helping. The food has been wonderful and a huge help in giving Michael a break here and there! We really couldn't do this without an army!

I want to wish you a very Merry Christmas and Happy New Year. God is everywhere! He provides us with everything down to the tiniest of details. I praise His name on high for loving us so much! May you get to enjoy your holidays to the highest of highs—the best you've ever experienced! I love you all and really am blessed by you!

Chrissy

Ten-year "We Still Do" vow renewal

DECEMBER 27, 2013

17 › Ten-Year Wedding Anniversary

I need to remind everyone that I have not always been who I need to be. I've been a person who has let my judgmental ways cloud my view and place large chains on my relationships. Before going into my surgery, I remember praying that God would break so many hearts in order for them to be transformed by Him. Little did I know that my heart would be one of those that needed to be finished off—completely broken.

I have had numerous relationships in my life where I could point a finger and tell you what they were or were not doing right. I could justify with the best of them. I could convince myself that I was where I needed to be and they weren't. Sadly, I've spent way too many years trying to fix relationships with the wrong tools—trying to fix them and not me. God has tried time and again to help me see it for the truth, but I couldn't get out of the way.

I've done some really cool things. I haven't been all consumed, but I do know I have been really wrong as well. Sadly, my relationships with some very dear people have been jolted or denied because of who I am. On Thursday, December 26, God changed me. Actually, He's been working on me for a long time, but today He got through.

When Lilian Grace came into my life and left, I was broken, yet it wasn't enough to finish me off. I needed more but couldn't see it. I thought that many of my broken relationships were due to people and their past and/or current choices. What I've discovered in my downtime post-brain surgery is that I'm a complete sinner. I am judgmental. I have let what I thought was truth rule me, consume me, and chain me from getting to a better, higher place with people and God. I have been miserable with many situations for years—hoping it would get better, but it didn't.

I spent yesterday doing a lot of digging and asking for forgiveness from people I love. Some of this goes back twelve years or more. God is precious in making sure my prayer before surgery was answered. He broke my heart the rest of the way. I hurt people I love with my words in trying to fix things that are not meant for me to fix. I hurt people I have made pay for things that I don't even know the truth about anymore or things that may have never happened. It all boils down to the truth that whatever happens to each of us in our sin is really between each person and God.

It was so freeing to be real with people I love and to really love them for who they are, whether I agree or disagree. The past is the past. I don't want to live in bitterness, anger, disappointment, frustration, hate, and judgment any longer. I want to be whole. I want them to be whole as always. I'm not the one who's going to make them pay for anything they've done, are doing, or will do. I want to know what it feels like to be free of my chains and sins.

I'm human, and I won't be perfect. I do believe that there are positive and negative consequences in life, but I also know it's not my job to make people pay. It feels good to let this go. I do know I'm going to try with everything that I can to give God my best and give it all fully to Him. I say again, I want to love people where they are and hope they get to where, who, and what God needs them to be. God is the man! He's got it in His hands, not mine!

My husband and I are celebrating ten years of marriage

today. We have been together twelve years, and I have not cried or begged for forgiveness as much as I have in the last twenty-four hours. Michael has loved me in all my ugliness, mixed in with my beautiful parts. He loved me even when I didn't deserve to be loved. I praise God that He makes sure to take care of us no matter where our hearts and souls are. God gave Michael the gift to love me unconditionally, even if he didn't want to. PRAISE GOD!

Christmas has not been what I wanted it to be. It's been really hard. Actually, brain surgery was a lot easier than the heart and soul stuff I've been working through. I'm just glad God listened to me and broke my heart so I could finally see the truth. I could finally see all my ways and get it right. I could finally get out of the way. I'm so thankful to family and friends who listened to me and let me share my heart with tears and sorrow.

We do have a long way to go. Forgiveness comes easier than letting it go. I still have to work at being the best version of myself, but I am relieved to know that it's all out there. If it's not, I know God will help shine a light on it. I'm always going to want to fix things, but I need to always remember to keep giving it to God to fix!

My mom and dad were wonderful today in bringing my dad's parents to me so that we could spend our own little version of Christmas together. My mom went all out on the food, and it was delicious in every way. Our presents from them and, actually, everybody were perfect this year. Piper got to have the best time this year. So Christmas wasn't how I thought it should be—but I can safely say God gave me something richer, higher, and deeper than I had hoped for.

I can't believe Michael and I will stand next to each other tonight at our ten-year "We Still Do" vow renewal in front of family and friends. I wish we could invite everyone, but there's not enough room. I ask that you pray for us. I know I'm still recovering from brain surgery, but I want to give Michael a special night. I feel like he's finally going to get the wife he deserves tonight as we renew our vows.

I feel like I'm so far from that young twenty-five-year-old girl who thought she had it together with all the answers. I still don't have all the answers, yet I'm finally getting smart about letting God have it all and trusting that He will provide what we need when we need it. I want to make God so proud and Michael too. I want Michael to be proud to keep calling me his wife.

Michael and I have seen so much pain and suffering in our short time together—many say it's enough. I can now say, "God, keep giving us what we need to honor You and help spread Your kingdom, to not be stagnant, to be able to continue loving unconditionally while forgiving one another, and to keep making it together while remaining in love!

I am truly the luckiest girl I know. I look in the mirror, and I see all my beauty, scars, and ugliness for the fullness that each is in my life. It's taken a lot for me to see, finally, that I've been the problem when it comes to many of the issues I've dealt with for years. I'm not here for a pity party. I just want you all to see that God's doing a miracle in all of me, not just physically. I'd be a liar if I didn't share it all with you.

I remember standing at the altar on Saturday, December 27, 2003, staring into Michael's eyes. God let me see the man he was going to be, and it was spectacular. I knew Michael was not perfect at the time. I didn't know all my junk either. I did know that God was going to be the only way we were going to make it. It still stands true today. God is the only reason that we are still doing this.

I praise God for Michael, no matter who or what he is. I trust God completely, and I thank Him for making Michael to be my perfect fit. In this life, nothing is guaranteed. I have to pray daily and work every day on my marriage, myself, and my relationships. I hope we get to keep doing this for eternity. May God keep us in this always, no matter what we face, because we are always going to face it here on earth. Praying God gives us all the ability to look deep, search, forgive, receive, and become new in Him!

I have to pray daily and work every day on my marriage, myself, and my relationships.

My husband loves this new song, "I Hold On" by Dierks Bentley. I thought it was appropriate to add here for encouragement. I'm thankful Michael holds on every day despite my strengths or weaknesses. I'm blessed that he hasn't given up on me yet. I hope the strides I made today bless us together and individually. God is so good! I wouldn't be where I am without God and Michael. They both make me stronger. I'd be nothing without them and their love.

Happy ten years of marriage to my husband and me, where life has taken us to extremes and we are still holding on to God and each other! I don't ever want to take this for granted. I love our story from the darkest to the brightest parts. I pray we keep going strong and never let go of God or each other!

DECEMBER 30, 2013

18 › Let Go, Let God

Letting go and letting God do His thing . . .

I need to write this before I hear my fate this week about whether I have cancer. I'm not afraid of either way this could go. God always has my everything. He is going to take care of me, no matter what. It feels good to have peace and trust in Him. He really does hold my future.

We finally have an appointment for my two-week post-brain surgery checkup. It's set for this Thursday, January 2, 2014, in Oklahoma City. My pathology report has come back, yet my patient navigator was not cleared to tell me the results—so we wait.

I have major praises, yet I'd like to specify two. One, we finally heard back and got an appointment. Secondly, they refilled my pain medication, which I desperately needed. I ran out, and the pain was really consuming me. Pain meds are working again—PRAISING GOD! I hate taking meds, yet I know I really need them right now.

Two weeks (as of tomorrow) have flown by in a blink of an eye since my brain surgery. I still don't think I've caught up with everything God has been doing in me and around me with others. I've been blessed to be a part of God answering prayer after prayer, not only for others but for myself as well. The ride has been breathtaking and beautiful to see unfold.

I'm no different than anyone on this earth. I'm just getting out of the way and letting God be. I've been very aware of my gut feeling (the Holy Spirit) and listening, which is paying off in huge ways. The rewards are too many to count. Many of us get so tired and rundown in trying to be and do for others. God's been showing me that He loves to pour us out in blessing others by being there for them. Plus, He wants to fill us back up to repeat. I always want to be able to be His hands and feet in this world. It's just the coolest and most spectacular ride to be a part of.

I am learning that burnout comes quicker than I like, and sometimes we don't see the rewards or results from our work. I'm not meant to fix things or people. He just needs me to be a vessel. God is working it out, whether it's instantaneously or years down the road when I may or may not see the results. Know that when you are giving and putting yourself out there, it matters—you matter. Don't forget to let God fill you back up, especially when you keep pouring out and not seeing the return. What you do is a true blessing, so don't ever give up.

There have been years when I never saw if I was making a difference or getting anywhere. Now He's blowing me completely away. I am so overwhelmed and consumed by what He is doing and accomplishing in many of us. It's just insane and magnificent. He keeps getting bigger and bigger. There is no limit to what He can do. I'm going to keep getting out of the way and listening to my gut more than not. I really feel on top of the world.

I want to continue to thank everyone who keeps stepping up and out of the way for God and us. You know exactly who you are and what you've been doing. I'm so very blessed to be on this journey with you. GOD has really stepped it up lately by answering much-needed prayers and providing for needs through our community. Thank you for listening to Him and giving of yourself. It matters! You matter! It's so cool to see it all unfold. Keep looking up and trusting Him.

We have been so blessed by people's generosity in showing up through phone conversations, prayers, visits, and food deliveries. I am horrible at letting people help me. Now that I've gotten out of the way, we see an abundance of blessings right and left for us and for those helping and/or being there for us. I am grateful for it all. I keep wondering how I got so blessed, and then I remembered God's been so good at making sure we are taken care of every day. I love how Big God keeps being.

I pray He does the same for you. It's so rewarding to get out of the way, let go, and let God lead. Oh, it feels so good! Praying that you always let God empty you and fill you back up for His purposes—repeat over and over again. You are loved by me and Him! You are amazing, and you matter!

JANUARY 2, 2014

19 › He Never Lets Go

We wait . . .

As I waited, I decided to listen to "You Never Let Go" by Matt Redman. Sitting here, imagining God never letting me go, brings an unwavering joy. God never will let me or any of us go. We must remember to praise Him through the storms and the joys—the lows and the highs.

I've been dealing with foundation tasks and problems. The devil has really been ridiculous in throwing curve balls. I have to admit, it's actually been a crazy, good distraction from my head pain and other post-brain surgery recovery processes. I do want it all to work out.

We are in the waiting room in Oklahoma City—just hanging out until we hear our fate. I'm not scared though. His love takes my fear and reminds me that, since He is for me, no one can truly be against me. I will praise Him no matter the results. I'm just ready to know how this is going to go.

Scratch that—I just weighed, and I've gained seven pounds in two-and-a-half weeks and my blood pressure is a little too high. After the morning I've had, this is no surprise. Well, know this—I'm ready for whatever, even with the weight gain and high blood pressure. As soon as we hear anything, I'll write another journal entry. I love you all.

God has got this! Keep trusting Him with me. He hasn't let me go. He never will! May the Bible verse below be loud in your mind and spirit. It rings true in my life as you have read through my testimony with the words I have shared in these entries and/or witnessed by watching our story play out in real time.

Memory Verse 40

⚔ *"Never will I leave you; never will I forsake you" (Hebrews 13:5).*

JANUARY 2, 2014

20 › Pathology Results

🎥 Note: This is a transcription from my original recording. To see the video, visit https://youtube.com/shorts/JVR-gGTJOl0?feature=share. Sorry for the quality of the video!

Hi, everybody! We just wanted to let you know that we are finished at the doctor's office. I'm not gonna lie—when I was sitting there, I knew that I was ready for whatever he was about to say. But I almost jumped out of my skin when he said the word that I really was hoping he would say. I made him repeat it again—and maybe again after that, because I just couldn't believe what he was saying.

But we can praise God now—it is benign! It's the best word that I could ever hear in my entire life at this point. I just want to wish you all a wonderful year. Just remember to keep your praises going up to God because He has been there this whole time. It's benign! I know the story isn't over yet for us, but I'm excited to see what 2014 is going to hold.

Just know that I appreciate you diligently praying and being there for us. You all have rocked it out, and we couldn't do it without all of you. So here we are praising God on high—it is benign!

JANUARY 3, 2014

21 › Tired

Tired is the word for the day. When we came home yesterday from such a wonderful day of extravagant news, I thought I would pick up Piper finally (the doctor said I could, but to use common sense). Also, I tried to do some things around the house and realized very quickly that it's too soon. Brain surgery recovery takes time. I spent most of today sleeping off and on, then eating in between due to exhausting myself with such little work.

Tonight, we got to watch the game with some friends, and I was so tired I fell asleep while talking midsentence. This makes me laugh, and I hope it does you too, because we all know how much I like to talk! It's been a long time since I've done this. I have to let myself heal. I know this, but my heart and drive want to jump right back into a regular life of doing things.

I'm here to say that I am without a doubt going to be taking baby steps when it comes to getting back into my life. I know some who have spent time with me think I've already been going crazy. I don't see it that way. I've been resting in bed while still talking on the phone, staying connected on the computer, and making things happen for the foundation. I have been blessed to be able to continue my passion for helping and being here for others, even if it means just communicating.

I am taking this time to really pray about where God has me headed after I get to a decent healing point post-surgery. I believe God is going to open and close doors where needed. I don't want to make something happen if it's not supposed to. I can do my part, and God will do the rest.

I do need prayers for the pain that I'm having when my medicine starts to wear off. It feels like the doctor is cutting at the two surgery sites repeatedly. It's been more painful at times than I'd like to admit. I pray this will dull over time and eventually go away. I'm not good at having to depend on medicine and people's help in my everyday life, so I ask that you pray God will push me aside and let others be here for me.

I'm so thankful that many of you have stepped it up and continue to help in any way that we need. It is a ginormous help for us. Michael can't do everything, and I am way more limited than I would like. I know more now than ever about what I do and why it matters even when others don't see it. It's painstakingly obvious to me, because there's so much I see that needs to be done in order for our family, life, and household to run smoothly.

I've been trying to say yes when others offer their services. I'm grateful that they include us in their chaotic or busy schedules. You all are true blessings. I'm realizing God wants to bless us and others on this journey. I need to step aside and let that happen. Here's to all of us getting out of the way so we can multiply the blessings in each other's lives. This life is not meant for us to do alone! Love you all!

JANUARY 4, 2014

22 › Wake Up

As I listen to "Wake Up" by All Sons & Daughters, I hope we each can wake up and see that God wants to heal us and make us the best versions of ourselves. This life is filled with junk, negativity, destruction, pain, and sorrow—all from below. God is filled with beauty, positivity, peace, grace, mercy, strength, and hope—all from above. We all have a choice called free will—we choose what we do, how we say things, and who we are. I know we all make mistakes, sin, and don't do what we could or should at times.

I do know that in all the pain we go through or even cause by our free will, God is always here to heal each of us. I am learning that when God changes us, we can't just talk about it; we have to show it daily by our actions. I've looked back at my writings in journals and the words people wrote to me. I still believe the lessons that came from those times—that we really have to walk our talk! Words are meaningless without action.

No matter how much I've hurt myself or others around me over the years, it takes time and freely choosing the better, healing path. Most things take time. I can't expect anyone to trust me, nor can I trust anyone else when trust has been broken. Allowing time and choosing to go in the right direction can help, yet I do have to walk my talk.

God really wants us to let His light shine through each of us. No matter what our story holds, He wants to use each piece of it to finish our journey with a miraculous ending where His will is done and shines brightly. It's all part of furthering His kingdom and making this world a better place while we are meant to be here. As hard as it is to accept, God knew when He knit us in our mother's wombs what our lives would hold—happy times as well as the trials and tribulations. He has prepared a way out of our free will choices. He's also set up every little detail to help us through anything and everything as long as we are choosing Him.

Wherever you are in your story, and no matter what we've done or what's been done to us, it's never too late. God wants to use our whole story to tell of His grace and mercy—to tell others everything about Him. All the goodness, hurts, pains, and darkest parts of us are included. None of us are perfect. My brain surgery cuts are a reminder that time is a big healer. The littlest task may require me to be still and sleep. This can relate to our walk as well. We have the power to step aside and let God heal all of us and others. It takes time. Some things take a lot more energy. We can be still at times, and He asks us to take steps in others.

I'm learning in my life that it's never too late to make things right. I can choose to step aside and let God heal things. I can't fix anything on my own. I have to allow Him to change the things in me that need to be changed. I have to be in the game in order for Him and me to win, making things right so that changes can alter the circumstances in my story!

One big thing that I learned before surgery was that I didn't deal with my own junk and projected it onto others. I'm just glad some have forgiven me, and we can start moving in the direction of healing our relationship. I can't expect things to be fixed and changed overnight. Trust is taken away quickly and earned back at its own pace—a snail's pace. My actions and words will have to line up in order for us to move toward healing. I'm willing to put in the work. Also, I will need them to do the same.

In my relationships, where others have been a major reason for brokenness, it's going to be hard when I know the other person isn't ready to wake up and see their part. We each have to learn to forgive ourselves first, then realize that we can find forgiveness through God. I'm going to keep praying and hoping that we will wake up, see what needs changed or healed, and move toward a wonderful, healthy relationship.

This life isn't easy, but we can wake up and not add to what we're already facing. What if we all chose to wake up daily, let God reveal what we need to work on or do, and lived that out? It would be a different world indeed. We would be different! Our story would be different. There would be richness, health, and peace.

What if we all chose to wake up daily, let God reveal what we need to work on or do, and lived that out?

I've been through my share of trials and tribulations in my life, but I choose to see those as stepping stones. I choose to see it all as a positive training tool for each mountain I've faced in life. Each part has helped change me, mold me, and make me who I am meant to be in God. Don't get me wrong—I would love to have not gone through any of it. I'm just glad God is continually waking me up so I can be present—letting His light shine through me (at least that's what I hope).

This doesn't exempt me from saying things I shouldn't or even doing things that are wrong. It just means I'm going to try my best to pick up my cross, let God lead the way, and hope His will is done. I hope I can erase my list of mistakes and not add any to it. I want my will to go and His to remain. I wasn't going to type this journal entry, but apparently, I needed to type it for myself. I also have been hearing story after story that has this journal entry all over each person's story. I can stand on this, because I've tried to change so many things and people in my life. I've been so worn out from nothing changing. It's not been for lack of trying, because I've tried everything I know to do.

I've learned that all we can do is work on ourselves to get right and whole with who we need to be with God's help. We have to forgive ourselves first, before we can forgive anyone else. We have to work through our own junk so we don't project it onto others. We can pray for situations and the people in each, but we only have the power to change ourselves and hope everyone else can do the same. Perhaps, then, change can happen. I stood on a lot of old junk, misunderstandings, people's false views, and the inability to change. I hope we can all wake up and find ourselves and our lives in a better place.

I look forward to complete healing from the brain surgery. It's wonderful that I've slowed down. It's perfect timing because I know many things my heart is going through will take time as well. I'm already seeing myself and my relationships changing. Sadly, I see the devil too often trying to destroy progress. I shout out loud, "In Jesus's name, be gone—you are not welcome here."

PRAISE GOD, our heavenly Father loves us so much He wants us to be the best versions of ourselves by taking care of every single detail. He wants each of us to be a part of His plan! He wants it all! I hope we can each be where, who, and what we need to be for Him. It's amazing to trust Him as He leads the way. I am blessed to be a part of His mission.

> *Praise God, our heavenly Father loves us so much He wants us to be the vest versions of ourselves!*

Every person who took care of me at OU Medical Center was the exact team needed to take care of me. Even if they didn't know or feel the importance of their decisions, they were meant to be. I'm grateful that God cares so much about me and everyone else. It's surreal and breathtaking to see His fingerprints. May God be with each of us in this walk. I love how He's working on me and others. PRAISE HIM ON HIGH!

Here's to each of us coming out on the other side of whatever we are going through and finding ourselves in a better place—happy, whole, forgiven, loved, and peaceful!

LILIAN'S CARINGBRIDGE

JANUARY 7, 2014

219 › Missing Lilian

It's crazy that Lilian was born in 2010, and it's now 2014. Typing out the number four at the end seems as surreal as everything else we've gone through as of late. I can't seem to wrap my head around the fact that she'd be turning four in four months.

It's been almost four years since we stayed at St. John's and the adventures we had during our stay. I see myself four years later, not recovering from a partial hysterectomy while being pregnant, getting ready to fight C. diff for six to eight weeks, or awaiting the fight for Lilian's first breath to not be her last, but rather recovering from brain surgery.

Wow, life can throw many trials and tribulations our way, especially when we are at a point where we think we may have fought enough or may have nothing left to fight with. I love how God shows me that we survived because He already knew what we'd be facing in this life. He has always known the whole picture, thankfully. He has had a plan since before my beginning and continues to have one in place to meet my every need.

Though I'm finding myself once again recovering from another trial or more, God remains the same through my story. He keeps showing up Big and revealing that there is no limit to Him. PRAISE HIM ON HIGH!

I miss Lilian Grace every day. She is an extension of my heart, no matter where she may be right now. I'd love to see her grow, learn, and do what little girls do. Plus, I'd love to see her and Piper do all the sibling things that siblings get to do, no matter how much it might drive me nuts at times. I miss it all.

Having Piper, I know what I'm missing that I'm actually not missing. I watch other T18/T13 parents fight daily for their child's care and place in this world. They work endlessly on getting others to see their child's worth and mission—especially their needs. They struggle yet are happy to do it all. Though I don't miss it, I would have done it forever.

I still stand on the day she left here—that she lived her mission out and got called home. I can imagine that He scooped her up and said, "Good and faithful servant—well done." She changed me by her battle, fight, and existence. She helped many of you and others. I praised God for our battles and our journey then just as I do today. His will be done, not mine. When I get out of the way, He is magnificent and makes the way better, richer, and brighter. He makes it all worth it, no matter what the journey contains. PRAISE GOD!

I pray, no matter how you feel or where you find yourself on your journey, that you can reach a place to praise Him through the storms. I pray you can stop and let Him work it out through healing and as he brings change! I hope you can see, no matter how it turns out, and know it was good and worth it. He has you and the situation in His hands!

Praying for your journey in whatever you are facing. Let God have control. See a change in your circumstances through a healing you never knew was possible—a renewing of everything! I can't praise God enough for using all my trials and tribulations to bring about the necessary changes of who, what, and where. I hope you can find a place where He can do this for you.

I really can't wait to see what's next because He's blown me out of the water. It all started way before Lilian Grace, yet I feel like I finally started listening, trusting, and stepping aside more when she came. It's just incredible. I see Him more and more every day, and it feels so good! PRAISE GOD!

Unspeakable joy

CHRISSY'S CARINGBRIDGE

JANUARY 9, 2014

23 › Video Update

🎥 Note: Here's a video update (transcribed). Enjoy! To see the video, visit https://youtu.be/k9Uc3yc1spA.

Hi, everybody! Sorry that I'm looking rather put together. I've had a rough couple of days. I tried to do some things I shouldn't have done and went to see people—ventured out. I kinda had to convince people to get out of the house because I was tired of being in the house. I realized that wasn't probably in my best interests, but I'm glad I did it anyway. I got to share a lot of cool God stories. I'm glad I got to go, but I'm also glad that I've gotten to rest.

God's been teaching me so many things. I've been trying to listen to that gut feeling, which I think is totally the Holy Spirit. I know some people do not believe that—that's okay. Bear with me—so far, it's been really cool when I've listened to that feeling. God's been working it out for a lot of things.

Some of it people have not understood. Some people haven't been as excited about my decisions and things. Some thought I was a little controlling, which I can be. Still, all the same, God has been good to me. He's been doing so many cool things.

I'm hoping I can get them all down (in writing) one day so I can share with all of you. Some things are not meant to be shared right now. I was thinking I needed to do a CaringBridge post. I kept trying to figure out what to type—nothing came. I was looking for a song because that sometimes inspires words to come, but it didn't. Then God—I could just hear Him saying, "Go to your Jesus Calling *journal that your step-grandmother-*

in-law got you for Christmas."

I looked up today, January 9, and it's funny. Those who have been talking to me will know how dead on this reading is. (I read the entry but cannot publish it here due to copyright issues).

Author note: The entry from the book was the perfect timing to remind me not to give up. When I line up with God, all things are possible. It won't be an easy journey, but it will be worth it when I seek His help and guidance. It's definitely worth reading.

If anyone knows me, I am a go-getter. I want to change the world. I want to do it right now. I am learning that His timing is everything. My timing has been wrong a lot of the time in my fix-it ways. I've talked about that before—even in my posts on CaringBridge.

I have been feeling a little not good—quite a bit of—not good. My pain medicine is running out, so I'm having to cut back, which is causing this side of my brain to have pain on this side of my head. It's typical. Keep praying that I'll keep moving forward. God has been so good! I am a miracle!

The thing is that I should have had so many therapies, like speech and physical—relearning how to do everything. God was good at saving me from that when He brought me back. I just get to be a part of that, and it's surreal. It's a little crazy.

He's really nuts. I love how nutty He is because I'm crazy too! There are so many people going through things right now. I just pray that you can lift my prayer requests as I pray for a lot of things happening right now. We have two boys who were in a car accident, and their families are going through a lot. Their caretakers—people taking care of them who are going through a lot. They have a lot going on. Pray for them and lift them all up.

We have T18/T13 families who have an abundance of

challenges and obstacles.

The [Jesus Calling] book lists three different verses: Romans 8:31, Psalm 46:1–3, and Luke 1:37.

Memory Verses 41–43

🗡 *"What, then, shall we say in response to these things? If God is for us, who can be against us?" (Romans 8:31).*

🗡 *"God is our refuge and strength, an ever-present help in trouble. Therefore we will not fear, though the earth give way and the mountains fall into the heart of the sea, though its waters roar and foam and the mountains quake with their surging" (Psalm 46:1–3).*

🗡 *"For no word from God will ever fail" (Luke 1:37).*

I've been learning that a lot. God—when things have happened to me, things that have really crushed me, and I could not see things changing—is working it out. I love it. He is here every day. I know why He wants us to have a daily devotional. That's the time where we are supposed to just talk with Him and re-evaluate ourselves.

Take a look in that mirror to see where you are and see where your relationships are. Every single day we have a million things coming at us—a million things. The devil—he is there. You can see him. I see him every day right now. He's popping up very quickly. I'm discovering his little tail end a lot quicker.

I also get to see God too. He presents things. They are like these little interruptions. They are interruptions with what our plans are—my plans. When I say yes to some of them—when I know my gut feeling is saying, "Just listen, you are not going to understand it right now, but I promise you that I will work it out." He has worked it out, and it's incredible.

I'm really hoping that you can get there. Know that I know there are some people worried about me. I am slowing down. Today, I need to take care of my husband. I'm going to love him. He has been a rock, but he is wearing down. I need prayers for him and for the other people who have been helping us. I think I have worn them out because when I have called them to say, "Hey, can you come back?" I think they are a little tired.

Please be with everybody. Other families are going through a lot worse than what we are. Just be with every single one of them. I know it takes an army for every single challenge—tribulation, especially when it's medical. It takes a lot.

I'm excited to say that those who have helped us by providing food have taken a lot of stress off Michael. Plus, I've been trying to do it, but it wears me out. I have to take a long, long—more than a nap—I really feel like I am sleeping. It has been incredible.

By the way, we were able to help out another family. We donated to another fundraiser—actually giving another family somewhere else food. Anyone who has provided food for us up to this point has helped another family get to be fed for probably—hopefully—a month. If not, it will be close to that because we purchased quite a bit of food. I'm so excited! So thank you!

It wasn't about us not having money for food but about the load off. Michael was realizing it—I was realizing it too—just what my worth is and his worth is. It takes everybody to keep the house going, happy and whole. I'm just so excited.

I've rambled enough but know this: I love you all and thank you for the continued prayers. I'm getting there. I still have a lot to face. I do have to stay slowed down, and I am doing that as best I can. People know me. I get crazy and want to take over the world and change it. Know this: I do appreciate every single *one of you. If anyone wants to come visit me, send me a message. We can set up a time. I know I can't have a million people in one day, but I can spread it out. That's just me protecting myself in that I don't have a lot of energy.*

Anyway, I love you guys, and just know that God is so, so good. I send praises up to Him. Know that I cannot believe that I really am getting to be on this ride. It's incredible and breathtaking. He's wearing me out with goodness. I didn't realize that I could be worn out with all His goodness, but I can. I have to rest in Him with all the good. Talk to you guys later! (Blows a kiss.) Love you!

JANUARY 11, 2014

24 › In the End

Not only do I love this song "In the End" by Natalie Grant and what it says, but I also love me some banjo!

There have been a multitude of tragic stories coming my way, as well as prayer requests for each of them. I've been sending prayers up and not always knowing what to say or do. I know I'm not alone. Once in a while, I remember that God knows exactly who I said I'd pray for, and I pray that He would give them precisely what they need. My ultimate prayer is that His will be done.

I've found myself tagging a few minor other details that resulted in asking God for what I want and need, which contradicts what my ultimate prayer has been. I catch myself and start a nice little talk with God about pushing my wants and needs aside once again. I'm human. We are all human, or we wouldn't be here. He sees the whole picture. He knows what gets done and where it will take us—the effect it will have on all. I want His will, knowing and trusting that He has the better seat, view, and master plan.

I wish I could tell everyone who is going through their own trials and tribulations that their own life or death moments, their own "I wish it could be this way instead of that way," and their "God, why?" moments can be fixed, but I can't. I can't fix them, change them, or make them what we want. I really don't want that at all! I can only trust that God knows what is best for all of us. I can only prepare as much as I can, even for the worst, and expect and/or hope for the best. It will get better in time.

We all make choices. We all live with our choices as well as other people's, whether we like it or not. On another side of it, we have to deal with what is going on every day of our lives, whether we want it or not. We can put blame on others; jump on the hamster wheel and get nowhere; project our own junk onto others; and be numb, not move, or do anything. Actually, we can do something. I want to choose to trust Him through the entire roller-coaster ride with His master plan, allowing Him to heal, mold, and shape me.

Our situations may be up, down, and all around. We may think something is never going to end. We may think we have a miracle of happiness and major hope, but things suddenly crash down and we see it as tragedy, sorrow, and disappointment because it didn't go how we prayed or wanted it to. Whichever way we see our journey, I pray that we jump into His loving arms and let Him drive our roller-coaster ride while trusting in His will. When I let Him lead, it's not as scary. It becomes a beautiful roller-coaster ride, where I catch myself amazed and my breath is taken away by all the glory and phenomenal coordination. Let's face it—life is full of positive to negative and good, bad, and ugly. Sometimes we focus too much on one side or the other. I don't want there ever to be false hope. I just want there to be hope, knowing that in the end, we win through Him and His will is done.

I'm working on baby steps for myself. As I have said before about my post-surgery recovery, I tire easily. When the smaller dose of pain med wears off, I feel exactly where the instruments held my head straight and still while the surgeon cut into my skull. I know my prayer request is so small and minor compared to those fighting for their lives. Prayer warriors, I need us to also lift up my prayer requests for those I promised I'd lift up—even the small ones. Pray God takes care of all involved and that His will be done, no matter what that looks like.

For me, I take my last narcotic pill shortly. I'm hoping Tylenol and Aleve will be all that I need for however long I need it after this one wears off. I've been working through my plan on weaning myself off, knowing that I was going to run out for a second time since coming home. I don't want to be on narcotics forever. I pray God will heal it all if that is His will.

With so many in critical condition right now, this journey is not an easy one. Everyone involved is doing everything they can for those we love and/or care about. God hears when two or more are gathered. I know in all instances there are dozens to hundreds of prayers going up. Deep down, we all want what we want, but reality always sets in. Our wants are not always what is best and won't always happen.

God has a beautiful plan. Trust me, I come from a journey where I lost my daughter to death on earth. I will reunite with her in the end—eternity will be a wonderful time to catch up where there is no pain or sorrow! Lilian died multiple times during her 103 days here on earth. Our roller-coaster ride with her and even my own health problems over the years (almost dying seven times) has been one that we could have never predicted. It was up, down, up, down—repeat! There were so many highs and lows. I couldn't keep up. God taught me in all these trials and tribulations, through the ups and downs, that He has me in His hands. His master plan has always been the best plan, even if I didn't like the results of many things in my life. I have not always known the why of the final results, but He's been really good to me, helping me see more than I thought

I could. Ultimately, we win in the end! Glory, glory hallelujah—we win in the end!

God has a beautiful plan.

Praying you jump into His hands, no matter what rollercoaster ride you find yourself on at this moment. Don't try to do it on your own. When we are weak, He is strong. God always provides! No matter the results of what you are praying for and hoping for, remember there will be a day of clarity, whether it be on earth or in heaven.

JANUARY 13, 2014

25 › Truth Is Truth

I am overwhelmed sitting here thinking about what God has provided and done for us. Everyone who has stepped up and out for us, I am forever grateful. You saw a need, and with your servant's heart, you made it happen. Not letting people help me or take care of me has been a common problem. I thought I could do it all on my own, which was a total lie. I'm thankful God has taught me to let Him bless all of us by spreading the load!

In my past surgeries and chaotic trials, I saw what was needed and made myself start again too soon. It was my job, and no one else could do it as good as I could. It made my healing process take a lot longer, and there were consequences for me. This time around, my body from the neck down is great. I have no pain or restrictions. From the neck up, it's a total mess.

I try not to complain or talk about the negatives in depth, because I really hope it will just go away. Guess what? It doesn't. I'm in a new situation that I don't fully understand. I have to lean on people, because if I try to get back to reality, my physical and emotional states suffer. I can't do what I want or need to do without major consequences for my health.

Brain surgery in two places is just ridiculous. Here I am! God has made me a miracle in surviving this without any therapies. I'm blown away that God has given me life instead of death. Here I am now dealing with the healing part: two locations of my head were cut into; my skull was drilled through to get inside—an actual breaking of the bone; deep inside, a hole was created and covered with a titanium metal piece; and some veins were repaired. Sounds simple, right?

Well, I did survive the surgery. I didn't have to do any therapies. I made it home after only two-plus days post-surgery. Yet I now get tired and sore just by brushing my teeth or trying to feed myself. I've gained thirteen pounds. I'm surviving on no narcotics for twenty-four hours, but I still have to deal with the pain. If I overdo, I am nauseous, sweating, dealing with bathroom problems, and exhausted from talking and increasing pain. I do not want a pity party. I just need to state the facts for myself and others who don't get it, because I don't share as much. Complaining about it doesn't change reality. Yet it does help me mentally.

My mind, body, and soul want to jump right back into life, yet my reality is that I can't. I'm healing. I went to a birthday party on Saturday. I found myself resting in a bedroom and on the couch at different times—sleeping for a long time. Sunday, I went to church but slept through the whole thing—no offense to anyone because I would have done it no matter what. That night, we went back to church for growth track, and I took my pillow and embarrassingly slept while snoring for most of it.

Today, I had an amazing sister from church think outside the box to come clean my house while my step-grandmother-in-law watched Piper. I slept off and on for most of the day—more snoring involved. That was after I had slept for ten to twelve hours. Is this frustrating for me? You better believe it. I am a go-getter, and I love to be active and take care of others. This is just a small bump—even if I think it's a mountain—in the road. I've got people I'm praying for who are fighting for life over death.

But I can't ignore my own stuff, no matter how small in comparison to the world around me. I've caught myself saying—though I hate to admit it—that I wish God could have just let me go home to be with Him. It seems like it would have been better for all. I know this is ridiculous talk, but let's face it—I thought it, and I said it out loud. I didn't want to share this tonight, but I can't shake it off. I feel like it could help some of you out there dealing with your own silent troubles! I know that I'm happy I'm here, but this isn't easy. I let it all weigh me down, and I get depressed. None of us truly sees how blessed we are until either we don't have it anymore or we are "paused" from our life.

I want everyone to know that I do love life, but even I can let it get the best of me. I have to stop listening to the lies and discontented hearts of myself and others. I have to keep listening to God's whispers and hold tight to Him. It breaks my heart that I can try to take care of as much as I can, yet it's not good enough for even me. Even with me being inside my body, I still hear myself trying to start sooner than I should. I catch myself believing what I think I'm hearing from others when, in fact, they may not be saying anything at all—it could just be my own voice.

The devil can get sneaky, but he doesn't win. I'm breaking free of those chains. I will listen to my body. I will be thankful that I get to rest in bed or on the couch, because it's about time I took some time to rest and heal the right way. I will know that this is part of a bigger plan. I am destined for some cool things to come, yet I need to recover. I will give it time, even if I catch myself screaming silently for myself and others to understand.

I'm reminded of a climber who lost his/her footing one night while climbing. The climber fell and didn't know what to do. In actuality, they were only inches away from the ground. I have to know that this could be my moment—maybe I'm only inches away from completing the healing from this or from a change in the journey. I will stand on the rock of truth and know that God will open and close doors for me. He will get me through this part of the journey. His timing is perfect. I just need to do my part. Healing is my part right now. I have to remember it's been only twenty-seven days since my brain surgery! Typing that seems ridiculous to me.

> *I will stand on the rock of truth and know that God will open and close doors for me.*

I'm praying that we all find contentment in our hearts and souls for whatever we are facing on our journeys, knowing we can lean on God through the small and large things in life—every day! No matter where you are in life, I pray you slow down enough to hear God's whispers and let God and others lighten the load. He's giving us directions and help all the time, if we only pause long enough to hear and follow. We are all works in progress. May we all find success!

PS: Thank you for the prayers! I do feel them and know God is answering them within His will. He has been so good to us and others. I am having a little rougher time than I like coming off my narcotics, but I know time will be my best friend and healer. Thank you from the bottom of my heart for continuing to follow our story, praying for our needs, and/or to those who have been able to help out in any way. This has humbled me in more ways than I'd like to admit.

JANUARY 16, 2014

26 › Holding Tight to His Hand

This week, I found myself getting deeper and deeper into a depressive-like state. Yesterday, I slept over eight hours—naps off and on all day long—on top of eight hours of sleep the night before (1.15.14). I even let someone drive my daughter to school without me, which is not like me at all! I've been in a state of mind this week where God has really helped me let go of all my control. It has not been fun for me, but I just didn't care. I was too tired, and my head hurt too much to care, yet letting go was much needed.

I felt so out of it, and my thoughts were not always positive ones. I wished, more than I should have, that God would have just let me come home to Him. I felt like I had disappointed many people and couldn't do anything right by trying to help out or take care of people. I knew the right answers to what and how I needed to be. I trusted God completely—still do—but how I was feeling was out of my control. I was fed up with a bunch of things, plus I felt like there were people against me and/or thinking I should already be back to my old self. I had my own horrible little voice telling me that I was worthless and out of control, while another voice was saying I should already be better, back to normal, and not needing any therapies—neither voice was truthful.

I spoke to two of my doctors—neurosurgeons—on the phone and had an office visit with another doctor. I have a bad sinus infection, plus I'm fighting a depression-like state. Depression is a natural, common side effect of brain surgery. Just hearing all three doctors in agreement made me feel like I wasn't losing my mind or battle. My main neurosurgeon said that I can drive and workout as long as I feel good and I'm not tired. Adding these should help in dealing with depression and getting back to a normal, healthier state of mind—thinking more positively.

I drove myself 1.32 miles to my doctor's office, which felt more freeing than a lot of things lately. I took my time and relished the simplest pleasure of driving myself. After finding out about my sinus infection, I drove less than a mile to fill my medicine. That trip to the pharmacy was like someone giving me a million dollars. I felt like a teenager getting to drive for the first time after turning sweet sixteen.

I stopped to get a drink at Sonic and go through the car wash before heading 1.3 miles back home. Oh, I didn't realize how therapeutic it would be to do this all on my own post-brain surgery. It isn't much for an average person, but it was everything to me. Though I'm exhausted tonight, it was worth it all. I know this is a small step toward getting my independence back, but it feels like giant steps for me. Another small step was that the doctor agreed with my neurosurgeon that it would be good to workout, which makes my heart happy. This means light walking and slowly trying out the stationary recumbent bike, but it's more than just lying around with my overloaded brain.

I'm hoping the sinus infection—causing major pressure on my surgery sites—is the cause of most of the pain in my head. Trust me, to those who might be freaking out that I might overdo everything, it's not possible. My body starts showing major signs of doing just a little with dark circles under my eyes, and the surgery sites start screaming at me along with shocks on the right side of my brain. So know that my body is smarter than my thought processes and strong will!

I need prayers going up that God will heal me and the depression-like state will disappear, the sinus infection will clear up, the possible buildup of extra fluid will vanish, and that overall my body will change for the better! I want to thank you all for thinking of me and lifting me up. I appreciate the honesty of so many of my friends and family for knowing that something wasn't right with me. In two to four weeks, we will revisit my state after adding in simple workouts and venturing out of the house with some independence. I'm hoping just doing those two things will really help zap the depression. Pills and I just don't get along.

I wasn't going to post my typed version and video (transcribed), but I thought it couldn't hurt! I'm including pictures of my two surgery sites to show my healing progress. Keep those prayers going up! Love you all!

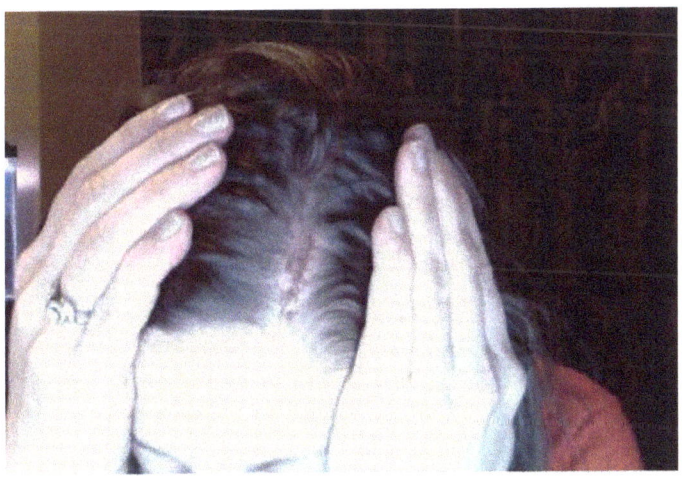

Frontal brain surgery site update

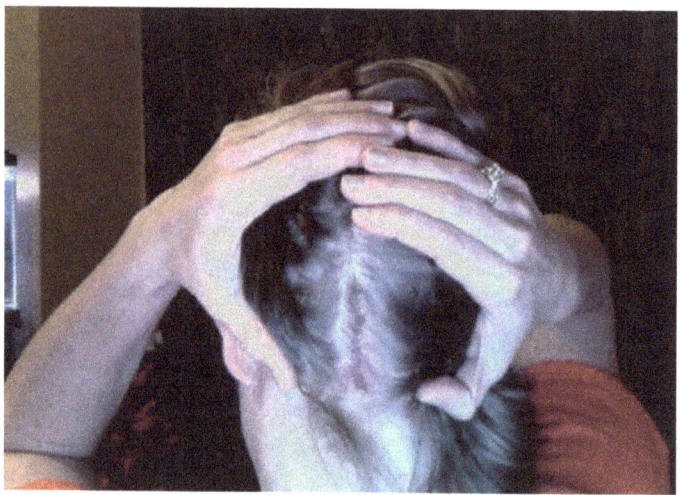

Posterior brain surgery site update

🎥 Note: To see the video, visit https://youtu.be/rJE3shUCrdA.

Hi, everybody! I want to try to give you as quick of an update as I can, but I was trying to type out a CaringBridge post, and I just felt like—you know what, I just need to do a video. I wanted to let you know with my last post I was very honest in what I was feeling, but I didn't get to tell you that I have had more thoughts of a lot of things. I felt like I wasn't being able to be enough for everybody. I wasn't being enough for myself.

I bypassed all these therapies because I didn't have to do any of those. It was brain surgery. I should be—you know—further along. I know deep down I need to take this slow—I know that. I want to thank everybody who has been worried about me or thinking about me. I want you to know that this is a big deal. After yesterday, I slept eight hours off and on in total with naps because I just didn't feel good. I felt like I just—I didn't even care.

I let some things—just whatever—you just do whatever, people. I don't want to do it. I have some wonderful people who love me who said, "Hey, this isn't you. You need to call the doctor and figure out what's going on." So I did. They called me back today. Actually, I had called two other doctors too. But my main neurosurgeon who did the surgery—he said that what I'm going through is very common. I do have depression—it's what it sounds like, and he said also I have something going on with my head with the allergies or sinus infection.

I needed to go to my main doctor here. I'm glad he said that. He told me that I could start driving if I felt like it and wasn't too tired. I could also start working out, which is really key. He said that would really help with my depression-like state. So I'm looking forward to all that. I did drive today, which I'm excited about, but I'm really tired. I don't know if you can see. I'm just really tired. I look really pretty here, and I sound awful.

My main doctor says that I do have a very bad sinus infection, so I'm trying to work through that. I think that's where a lot of my pain is because it's pressing in here (hand on head) but mostly right here (moves hand slightly back to the side of head). I wanted to show you how my scar is healing. That's the one where they went and drilled a hole in that third ventricle to help with the hydrocephalus. They put a metal plate in there.

And then—hopefully you can see it—that's the main one. I have no idea if you saw it, so I'm hoping. If not, I will have to re-record. But anyway, this is where this hurts pretty bad, and it feels like he is just cutting—and right here (points to the other surgery site). We also noticed that in my right ear that he (the doctor) could see some pressure—like extra pressure—something going on. I'm hoping—hoping—hoping and praying that if we take care of the sinus infection that it will help a lot with my pain.

I do not want to be on any narcotics anymore. It was hard for me coming off them. I've never taken narcotics for that long. I really only take them for about a day or two because I don't like how I feel. But I really needed them. I'm glad that plays in the part of the depression-like state. He and the other two doctors agreed it sounds like I have some depression, and it's nothing to take lightly. We've actually discussed that I would start working out a little bit—really light. It's not like I'm going to get to do a lot, so don't worry out there, people that are freaking out right now. I can't do a lot. I'm going to do what I can.

I did drive today. I drove myself to the doctor's office so I could see what I had. It was a little over a mile away. I went to the pharmacy and got pills. It was so nice. I'm not gonna lie. I felt like a teenager who just got her license when she was sixteen years old. Things we take for granted.

It was just nice to get to walk around the store and not have someone right beside me because I've had to have people with me a lot lately—so that was nice. Then I got to go to Sonic and get a drink. I felt so independent. I know it's like a little drink that cost me a dollar, but I didn't care. I went through the car wash, which I was kind of scared of because it was a tight little area. I thought, You know what? I'm cleansing everything. I'm just cleansing it off. God, just take it because I'm tired of just feeling like I just can't do stuff. I feel kind of like I'm trapped, but I know I'm not.

It does take time. I need you guys to hear that from me. I know because I've had some people really scared for me, and you shouldn't be. I promise what I'm going through is natural. This is a natural thing to go through, and just know that I'm aware of it. If this state doesn't change after adding a couple things of independence for me, then I'm definitely going to go to the doctor again to get the medicine that I need, because depression is not something that you joke around with. It is very serious.

When I'm going through what I was saying out loud about wanting God—wishing—He would have just taken me, I heard it, but it's like I'm trapped inside going, "No, I'm really okay. I've really come so far. I'm so much further." But it doesn't matter what I'm saying inside because I can't get it out. I had some lovely people who I talked to the last few days trying to get through to make sure if it's in my head or something else that is happening.

I will say the doctor said this is perfectly natural. This is what most people with brain surgery go through. There are a few people who get away with not having it. I'm just not one of those people. I'm on the other side of it too though. I haven't had to have all the therapies like everyone—some people. A lot of people have had to relearn how to walk, how to talk, how to form sentences, and how to say a word. They don't even know the words.

My other symptom that I do have is short-term memory (loss). Who knows if I've had that before, but it gets frustrating! Michael told me one day to stir the soup, but I didn't. He got really mad at me because I didn't stir the soup. I'm like, I didn't even remember we had soup cooking, so that was my problem. Then, so many days later, I'm like, "Oh my gosh, he told me five times to stir the soup, and I didn't." I guess if he really wants me to do something, he needs to tell me five days before, then I will remember it on that day. Anyway, that's a little humor because you have to have a sense of humor in this time of life.

I wanted to tell you all thank you so much for praying for me. I do ask for some specific prayers right now: number one, that God would heal my sinus infection that's putting pressure, which is causing a lot of the pain. I think a lot of my pain will go away once we take care of the sinus infection. He (the doctor) said it's been building up for a while. It's really in there. I can feel it. It's rough. Also, that God would help me with the depression and that it would go away. That He would heal it because it's no fun going through it.

Anyone out there who is going through depression, I prayed for you right now because it is not fun—a lot of things you really have no control over. You're like trapped inside going, "Wait a minute—I know what's right and what I should be doing while knowing it's great and God is good." But it messes with your brain a lot.

(Another prayer request) Also, I know that I've got really small veins in my body, so I need God to work on those. This is why it takes me so long to bounce back, because I have poor blood vessels. I do have my left arm where they had tried to put a main line. It's caused some of my nerves to mess up—electric shocks (in that arm). I know my neck on the right side here (points to location) is really tense, so he told me I need to start stretching it. So just pray that I'll do the right stretches and not injure anything. Really, the main things are depression and infection—it's killing—it's kicking my tail end. We will just put it that way.

Sorry, this is going on longer than it should. But I will say that God has been so good to me. He gave me—I went ahead and looked ahead on January 18, and it just spoke to me about what I'm going through right now. (The reading of Jesus Calling, January 18, is not transcribed in this journal for copyright reasons.)

It's so true—no matter what's going on, God has always been good to me, and I know it. I think when my husband has got it together, I really keep it together. But whenever I see him crumbling, I lose it a little bit. I do depend on my husband a little bit more than I think I do and I should—he is our spiritual leader of our household. But I know whenever he's—everything's kind of spiraling and stuff, I start really losing my ground a little bit. But I know that I'm still on the solid rock of God—he's going to get me through anything.

This is just a little bump in the road that has sometimes felt like a ginormous mountain. If I can tell you anything about what you're going through in life, hold on tight. God has got you. He is taking care of you. He has a plan for you, just like he has a plan for me.

There are going to be times when the devil just tries to hit you in every single direction along (the way). He did this week. My daughter's sick right now. She had an almost 102-degree fever tonight, so we will have to take her to the doctor in the morning. My husband has been kind of out of it and stressed. I could see it. I hate it for him because I don't want him to be stressed. He's gone through so much with me with my health and just our lives together—we lost a child. He's been there through the whole thing. I am so thankful that he's still by my side because he could have left me like anybody else—a zillion times, I feel like. I'm just going to pray a prayer right now:

Dear Heavenly Father, I just thank You so much for loving me—always loving me. That love never goes away—nothing can separate that love from me and You. We just thank You so much for everything You have done, Lord. You just keep showing up. I know there are so many things happening right now. I just pray Your will be done. You know, sometimes whenever You heal us—sometimes that means we get to come home with You, but then other times, we get to be here. Lord, You know when we're supposed to be here or not—I just thank You for that.

You've got our backs. You are guiding us through this life, Lord. I just pray You'll heal each one of us in what we are all going through. We are going to get there, Lord. You are going to make it happen. I just praise Your name and lift You high in Your wonderful and beautiful name. Amen.

I love you guys. I just thank you so much. All the people who have come and helped me—let me tell you what—it is hard for me to let people help. You have been so gracious in helping us—providing food, cleaning, and doing stuff for Piper. You've done so much. I'm just blessed. We've been so fortunate to have so many amazing people—especially those who are praying where you are. It's phenomenal! I do feel the prayers. God's been really—when I catch things—He's like, "Bam, let's do this." Like, we're not going to stay in this state for very long.

I'm thankful that I'm going through this because I do need to let go of the reins. There's a lot of people I can trust, and I need to just trust them. I can't stop stuff from happening. I just have to trust that God is going to get us through it—whatever comes and hits us. So anyway, thank you guys so much. I love you (blows a kiss).

JANUARY 20, 2014

27 › Walk on the Water

Praising God . . .

I continue to be super blessed by so many people helping me. My biggest helper this past week has been my mother. It was hard to say goodbye and let her get back to all the other people she helps. God has been moving and working tremendous miracles in my and others' lives with the healing of our hearts and souls—more needed than I could have ever thought.

On the post-brain surgery journey, I've had many side health projects that have gotten in the way of healing. Yes, health projects sound better to me than sicknesses or setbacks. One of my side health projects has been a sinus infection. It's nearing the end of its stay, which is helping in all areas of my life—mentally, emotionally, and physically. My head/skull pain is finally starting to lighten, which is a big relief! PRAISE GOD!

My daughter Piper's health is improving, but it has been hard on her and everyone else. We fought her fever for four days. I've kept her home today from school, just in case. Not only is it hard to be sick and have your baby sick, it's hard to do it post-brain surgery. My mom and husband were life savers through all that we've been facing. I forgot how bad a sinus infection can be on a person, but adding my other healing and dealing makes it way worse for me. I'm praising God that this too shall pass! I see the light at the end of the tunnel.

I now understand why it is harder to get back to normal

life. In my healing, everything takes a lot longer and requires energy just like running a marathon, because my main station was messed with. I'm sure there are many who would love for me to be back in full swing, doing all my jobs, but I have to take naps throughout the day in order to function. Since I am finally taking it slower, I am getting stronger!

I am finally accepting that God is using this to coordinate and bring in full force a healing program that has been in progress for years. Plus, I'm getting some rest. I didn't know I could ever really accomplish this in my life. I see significant changes and victories in my small steps, which makes me very happy. God has been so good to train me with lessons through life, as well as heal me from all my brokenness.

I've been doing more devotional time while focusing on what, where, and who God intends for me to be. I'm praying that wherever He has me going and/or whatever He has me doing that I'll continue to trust Him as I work on a more balanced self and life. Again, I cannot thank you enough for your thoughts, prayers, and/or help during this season of my life. You have helped one of the most stubborn people I know—me. God has been gracious and merciful in answering prayer after prayer while working on me. Thanks for being obedient and communicating with Him on my behalf!

I've found some of His answers to be very humorous but totally needed. Remember that, when we pray for others, He'll make sure to take care of us as well! I love this about Him! I'm happy I've gone through the bad, the good, and the ugly. Some adventures I could have done without, yet God has used them to teach me lessons and chisel away my imperfections. In my healing, I'm letting this be not necessarily a restart button for my life like I originally thought but a chance at finally being ready to walk out on the water as my journey shifts and heads into a new chapter. I'm glad He keeps getting me to a place where I can see what He's doing! I love seeing how God works it all out!

I'm getting ready for when I walk out on the water again for my next assignment while learning more. I can see how He brings all my experiences, adventures, and lessons into a magnificent mixture to help me get to where, who, and what I can be. I have been very active in my grieving journey, and it makes me happy to know all this hard work is paying off. Lilian Grace taught me that God has been trying to talk to me, work on me, change me, and use me all along.

I can only imagine God shaking His head, stating something to the effect of, "Baby girl, I communicate with you all the time, if only you could be still and just breathe. I know you hear me, here and there, through things, but I want to help you with everything. I communicate with you 24/7. I place people and things in your life to help you out. I love you unconditionally and have plans for you that are far more than you could ever imagine." Just thinking about this and looking back at my thirty-five-and-a-half years helps me see just how much He has done for me. I've been fortunate to do some amazingly wild things for His kingdom and His children. It's really cool and extravagant, to say the least!

In knowing my life has changed drastically over the last five weeks, I realized He's given me a multitude of opportunities to rest, review, and restart over all these years. The only problem before was that I always found myself learning many lessons yet still trying to be the previous version of myself—holding on oh-so-tight. I will not ever be the Chrissy I used to be because I am a better version of who I need to be for Him.

This brings me to the fabulous song "Walk on the Water" by Britt Nicole. Since I was a little girl, I wanted to be a vessel for God—doing His kingdom work. I love getting people to their full potential by helping them reach their best version in this life. I have been fortunate to play small roles for others. I look back and praise Him for how He used me, even when I wasn't where I could be in Him. Even though I had some amazing times doing His work, I also see when I wasted a lot of His time.

Over the years, I've been a people pleaser. I've struggled with my worth and forgiveness for broken promises between God and me. The depression I've experienced through this surgery did not start post-surgery. I have a feeling it's been deep down for some time. Looking back, I see how much God wanted me to see how worthy I am—beautiful, inside and out, and priceless. He paid it all for me when He sent His Son to die on the cross for my sins! PRAISE GOD!

Many people have asked me where I think my journey is going, and I will give you an answer. I am going to try to put myself out there while praying God opens and closes doors where needed. I'm excited that God has given me time to review and recognize how He has gifted me. I don't have to rush. I just have to take a step out on the water. He'll do the rest.

If there is any advice I can give, I'd like to give some here—random at that:

- Don't settle for a life that you are just getting by with. God wants more for you than that. You may not be using your full potential, or maybe God needs to do some work in you that you may be ignoring.

- When God gives us time to rest—even if we don't see it that way—take time to rest, and slowly find your new balance. This one I'm finally getting.

- We can be angry, bitter, or miserable, because we have focused on things of misunderstanding, falsehood, or misconception. Face all of them—deal and let go—so you can live a life of contentment, sweetness, and happiness.

- If we feel like we have been wronged or just fed up, why not go to that person and get it straightened out? I think this could resolve 85 percent of our struggles or problems. Most of the time, there's a misunderstanding, falsehood, or misconception at play!

- If we can't get over something, perhaps we need to turn the mirror around and see the problem—ourselves. Not every time, but more times than we would like to admit.

- Our world or life could be richer and better if each one of us could let God heal us and make us whole again.

- If you don't like what is going on, perhaps you are meant to be somewhere else. I know that when I am not willing to move, God will eventually move me through my circumstances. I usually don't have a choice after my circumstances drastically change.

- I've learned that the grass is greener on the other side, which requires a lot more work and maintenance. This goes for anything in life. Having my own business and being a stay-at-home mom are tough to do, and money doesn't fall into your lap.

- Each of us is worth everything in God's eyes.

- If I get myself lined up with God and right with Him—forgiven—it doesn't matter what everyone else thinks, only Him. We all, and that includes me, can be too quick to judge and can hold past sins over each other's heads and even our own.

- If I do all things through Christ, He gives me strength every single time.

- Life is not a guarantee. We take life and things for granted until they are gone or we have to take a break from them. Cherish even the smallest things in life because you never know how much you'll miss it.

- If you don't deal with your issues or junk, it will follow you everywhere and in everything that you do. Sadly, we project our junk onto many people and expect it to be okay.

- When making decisions in our lives—good, bad, or ugly—imagine your choices being played on the big screen at church for everyone to see. Would you be happy with your choices or completely disgusted? If anything you do can't be played on the big screen at church, should you be doing it in the first place?

- Life is always easier when I am real with people and not trying to be someone that I cannot be.

- Communication will save your life and everything in it! It is a major tool in keeping my marriage going through all the craziness.

There are so many other lessons to share, but these made the list. I just felt like putting it here. Many of us are going through our own battles and transformations—just remember to hold on to God.

I found a perfect nugget for many of us today that's in my *Jesus Calling* devotional. Go read the January 21 entry. It touches on our desire to want only God and depend on Him. When we trust Him, the fear of falling fades away. We are safe. Here are the two verses from the reading:

Memory Verses 44–45

"The eternal God is your refuge, and underneath are the everlasting arms. He will drive out your enemies before you, saying, 'Destroy them!'" (Deuteronomy 33:27).

"Neither height nor depth, nor anything else in all creation, will be able to separate us from the love of God that is in Christ Jesus our Lord" (Romans 8:39).

Praying for all of us to let go and let God do what He needs to do through answering our prayers and shaping us into who, what, and where He needs us to be. We are made for more when we allow Him to change us. Will you walk out on the water with Him when He calls? You will lose only what is not serving Him, others, and yourself.

I praise God for caring about me while taking care of me! Be brave in knowing that God is for you, and nothing can separate us from Him. Love you all!

JANUARY 27, 2014

28 › Waking Up

Ever have a wake-up moment when you realize you've gained way too much weight and/or that your light bulb covers are not tan, just dirty? Well, I'm a little over six-weeks post-brain surgery, and I feel like I'm waking up to a whole new reality. I've gained a total of sixteen-plus pounds over the last two months. My light bulb covers will be cleaned one room at a time since they aren't a tan or cream color—it's called dirt!

How many times do we let life get in the way and drag us down? Too many!

I'm a little over six-weeks post-brain surgery (short-term memory loss catch), and I feel like I am getting my life back a little bit each day. I still get really tired and sore if I overdo it, but I am finding that I can do more than I did the previous week. I have to rest a lot more than I'd like, but I see it as a vacation in between trying to do basic chores. Thanks to a new close friend for suggesting that I keep track of what I'm doing and what I'd like to see myself doing, then look at the list the next week to see where I am. It's been an essential tool for me.

The pain, steroid, antibiotic meds, inactivity, and overeating—stress eating—have played a role in my weight gain. Today, I started a twenty-four-day cleanse to get me back to reality while slowly beginning a walking program in the house—I'm slow, but I'm moving. After one day of eating better and adding in major vitamins, I see this is a smart move for me, my husband, and everyone around me.

I have discovered over the years that there is a magic number where everything fits better and I feel my best. Gaining all the weight hasn't helped my depression-like state or my overall health.

My sinus infection turned into bronchitis with a major head cold mixed with allergies and a couple of other unmentionable side effects. My husband and daughter have had their own health struggles, so I am slowly going to disinfect the house with many helpers. I always knew helping others was good for me, but I never have let people really help me much. I seriously could not do my life now without many of you. I thank God for helping me see the light!

Please continue to pray for us, especially so that we can have a household without sickness. It's been hard. I know that myself, along with many others, are sick of being sick. Someday, I will look back and smile, knowing we survived and thrived after this season. It's just hard to see past some of it now. I've had to miss some very important moments, but I know that I'll be back to some of it before long. Also, pray I keep things slow by listening more to my body. It's been doing well at letting me know. My short-term memory loss has been in and out. It seems like it's getting better, but there is room for improvement.

I pray that we each make a reality check and let God make changes and adjustments where needed. I don't want to catch every illness under the sun because I'm unhealthy. I have a mission to do one thing at a time. I have the power to eat better and work out slowly—to be healthier. Here's to all of us continuing to reach our full potential in all aspects of life!

FEBRUARY 5, 2014

29 › Seven-Weeks Post-Brain Surgery

I've included an update video (transcribed below) with pictures. Enjoy, and love you all! Thanks for the continued prayers!

🎥 Note: To see the video, visit https://youtu.be/S0qs3WmsbKw.

Hey, everybody! I just wanted to give you a quick update about everything that's going on. I'm seven-weeks post-brain surgery. I feel like I've come a long way, but I still have a ways to go. I'm still dealing—as you can hear—with a stinking sinus infection that will not go away. Please, prayer warriors, pray that it goes away and stays away. I'm tired of dealing with it.

I've now—I'm on—I went ten days on an antibiotic and now ten more days on another antibiotic. It's just driving me nuts. Then I went—without thinking about it—twenty-four hours without extra-strength Tylenol, which I was doing every six hours at 1,000 milligrams. That mattered. I'm back on it—started that again this morning, so I'm hoping that it gets better.

They've got me on this spray stuff. Hopefully, that'll help with the sinus infection along with the amoxicillin. Just pray—my stomach's been having issues with everything. I don't know if it's just finally catching up to me—just everything. I've been trying to do a detox program on top of it to try to just help cleanse everything out.

I'm a stress eater, so that hasn't been good. I gained up to twenty-two pounds total since before the surgery. I'm down a little bit now after working on that. For my body, I know when it's at a certain weight that I will catch everything, and I'm just miserable. I know I'm still—it's so different for every one of us. But know that I know that for my body, and it's been tough for me. But I'm a healthy eater. I'm still doing things. I'm a stress eater. I started just grabbing everything and anything. It could be the most random things. It wouldn't matter if it's been there for months. If it's not expired, it's going in (my mouth). So pray for me that I will have some obedience in watching that—it would be nice.

I just want to thank everyone again because I know we're each going through our own problems. I'm praying for everybody, especially those that watch this—that God will just be with you and everything that's going on. You are not alone.

I've definitely been fighting—I catch myself saying crazy things to myself. I'm sitting here going, No. God thinks this of me. God thinks that. God loves me. God thinks I'm worth it. God thinks I'm beautiful. Know that God's been really good to me in working with me through a lot of things. I'm excited to see—you know—all this that he's doing. It's been helping a lot of people, so I have to praise Him for that. I can't be upset. I have had to miss a lot of things that—it's hard for me because I feel like I'm missing out. I'm like that two-year-old who doesn't want to go to sleep, like the two-year-old I have who does that. But it's been good.

I think about Stevie Crowder's family. If you're watching this, she is and will always be a superwoman to me. I don't know how she did it. Sorry, I'm gonna try not to be emotional, but she was amazing. I didn't get to talk to her personally, but

RAINBOWS AND BRAINSTORMS

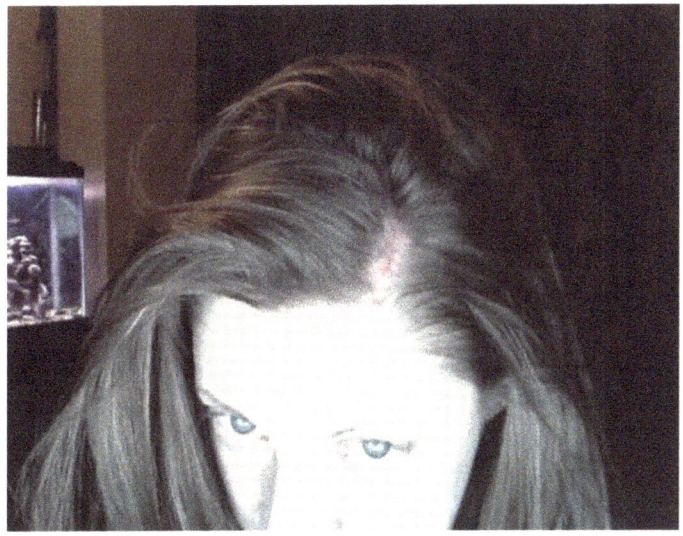

Frontal brain surgery site update

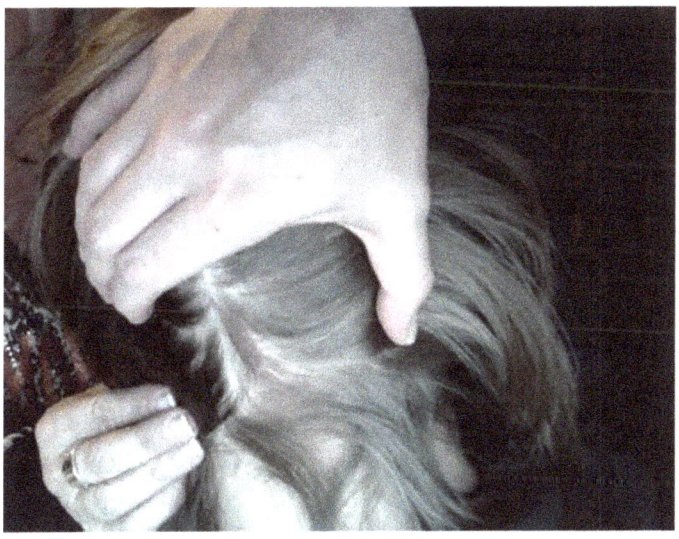

Posterior brain surgery site update

I knew by the things she would post—the pictures I'd see. Brain surgery is the hardest thing I've ever gone through, and I've lost a child. It is not easy. It's been difficult, but it's been good for me too. Because I see where God—the things He's wanted to work on me, He's working. He's maturing me in so many areas of my life.

I look back now at my past and go, "Wow, I bet some of my bosses—so many of my people I dealt with—were like, wow, she really needs to get it together. You know, she has it together on so many levels, but then not on so many levels."

God's been good to me. I see my life coming back like 180 degrees, but I'm in a different place now. I know dealing with Lily was good for me. It stripped me of things I needed to be stripped of. This brain surgery is really shaping me and helping me know that I can—I'm capable of doing a lot of things. I'm just not meant to do it all at once. That's something I continue to work on, but God's been good to me.

I've been able to tell people no a lot lately, which I hate. But it has been good for me too, because life goes on if I can't always do it. I'm excited to see where I'm going to go with all this. It's just crazy. Like I said—thinking back to Stevie and knowing her brain matter was cut into and mine wasn't. I just had the holes drilled in my skull, and I can feel it—it throbs.

Today, I was trying to do some stuff, and I had to like— whoo—stop for a minute, and people looked at me like, are you okay? I just said yes. I just—it was throbbing hard, and I have to—it's just part of it. I don't know how long that'll last, but I do know I'm so much further than I was.

If you would have talked to me two weeks ago, I would have thought that this is never going to be different. I am going to be stuck here forever. I've talked with some other people, and I know that we always want everything now. We want it quick. We want it easy. It's not meant to be easy all the time. I'm glad that God is working on me. He still loves me enough to deal with who I am, and He wants me here, so I'm excited! I look forward to seeing where He has me going. I'm praying a lot.

Please pray that God will put me where I'm supposed to be—there are lots of options at this point. I'm just kind of getting myself ready so I can move whenever He says it's time to move on whatever it is. Anyway, thank you so much for just constantly being there for us, even if I don't physically get to talk to you. It means a lot to know that you are here. Know that whatever you're going through, God's got this—He's got it. Just put it in His hands. It's a lot easier because I try.

I went a week—over a week or so—not trying to read Jesus Calling *because I was afraid to read it. I'm glad I did because it was the stuff I needed. It was good stuff. Anyway, I love you guys (blows a kiss) and thank you so much. Hey, I'm getting there. You just never know each day. I kind of go through it and think,* Hey, it's going to be a good day, *and then I sleep for three hours. So you just never know. Anyway, He's got me in His hands, and that's all I know. I'll talk to you later.*

All smiles on Valentine's Day

FEBRUARY 14, 2014

30 › Eight-Weeks Post-Brain Surgery

Hoping everyone is having an extra special Valentine's Day. No matter what state you find yourself in, know that God loves each of us unconditionally! Enjoy the video! Love you all!

🎥 Note: To see the video, visit https://youtu.be/Mv90tVtyaIE.

Hi, everybody! I just wanna wish you a happy Valentine's Day. Wednesday—this past Wednesday—marks eight weeks since my brain surgery. I wanted to give you as quick of an update as I can. I did a seventeen-minute video a couple of days ago. I was gonna post up, but I am not going to post a seventeen-minute video.

I just wanted to let you know the things that I'm still dealing with. I'm still dealing with weight, which is fine. I've been doing some things that are not helping the situation, like eating, and I can't work out like I used to, so that's been interesting. I have added a little bit more intense of a workout compared to just walking around my house that has thrown me back a little bit. I have to make sure that I'm resting on top of that.

Also, my head right in here (pointing to the area)—still—it just likes to hurt off and on a lot. I thought I could try to spread out my Tylenol—the extra-strength Tylenol—and that's not happening. It's still painful. Best way to describe it would be, when one of your limbs is numb and you are trying to—and you accidentally hit something—that electric shock shocks through, and that's what my head feels like a lot. I know that once in a while when we are riding in the car and I try to lean back, it hurts to have it even hit the seat. So right now, I'm having that where there's some pain, but I obviously put some makeup on and did my hair today. It took a lot out of me, but that's okay. It's part of it—I'm realizing that.

A few days ago—a couple of days ago when I actually recorded, I was talking about being frustrated and knowing that I just wanted things to be different. I'm tired of it being like this, but then also, I know God—His own—has been teaching me that I need to be patient. I need to be still, and that is not easy for someone like me. But what is really great—I was getting very frustrated, and I had a prayer that God would please help me because I am really struggling.

This is what He gave me. This is something from February 7 in my Jesus Calling *book that I hadn't read. I had to go from the (January) eleventh to the (February) seventh, and this is what treasure was waiting for me.* (The reading has been removed for copyright reasons. The summary is about coming to God for rest and renewal when things are rough and you are worn out. It brought reassurance and peace to my spirit. He reminded me that He has every detail covered. I may feel like I'm alone, but He is always working to make it right and provide for every need. The suffering never feels good. He wouldn't allow it unless it was necessary. I encourage you to read it.)

Really? I cannot say there is not a God. He is always taking care of me. I've been noticing a lot of people around me who have been going through so much pain and sorrow. There are lots of life changes happening for people, with relationships ending and new ones beginning and job changes. I know right now people have been asking me, "What are you going to do, Chrissy?" The answer for this very moment is that I've got to make sure I continue to get my act together for my family—for myself.

I know that not eating right and not getting to work out that I've now—I'm twenty pounds for sure still. I've been doing a detox. But when you do a detox and you're still eating out and doing things like eating sweets, you're not going to get anywhere. I'm not gonna lie. I've needed the sweets. They've helped for a short minute. They've helped me feel a little bit better about everything that's going on—the frustrations I have because it's not easy when you're so active and you can do everything you want, and then you can't.

So I have to take one day at a time—one step at a time—and know that God really does have this time for me. He's blessing me with time off from everything. I've got to accept that and know that this is just a small step in my life. I've got the rest of my life, so if I can accept this—be content in this—He's working it out. He's getting things ready.

I've got about ten pounds I could go down. I'm just really waiting for Him to tell me, because God is not a God of confusion. He will definitely let me know. He's taking care of me. He's got me in His hands. I'm just so thankful for that. It's like the best Valentine's gift anybody could ever give you. Number one: God gave us Jesus—He died on the cross for our sins. When we come to Him, we have eternity. He also takes care of us every single day.

God is—I'm sure—very entertained by me sometimes and probably frustrated at other times, but I'm just glad He loves me unconditionally—that's everything to me. So if I can give you anything, number one: please pray for me that I'll continue to let God let me—that I will be still. Number two: I won't overdo it. I've done really good at trying to balance. This week's kicked my tail end a little, but I've been trying to—I've been kind of all over the place. I just—pray that I'll keep trusting

Him and letting Him take care of me.

Like I said, He's been lining up my life. I know the possibilities of my life—it all depends on other people. I'm just kind of sitting here waiting to see what He wants, but I'm also healing. I'm still working through that. It's just been two months. I'm so much further than I was. I just love you all for continuing to lift us up in prayer. That sinus infection is finally starting to go away. I feel like we're getting somewhere, so just pray that we'll have continued health and that I'll still make these baby steps. God is good. I really am blessed. I've met a lot of people and gotten a lot of cool God stories along the way. Thank you, guys, so much, and I love you. Bye! Happy Valentine's Day!

Piper's Valentine's Day nap

FEBRUARY 19, 2014

31 › Nine-Weeks Post-Brain Surgery

Love you all! Thanks for continuing to be here with us and lifting us up! God is so good!

🎥 Note: To see the video, visit https://youtu.be/slQSIDJnnzw.

Hi, everybody! It has been nine weeks since my brain surgery. It's surreal to say that I'm surviving and thriving from brain surgery. I'm so blessed! Thank you so much for all the prayers and just thinking of us, lifting us up. It has been crucial to help me get to a better place. I've had my highs and lows. I feel like—you know—the changes I've made so far in the last twenty-four days have started to help me.

I've been reminded of some things that I still need to work on, which are good. I've added the infrared sauna, and that's helpful to pull some toxins away that I needed (gone). I drove myself to Cushing and back, which was really a huge, huge stride in my life. I was so excited that I got to do that. I also have been working out every day now. I was giving myself some breaks, but now just a little bit here and a little bit there. Yesterday, I did real light, just walking. Still, it's better than nothing, and I'm so excited that I can say that I can do that and not feel like I'm dying.

My head still hurts, but that's part of it. I'm trying to do what I can—know when to rest. I took a nap yesterday because I knew I needed it after two days of working out. Yesterday was a lighter day. I know that God's not done with me. He's got a ways to go on me, especially my heart. I've been reminded this week of things I need to work on with people. I've been in a place sometimes where I just don't care. I don't want to care about the situations that have been happening. I kind of want to just ignore it.

But guess what? When we ignore things, it doesn't go away—it's still there. Just like me, ignoring my situation of eating whatever I wanted these last couple of months since my brain surgery, I gained twenty-two pounds. Obviously, my ignoring what was going on with me did not help. It just made things worse. I do know that I am trying to go in a more positive direction on some things that I need to.

I've come so far with so many people. There've been so many relationships in my life that have been patched up. Not even patched up—healed, made better. I feel like we're in a good place. If I can help you in any way with any of this, know that you have to try. You have to give it to God. I will say number one: the Jesus Calling *book has been phenomenal. It's been what I needed to read a lot, even if I have not wanted to.*

Also, Mandisa—ahhh—she's just awesome. She has a song that I've been listening to a lot—I love it. There's another one, too, but this one I wanted to really read the words to you. It's called "Press On." (The words have been removed for copyright purposes.) *It's a great song. I'm telling you that Mandisa has some phenomenal songs. They have been good for me to listen to. I know for me—my encouragement to others is to make sure you're putting soul food in through music, through reading, and through going to church—it helps. It's helped me so much.*

I'm still, like I said—I'm not perfect. I still have people I don't want to talk to that I'm like, I just can't. I just need you to stay over there and do your own stuff that you've been doing. We'll get there someday. It's not a good place—that's showing conditional love, and I don't want that. I want unconditional love like God has given me. He's given me unconditional love. He's given me forgiveness.

My encouragement to others is to make sure you're putting soul food in through music, through reading, and through going to church—it helps.

I know when I see someone not trying like they need to be—it's harder. Like, I can say for myself, it was hard for me to see that I wasn't trying. I just didn't care. I'm glad God's got me to a different place right now. Like I said before, I've got a long way to go. I'm not perfect. I will say this: the church is a hospital for sinners. I am a sinner just like everybody else—nobody is exempt here on earth until we die and go to heaven.

Anyway, I wanted to give you that quick feedback. I love you guys, and I just thank you so much for continuing to be here on our journey. I'm going to press on. I'm going to do this race. My life right now—I feel like—is really a marathon training. It's one day at a time—one step at a time, sometimes even. I can't go mile for mile because I'm not at that place now. I will be—I have a feeling. I'll get to run again. I can't wait. I feel like I've come so far.

I praise God for everything. I wish you all good luck in what you're going through on your own walk. Know that when you try to ignore the situation—whatever you're going through—it's not going to go away. It's going to still be there, and it could get worse. I love you guys!

MARCH 3, 2014

32 › Eleven-Weeks Post-Brain Surgery

All I've wanted to do is to be back to my old self since brain surgery, but the truth is that I don't want to be my old self. I want to be a better version of myself. I want to keep letting God mold and shape me into who He has always intended me to be.

> *I want to keep letting God mold and shape me into who He has always intended me to be.*

Wednesday marks eleven weeks since my brain surgery. I've looked back at the beginning of this CaringBridge account by reading the posts and watching the videos. I guess God intended for me to see how far I've come. I've been very emotional but so grateful for God's grace and mercy. I know exactly how I felt when I said my goodbyes on surgery day, what it felt like to wake up, and the struggles I've had since. This journey has been unique and at the top of my list for trying to survive it.

See, losing my daughter, Lilian Grace, was the hardest thing I had ever gone through before the brain surgery. Trust me, I've had many journeys to choose from, yet it was number one. I will say that brain surgery has been worse than even that. Lilian Grace's death is something I continue to live through, yet it hasn't confined me nor kept me from doing life. Brain surgery stopped me. It's the one thing in my whole life that actually stopped me. I had no choice but to physically do nothing—to think, to process, and to move into a different place right where I was.

I finally had to face a different kind of grief and trial. When you only have the option of being still and not moving, it makes you face everything. It all catches up to you. There's no running, training, distracting, or anything else. There's only one way to face your reality when you are stopped—straight on. It's the hardest thing to have to face all aspects of reality, no matter how much you didn't want to and no matter how much it could hurt.

There's a song that I wanted to listen to before I even knew I was facing depression from the surgery. I was drawn to the song over and over. One Sunday at church recently, my wonderful friends (Shad and Rachel Foley) sang it. I cried over and over. The song had multiple meanings for me: one was from my perspective to my old self and another to my relationship with God. The song is "Say Something" by the Great Big World and Christina Aguilera.

In the song, for myself, the depression was fierce and life-sucking. This song helped wake me up. I was losing myself and didn't want to be here. I had given up, and I didn't trust myself any more in what I thought or wanted to do. I let people help me, and thank God I did. I needed them all. I was drowning and had forgotten how to swim. It all was way bigger than me, and I couldn't see myself getting any better or for things to change.

Thank God, I was wrong. My willpower didn't give up. I said something and woke up, realizing things had to change. I needed to do the opposite of what the voice of depression was saying to me. I needed to start saying something to that crazy voice inside. I needed Chrissy, who had survived all those other trials and mountains with God's strength.

I can sit here and type a wonderful statement for myself, God, and all of you: I am surviving and making great strides in recovery. I didn't give up on myself. I got up again and dusted myself off. The pain still comes and goes, but I can actually do things. The sinus infection is gone. I'm doing preventative things to keep it all under control. God has blessed me with intelligent doctors who have helped me tremendously. PRAISE HIM ON HIGH!

I've been working out a lot to help fight depression naturally. The infrared sauna is helping me relax and remove the toxins that had built up in my system. I'm on an allergy spray to keep the sinus infection away. I'm doing acupuncture again to help with healing and hormone therapy, which is already showing that it's working. PRAISE GOD!

About the song and how it applies to my relationship with God: I pictured God singing this song to me. I know He will never give up on me, but that doesn't mean I get to take Him for granted. He loves me unconditionally and forgives me always, but I can't take that for granted either. I want to make sure I make Him proud. I know that I will more than likely fail people at some point, yet I don't want to fail Him. In all of this, I have learned that we all have work to do.

This past week, I was blessed by two amazing women at two different lunches. Many things were discussed, and it made me ready for my weekend and the next steps God has prepared for me. I can't wait to see what God has in store for me and all of us!

This past weekend, I attended two celebrations of life and a fiftieth wedding anniversary in Cushing. It was so wonderful to catch up with so many classmates, friends, family, and church family members. I didn't realize how much I missed the face-to-face encounters with everyone and how much I needed to see many of you. It reminded me of how lucky I am to have incredible people in my life.

God is so good at giving me blessings and helping me see where I need to go. Sitting at the celebrations of life was surreal. You all could have been at mine just eleven weeks ago, but God had a different plan, for which I am grateful. We all have a purpose, and He knows when our time is done. I'm thankful that I still get to live out mine for longer! I remember many of you telling me that God has even bigger things for me. I'm starting to see those things come about, and in time, I will get to share.

I get to do this life—it's so cool! God is really good all the time, and all the time He is good! Thank you from the bottom of my heart for caring, praying, and/or thinking about me and my family. You've helped me in more ways than you will ever know. Always remember to say something to God and yourself throughout all that you face. Don't ever give up! God is working it all out! Love you all!

MARCH 30, 2014

33 › Finally, an Update

Finally, my first post in a month—enjoy!

I can't believe it's been a month since my last update. Thank you to everyone who has sent me texts, emails, and Facebook messages—even called to check on me. This past month has had a lot of ups and downs, but God has been taking care of me through it all. Praise Him for not giving up on me.

I'm typing this at 2:07 a.m. from Cushing (posting from home now after eleven at night on the same day). This weekend was not what I had planned, but it makes sense lying here in the guest bed at my dad and mom's. I hadn't planned on spending the night, but things changed. I felt like it would be beneficial to stay. I've learned when I get a strong feeling from my gut that I should listen, so I did.

Unfortunately, my aunt lost her mom this past Friday night, and it got me thinking about a lot of things. I saw my niece play soccer. I got an awesome, much-needed two-hour-and-ten-minute walk with my sister-in-law, Kristen. My mom and I got some major quality time, which we both needed.

My dad watched the Man Up weekend movies on the Up channel last night. I ended up watching *Courage* and *Grace Card*. Both of these movies were meant for me and made me emotional (no surprise with the way I have freely been shedding tears lately), but this crying was different. I could feel a release and emptying happening from this cry fest. These movies added to this month's journey of silence from my blogging in giving me no choice but to type this for you all to read.

I felt led to punch in two different dates into a between-dates calculator, and craziness happened. Today marked 103 days since my brain surgery. I bawled my eyes out—not for the pain in that number but for the reminder that God is so specific and knows me so well that He gets more than specific about helping me and guiding me. My journey with Lilian Grace was hard. At times, it felt short, yet longer on other days. Guess what? Since my journey from brain surgery began, I've felt similar things and feel the shortness and length of the recovery. Both 103 days at this point have gotten me right back to where He needed me to be, especially with today being our last day at our old church building where we got to bring both girls to share God's place and people. (Today was crazy emotional, by the way.) Letting go of a place is not easy, but I know God has incredible things planned!

See, I'm realizing that we really do have the answers, usually on the first instinct—that gut feeling—and reaction to a majority of things in life, yet we have a hard time following through with what we discover. What's wild about how God works? No matter what we choose, if He has a plan for us and we really want to follow it, then He will always bring us back to it, no matter what situation or part of the journey we are in. He's magnificent in that He never gives up as long as we are willing to look to Him. Bear with me, because I need to take us back some weeks:

March 2: I was asked by two wonderful friends to officiate their wedding, which means I needed to be ordained. I realized that many other projects I'd been dragging my feet on would benefit from me taking this leap of faith.

March 9: I spoke with my pastor about getting ordained. I felt like, *Who knows what might come of it?* But I was going to trust God. I know I've been called to do more than just sit here. That night, Michael and I attended the Winter Jam concert—amazing! I thought of my "reset and live" strategy for a business or project idea that involves resetting ourselves along the way so that we can live the life God intended for us to live!

March 10–13: I decided to start going down my roads of opportunity to question and see if a door was open or shut at each place. I have discovered that, while there are lots of roads I could travel down, I don't want to go down just any road. I want the one He has planned out!

March 14: I needed a Bible study. I do one every year with my personal business, and several women have asked about our next one. I wanted one covering freedom, but Beth Moore was too expensive for me—I'm not making any money right now—so all roads thus far were closing. I have felt stuck for some time and started talking out loud at the Christian bookstore to God and myself about it all. Piper goes, "Momma, look!" I look over, and of course, a blue box with large letters across it read STUCK Bible study. Sure, and of course, it's the one! It only took me several trips to Mardel to get this one on this day! Key—give it to God and let go! He rocks at making it happen!

I listened to all eight sessions that day in the car. I paused it while I checked out a location for a possible storefront for my business (if I'm meant to open a storefront), which ended up being $1,400 base rent. Hello—no! Another door closed, but the Bible study door was open! Surprisingly, I got a call out of the blue from one of my passions with a possible job opportunity working with teenagers—I felt craziness mixed with happiness. I'd been waiting for any opportunity to work in my field again, and here was a potentially open door. I wasn't sure if I'd still have what it takes to work with teens anymore, so I prayed.

March 15: I volunteered with my dear friend, Kris, at the Newsboys, Third Day, We as Human, Skillet, Mandisa, and Brandon Heath multi-concert, working at the Brandisa booth with teenagers—loved it! I was in my element with people, young and old, talking about God and life. I really bonded with the teenagers, so that door was staying open.

March 16: I wasn't going to go to church since Piper hadn't been feeling well. Michael and I wanted her healthy for a visit to her aunt and uncle's in Washington over spring break, so we went to separate services. When I told him that I was just going to stay home, he said I had to go, and it would be good for me. Let's talk about the sexiest that he has ever been telling me to go to church—whoa! He was so right! There's so much to the story, but God was moving there. There was a fabulous baptism service, but most importantly, God gave me the answers I needed through Pastor Matt. He said that if you're needing to know what to do or where to be, go back to the last place of clarity from God and start from there.

Mine was at Lilian's celebration of life (a little over three-and-a-half years ago). That day, when I spoke at her celebration of life, I felt on fire and in the ultimate will of God. I was in my element and linked completely to Him. I could almost physically feel myself stepping on the devil's face. It was insane yet a natural high! At that moment, I knew more than ever that I was supposed to do ministry to help people reach their full potential. I saw myself speaking everywhere, writing kids' books, leading studies, and training people through fitness. I volunteered at the church, and life didn't seem to play out like I thought it would, so I started my own business to minister through workouts and Bible studies by being real and trusting Him.

After sharing my heart, this passion hasn't left. I feel that same fire I felt the day we celebrated the life of my baby girl. I'm praying for God to help me know what exactly should happen, but I'm enthusiastic and inspired by the open door in the ministry that is taking place in the near future.

Two weeks after my major discovery in Pastor Matt's service, we flew to see family on March 16. The flights increased my depression and pain. It was hard on me, but even harder on those around me that had to experience me at a different level. I still made myself do the opposite of what the voice of depression wanted, so there were some wonderful moments. Along with those moments was a lot of confusion, flipped upside-down scenarios, disappointment, hurts, and sadness.

Amazingly, I did end up with more cool things happening, with God helping me see that I haven't lost the gifts that He gave me at birth, and I am passionate about certain things for a reason. I won't be living out my gifts and passions exactly how I thought I would, but the journey God has me on is going to be bigger and better than I could have hoped for. God has placed me among some of the most talented and godly people who are trusting Him and bringing so much to everyone. I'm lucky I'm going to get to work alongside them at some point!

The elements of distraction, chaos, hurt, confusion, and disappointment will always be there, yet as long as I trust

God and remember to bring it all to Him, His plans will prevail. I'm lucky and blessed that I am called His child. I can't control people or circumstances either, but I can control my attitude and behavior. After a couple of weeks of thinking I've lost relationships and perhaps direction, God is working it out and showing me I just have to keep connected to Him. Things happen for a reason. I feel that my situations and trials over time have really been God placing me in the fire to make me shiny again so He is able to see His reflection.

It's exactly three in the morning. I remember on Lilian's 103rd day at 3:00 a.m. when I was awakened by Lily coding and the song "No Air" playing on my phone. Lilian had earned her wings at that moment, but the staff and life-support machine kept her going until later that day, when we finally had to turn it off. I remember for many months after she passed that I'd wake up at that exact time on the fifth of every month. It was terrifying, but I'm at peace so much later. PRAISE GOD!

How many of us keep getting in the way? What if we could really let go and let God create His masterpiece in us? How much healing would take place? How far could we be from where we've been? What could God accomplish if we were healed and did what we were meant to? What could change if we took His hand and got out of our personal gutter?

I think God really has been good to let us know. We've been good at either not listening or doing what we want to do instead of what we should be doing. It's easier to long for something than to live it out—like being a spouse, parent, or coworker—the list could go on and on. It's crazy to think just how simple and life-changing His answers are for us.

I'm still dealing with a multitude of pain inside and out, but I'm not going to let it be the focus. When I was single, I couldn't stop thinking about being married. From the time I was first married to having our first child, I couldn't stop thinking about becoming a parent. When I went through brain surgery, I kept thinking about when the healing would be done. What I could and should have been thinking is, what can I be doing with the time and freedom I have right now?

> *What can I be doing with the time and freedom I have right now?*

See, being single allows for freedom to do wonderful, unique blessings for others and God without having to take care or ask permission from a spouse to do it. A time without children allows your schedule to be open and "come and go as you please" with rarely any restrictions. There's no little person depending on you for their every need. Being healthy gives you freedom for almost everything. There's no healing that restricts or keeps you from living life. There's no downtime. You are able to do anything. Marriage and children are not meant to be a prison—neither is getting those things right now as well.

Ecclesiastes has it going on for the "time for everything." I painstakingly understand it more now than ever before. When we aren't getting the desires of our heart, it is for our own good. God has other things in mind before we get them. I wish I could take back the time I spent crying, wishing, praying, and pining over the desires of my heart that I was not getting right then. God needed me to use the time wisely for other reasons—to serve differently without restrictions and major commitments.

Fortunately, I didn't miss out on everything. I was part of fabulous ministries and tasks He had just for me. I feel that I could have multiplied His work more instead of dragging the journey out. He's been so patient with me and continues to be. Hopefully, I'm learning much faster after three-and-a-half decades. I'm not going to let my longings get in the way of being content in the fact God has me right where I need to be in this season of my life. I want to enjoy and soak up all the riches this season has, even if it's not always fun! I'm going to keep dancing in the rain and figuring out how to smile, no matter what!

I'm not going to let my longings get in the way of being content in the fact God has me right where I need to be in this season of my life.

After rereading the above, I get to add about the fabulous day God gave us today. God blew me away, as He often does. At church today, we sat by the last neighbor we had when Lilian was alive. She's been through her own journey, and God was just wild enough on my 103rd day since surgery to seat us next to her, plus made today our last service at a place where we have been so connected to Lilian. Our church is moving from our old building to our brand-new one after years of being in the desert. It feels like we are moving to our promised land.

We all experienced a rush of emotions. That building holds many buckets of tears, lessons learned, growing pains, phenomenal worship moments, and a bond between us where both of our girls got to be in front of the church. It was rough. We even had a candlelight service—crazy and beautiful that God loves us so much that He planned every last minute and made sure I knew He was the Planner, Healer, and Creator.

As we took our last picture holding our second baby girl almost at the very same spot that we held her big sissy, Lilian, I choked up. I am blessed more than I deserve. We all have the opportunity to let Him be in our everyday walk. He shocks me while blowing my mind on a regular basis. I'm so glad He thinks of everything. Only He could plan out how today went and what all was represented, down to who we sat next to, what songs were played, and how things needed to go.

Tonight, we did more training for the new building. Sitting there in the ginormous building (our old one was really small), I was reminded of my friend Karen's words this morning. She knew that us leaving the building was going to be hard, as well as for her for different reasons, but she reminded me that Lilian was waiting for us at the new building. The new building already feels like a new chapter and a place of serenity, solace, and refuge. I hope that wherever you find your life that you know you are never alone. Your life matters and is a perfect puzzle piece that fits in this puzzle of life!

I'm still going to struggle, but I know I won't forget who is holding me and my future. The future looks bright. After telling my husband last week that I was sorry God brought me back and there was nothing I could do about it—sorry he didn't get relief from me—I realized that depression is something I have to face on a daily basis. It's possible to recognize, fight, and beat it, but it's a daily walk for me at this point. I am happy to say I'm further away from that statement I said to him when I was feeling horrible and drowning inside, but I'm also remembering to trust God and fight!

Here are some fabulous songs that moved me through my tears last night:
"Healing Begins" by Tenth Avenue North
"Your Love" by Brandon Heath
"Sound of Your Voice" by Third Day

What's great about these songs coming from the movies I watched? I got to see all the artists perform the songs live! God just keeps giving all the time—He's so Big! Thanks for hanging in there and reading this. I pray that God keeps working on us and getting us to where we need to be. If only we could reset on a daily basis in order to live the life He has always intended us to live, then this life could be enriched and help us prepare for a much longer life in eternity. This life on earth is a nanosecond compared to eternity! Love you all!

LILIAN'S CARINGBRIDGE

In loving memory of Lilian Grace

Never forgotten

MAY 19, 2014

220 › Even If

Time keeps on ticking, plus Lilian's next race info . . .

I can't believe I didn't get to post on Lilian's CaringBridge for her birthday. I know life has been in full swing, but this has been a first. I'm not sure if that means there's been too much busy work. Life does move on, and some things might get left where they've been.

This year has been a wild ride for us. I still can't believe Lilian Grace would have been four this past April 25, 2014. There has been so much jammed into these four years that seems to have made it feel like a flash. Sometimes I struggle to remember what in the world we've been doing. I guess that means we are living life to the fullest and working through each day that comes our way. I think it's called survival mode when raising children. Our second baby girl is now two-and-a-half years old.

My heart has been moved all around for others. I sadly have witnessed and heard of many losses of unborn babies and children from newborn to a young age. None of it ever gets easier to deal with. My heart aches and the tears roll continuously as theirs and my heart breaks even more. I've been telling so many lately that I do not trust this life here on earth, but I do trust my heavenly Father to give me exactly what I need with what has been given.

I've been reminded time after time that God's timing is perfect, even if we cannot understand it. I remember getting frustrated with that statement, because it used to not give me comfort at all. Yet now that I have a closer relationship to God through all my wild rides of this life, I get it—I get Him. He really does know what's best for us. It just makes for a tough time to process and get to a better place at times.

If I can give anyone any advice, it's to hold on as tight to God as you possibly can. I remember holding a pillow and squeezing the life out of it just so I could physically imagine Him holding me—oh so tightly! I know I've said this repeatedly over the years, but sometimes you have to say over and over, "I trust you, God! I trust you, God!" Say it until you believe it! You may feel anger at first, but when you realize that God isn't doing this to you, it will change, and you will change. God wants the very best for us.

I do know this much—He has been the one constant in my life who shows me graciously every day that He does exist while loving me very much. I only succeed and continue to be, all because of Him! I'm praying for all of us who have experienced loss in many ways in this life. I know many of us are living a life that wasn't the original plan we had, but God is so ginormous in making it way better than we could ever pray for or imagine. I'm praising God for helping us heal and grow stronger while surviving and thriving!

"Even If" by Kutless is a song that was brought to my attention for those who might need it. It may not feel like the healing is going to come, but you will wake up one day, finding that you need just Him. Love you all!

I can't forget to let you all know about the Fourth Annual Warrior Princess Trail Run set for Saturday, August 2, 2014. For more information, visit http://www.warriorprincessfoundation.com/.[19]

---

[19] Note from author: This website is no longer active.

Early Bird Race Registration May 1–25, 2014:
- 103 Minute Trail Runner: $35
- 1.03 Miler Fun Run/Walk: $30
- Shadow Runner (includes shipping): $35
- Lily's Angels (Non-Runner Supporter Shirt): $15

Race Registration May 26–July 10, 2014 (Shirt Guaranteed):
- 103 Minute Trail Runner: $42
- 1.03 Miler Fun Run/Walk: $37
- Shadow Runner (includes shipping): $42
- Lily's Angels (Non-Runner Supporter Shirt): $20

Late Race Registration July 11–July 30, 2014 (Online):
- 103 Minute Trail Runner: $50
- 1.03 Miler Fun Run/Walk: $45
- Shadow Runner (includes shipping): $50
- Lily's Angels (Non-Runner Supporter Shirt): $25

You will be able to register via hard copy registration form with a money order/check payment at RunnersWorld Tulsa starting May 26–July 31, 2014.

Remember to register early to guarantee availability of a shirt. Your size is guaranteed if you register by July 15, 2014.

If registering online, there are additional fees from Eventbrite added to your order. To register online, visit https://warriorprincessangelrun4.eventbrite.com.[20]

---

[20] Note from author: This link is no longer active.

CHRISSY'S CARINGBRIDGE

Forever love

APRIL 10, 2014

34 › I Can Just Be Me

Perseverance . . .

The word for the moment is perseverance for my past, present, and future. It's fair to say that most of us could use some perseverance when living out our lives! Here is the online definition:

per·se·ver·ance, pərsə'vi(ə)rəns/ noun: Persistence in doing something despite difficulty or delay in achieving success.[21]

After speaking for a second time at the University of Tulsa about Lilian Grace while recovering from brain surgery and being here for some friends who lost their sweet baby girl at twenty-one-weeks' gestation last week, I was reminded that it all requires processing, even if it's for the good and makes me happy doing it all. Every day in my recovery and grieving journey requires the above word. I have many days that are good ones, yet I have moments laced throughout the day where it's not so good. Though I've come so far in my recovery and grieving, I need to remember that the small techniques and methods that I use on a daily basis really make or break the good days. People ask me all the time how I'm feeling, and it's hard to answer them sometimes. I feel pain and tiredness fairly often these days, but I don't let it stop me.

---

[21]https://www.google.com/search?q=perseverance+definition&rlz=1C1VDKB_enUS987US988&oq=perseverance+definition&aqs=chrome..69i57j0i20i263i512j0i512l8.7475j1j7&sourceid=chrome&ie=UTF-8

I found a great quote on the web from Michael Jordan: "I can accept failure, but I can't accept not trying." It is so true! There are going to be hours or days where I'm either failing at my recovery or rising above it. It's important that I keep trying. That's key for all of us, no matter what mountain, trial, or tribulation that we find ourselves facing. Most days, I struggle with pain and tiredness, but I don't want to let that stop me. I don't let it stop me. It's incredible how God has trained me. I'm able to step up and knock it out of the ballpark! I've been able to volunteer at our Solace Cafe, which has been a fun time like no other. I've partnered with a couple of opportunities recently and worked with teens and their families. PRAISE GOD for giving me the perseverance to go big!

Surprisingly, I've been able to integrate back into life when I'm doing my daily devotionals, eating right, pacing my schedule, and working out. It's common sense, yet not commonly practiced. Maintaining a busy schedule is exhausting and gets me nowhere. I'm glad God's mercies are new every morning. I realized a few days ago I need to reset and start paying more attention to the basics.

There was this chair. Isn't there always a chair? For those of you who've known me a long time, you know chairs and I don't get along. It was my fault, and I was the one injured. No chairs or walls were harmed, just me!

I was on a girls' night away trip in the middle of nowhere, and I had used this heavy wooden chair to put under the doorknob at the inn where we were staying. I thought it would give us extra protection since there wasn't a dead bolt. The next morning, I had to get something out of my vehicle, so I moved the chair to the side. When I came back in, you would have thought it was my mission to take out the chair. I was so distracted and oblivious to everything that I bulldozed over that chair. Too bad no one was filming this epic moment in my life because I probably could have won some money on *America's Funniest Videos*!

All I could think of when I was pretending to be a defensive lineman taking out the quarterback was that I needed to protect the head—protect the head—since the doctor said that I needed to avoid getting hit in the head for at least a year. Oh, I protected the head. If you could see some of my bruises now, you'd wonder what the other guy looked like. I thought for a little bit that I broke my leg. I have bruises on my right upper arm, elbow, upper arm, and above the wrist; left leg above the knee with the largest bruise thus far; right lower leg, where there's a minor laceration and swollen knot; and soreness all over. I'm actually lucky that this happened.

What?

I know it sounds crazy, but it has been another wake-up call that I needed. It really does matter that I continue the small things that add up in my recovery. Paying attention in life matters as well! After just two days of getting back on track, I am reset and ready to live out this next chapter in my life. God's giving me some wonderful opportunities to use my gifts, talents, and degree again while still getting to be a flexible mom for my sweet baby girl.

Though I truly have the all-or-nothing personality, Lilian Grace and my brain surgery have adjusted and altered me. I still want to do the all-or-nothing as life plays out, yet God is making sure I get a balance in between my trials and errors. I'm excited about the future that He has prepared for me, and I'm ready to just be me! In the midst of battling depression and brokenness, I know God is who He says He is. I have to continue to let it go as my two-and-a-half-year-old sings and reminds me all the time now—thanks to

Frozen! I need to let God be my God so I can just be me.

I am a vessel. I am only successful when I step aside and let His light naturally shine! He's made me into a leader who is gifted and talented at helping people reach their full potential as long as I get out of the way. Me on my own doesn't work in this life that I'm living. He goes before me and makes a way that He etched out for me. PRAISE HIM ON HIGH! He's always by my side!

God reminded me of two perfect songs, "I Can Just Be Me" by Laura Story and "Whom Shall I Fear (God of Angel Armies)" by Chris Tomlin. I hope you can listen and enjoy them. I love music and how God provides treasures within the lyrics to assist me throughout my journey! We sing the second song at church often, and it now has an even deeper meaning for me—rising up and not fearing as He leads. I pray that each of us can remember to be a vessel and let God do His thing! His angels are right by our side—fighting for us while protecting us! We are in His hands. We aren't meant to try to do this all on our own. He's way bigger and better than we could ever be. He knows EVERYTHING!

Seeing ourselves as a vessel can help us make sure we take care of this body He has created for us. This is one I really need to work on, because I've been a crazy lady when it comes to food lately. I've been reminded continuously that I eat more when the pain is greater, so I'm going to work on making sure I take steps that help alleviate the pain. When I eat less, I'll spend less as well—another problem taken care of! Boom! Now for the hard part—I need to step aside in obedience based on the lessons that God has taught me for thirty-five years plus. I'm glad that I am not alone!

APRIL 17, 2014

35 › Good News

God is here every day and all day—sharing good news . . .
Forgive me for the length of the video—it's seventeen minutes and twenty-five seconds. If you get that much time to watch it, you'll see that I catch you up by sharing what God has been doing. God is so cool! I know life can throw many things at us, but it helps to see that He works it all out. He's working on great things in my life, and I'm glad He's leading. I just pray I keep getting out of His way. Training and applying lessons learned is the current theme of my life. Wishing you all a very blessed Easter!

Lots of love,
Chrissy

🎥 Note: To see the video, visit https://youtu.be/mDRN-eXMmGw.

Hey, everybody! It's been four months since my brain surgery—a hundred and twenty-one days. It is crazy what I'm going to get to say to you, and I'm so excited! It's been a crazy ride with everything that I have faced. Who would have thought that I would get to share this with you? (Not I!) Before everything that's happening right now—people who have talked to me, who know what I've gone through—the struggles and the changes. Brain surgery really stopped me.
I had to deal with a lot of stuff from me and Lily that I didn't even realize I hadn't dealt with. It's been good for my heart and

soul. *I feel like God, as a silversmith, puts you in a little fire. It's not like He creates these, but He uses it to help refine you. He wants to get us to where He can see Himself—His own image—in us. I'm not perfect—I'm far from it. God is still working on me.*

It's just cool that I get to be a vessel and let Him work. I hope I get out of the way more than I get in His way, because—let me tell you—I'm good at getting in His way. I know a lot of us are! A cool thing is that my life has changed quite a bit. Before I tell you that, I have to let you know where I was.

Before (my brain) surgery, I was working at a cafe. It was craziness. I'm telling you that I will never, ever complain about the food industry again, because I know what they go through—just a little bit behind the scenes. They work their tails off—they do. Secondly, I worked at a preschool. They work all day with our children, helping feed into them, teaching them, and helping them be better—that's what I'm hoping for all teachers.

My daughter has wonderful preschool teachers who really do that. One day, Piper came up to me and was saying, "Your name is Chrissy." I'm like, "Yes, it is." She said, "Daddy's name is Michael." I'm like, "Yes, it is." Then we had to talk about who I am to her. "Well, you're mommy, but your name is Chrissy." I'm like, "Okay." She's two-and-a-half, so I'm like, what in the heck have they learned? They had learned our names—that we were real people. I thought, That's really cool that she knows that we are real people in this world, and that other people see us a different way than what she does. We are her mommy and daddy, but we're also Chrissy and Michael.

I just thought, How cool is that! *A little reminder from God above that I am—I am Chrissy, but I'm also a mother. I'm also a daughter. I'm also a sister. I'm also a friend. I'm a sister from another mother. I'm also a worker. Those are who ... just things that describe what I do, but really, I'm Chrissy! God gave* me Chrissy—*that is my name. There was a little topic of this on one of my devotionals that really talked about God being Yahweh—that really is His name. All these other names we have for Him are what He does and who He is. I thought that was cool how that linked up, and God's been doing that a lot for me lately.*

But what's really cool is, I—before—when I came back and I went through the depression—I've been trying to get back on track. I've been trying to lose weight—that's still been a rollercoaster ride, because that's life. I wanted to go back to my previous jobs, even if I knew it was crazy and just all over the place. I still felt like I was drawn to go back. Every time I would try to go back—and I was going to talk to my bosses that day—I was determined to go in and talk to both of them—but I would hurt so bad. The pain would increase. It would be awful. I'd be like, "Okay, I can't. I'm not ready." What really was happening was that I wasn't meant to go back.

It was hard for me to accept, because I thought, Well, I've got to be doing something. *Right before spring break, God gave me an opportunity. I'm excited, because if you would have told me that this is what was really going to happen, I'd be like,* Oh, it's probably not, but that's okay. You know whatever God wants from me, then I'm going to do it. *I can tell you, number one, I will be, at some point in time, doing some sort of women's ministry somewhere. I'm hoping it is at my local church, but I'm just leaving that to God.*

What's cool is that He's training me in the meantime while I'm waiting to do some other things that I love to do. Number one, I'm actually an OSU (Oklahoma State University) Extension employee again. I'm a program assistant with a grant that we are doing—the Juntos 4-H grant program. It's a little crazy because I only get ten hours a week. So I have to make sure that I'm really focused—only doing ten hours but also trying to do what is needed for the program. I'm getting to do the one piece that I absolutely—if you could have—if I had to choose from any of it because I loved it all—this one little piece would be what I love the most. God's giving it to me, and I'm so excited.

This week, I added that to my life—ten hours; then I added in working at the cafe more than what I've been—twice a week. I was still trying to do my workout. We joined a gym—the Sky Fitness gym—because it has childcare. I can cut out some of the problems that I had—God helped me know how to make this happen, so Sky Fitness gym does that. When I'm working out every day, I am—it is good for me.

I will say, though, I took two naps this week. Monday, I slept at the car dealership place because my poor car needed work. It has not had its TLC (tender loving care) lately—so I had to do that. I spent a little bit of money because there were a bunch of things that needed to be done. I slept the whole time in the lounge. But before that, I had met this lady. It was a weird, quick run-in where she said something to me. She is going through a divorce. She ended up praying over me and using her prayer language. I slept, so apparently, I needed the rest anyway, but I snored. The guy that woke me up—I know he was like, "I'm sorry that I have to do this to you in waking you up, but . . ." I said, "Oh, it's good." I had a little slobber. I was like, "Wow, I really needed the sleep."

The next day, I slept again. I had gone to Muskogee, Oklahoma, to do my paperwork. But it was cool because I had forgotten my social security card here at the house with my checkbook—which is what we needed. I ended up having to go to the Social Security office. I was laughing, because the young lady that got hired for another position that I will be working with—she is Hispanic—she had all her stuff. I said, "Hey, I'm just making you look good today"—that's number one. Number two was the lady that I met at the Social Security office—we were supposed to meet. It was crazy! God had some awesome information for her, and here I am just saying it out to her. I was so happy after I walked out of there. I told my boss that I was like, "Wow, this is crazy. I was supposed to meet that lady. I'm glad that I forgot my social security card."

When we look at life and when things aren't working how we want them, think about that maybe He's got a better plan. Now we can have the other side of it because there is a war going on. But I'd like to see, first—you know—what is God doing with this? He's training me. Just like at the Solace Cafe. I love it. I love the craziness of it. It's like I've got to calm people down though. Sometimes, we get a little crazy, and we think we've got to have all this, all the time. People have to learn time too. There's a time for everything.

Just like with my two-and-a-half-year-old daughter. We talk about Ecclesiastes a lot—off and on. I remember hating Ecclesiastes sometimes—I'm like, Really? You're just going to tell me there's a time for everything? But there really is. *Just like me forgetting something. It turned into something—a divine appointment that I had no clue was going to happen. I'm so excited that I got to do that. I love it, because this job is training me that I have only so much time, and I've got to make that time worth it. I've got to make it happen because I still want the quality and the high expectations for myself to be met, but I have a timeframe.*

Just like when I do women's ministry, I'm going to have to do the same thing because as women, there's so much that can happen to us—so much that is needed. I've seen from other women's ministries how you can get so overloaded or overwhelmed. I don't want to do that to my family, especially if it's just a volunteer thing. I'm owning it that this is what God is—He's training me.

I've decided in life, whenever you're going through stuff and something is happening, you're either getting trained yourself or you're using the training He's given you. It makes life a lot easier. It's still going to be stressful, and I'm still going to have moments. I did cry on Tuesday after I had woken up, and I was almost late getting Piper to dance. I was just like, Oh my gosh, this is how—what have I done to myself? I have added all this new stuff. God, what am I going to do here? I'm going to have to calm down. *Well, this is what he gave me . . .* (Excerpt has been removed for copyright reasons. The summary of the excerpt was God reminding me that He is my protector and comforter. I felt God leading me away from my negativity and reassuring me that He is always here. I needed to look at my situation as an opportunity to grow and gather more training tools.)

Really, I just read God's answer to Michael and was like, "I needed Him to say this on this exact day from a lady who wrote Jesus Calling, *Sarah Young. How long ago did she write this— you know?" It's fit for that same day that I was freaking out when I was going, "Oh my gosh, Lord, what have I done? I need to slow down. I can't do this. I'm tired. I'm going to have to change everything. I just don't know if I can do everything at the same time." Here He is just going, "Baby girl, I got it. This is good for you. This is part of my plan." I'm excited that God is doing crazy things. Yes, there are going to be days that are not good—trust me.*

I was having a conversation with a couple of people today. I said, "You know, I think whenever I see people when they're praying so hard, and they want something to change so much— you know, sometimes, God's answer is no." It is not easy to accept no from Him—it really isn't. Sometimes, it's worth it because He sees the whole picture. We have to trust Him. Keep moving and going in a direction—hoping. God will help you if you keep praying.

God put everything where I needed it to be. If I'm going down the wrong direction, He gives me a fork in that road so I can go down the right way that He wants me to go and where He needs me to be. I could have freaked out Tuesday morning when I was sitting down and I realized that I had forgotten my checks. Well, then, I didn't realize that forgetting my checks meant I was forgetting my social security card—which was a big deal. I didn't freak out. I thought it could be taken care of if I called the bank and got the routing number. I found out that I had to have the check. Then I realized that was where my social security card was. But in that moment, I didn't freak out. I just stayed calm and was like, "God, life happens, and I can't change it."

I know it's everything that I've gone through that has really helped shape and mold me, but there are days—don't get me wrong—that I'm not going to get it right. Just pray for me on those days, even more than you do on a daily basis.

I want to thank all of you. I know Lily's birthday is coming up next Friday. It's just crazy how four years have gone by so fast. I love her. I miss her, but I'm just so grateful for her and what God used her for to get to me and so many others. I'm so blessed that I've had that opportunity. Just like Sunday being Easter, you know, to really think about being up on a cross, being pierced through your hands and feet while having a crown on your head when you're bleeding to death, and you have a conversation with your Father. He tells you no. (Jesus) *is like, "Why, oh, why, have you forsaken me?" Yet God didn't save Him—didn't rescue Him from that cross— because there was a plan.* (Jesus) *had to go through what He went through so we could have eternity—that's just incredible.*

It just blows my mind to think that all the pain I've ever felt—just how much more magnified that was (for Him). *No* matter how much of a mistake—all the mistakes that we make—He was up on that cross. He fought hell and got the keys. All we need is Him so we can have eternity. Let me tell you, I'm ready for that day when we get to—when He comes home again and gets us. We get to just go.

I remember reading a story on Facebook just last night. I think—about a painter who talked about when you knock that He'll answer. The thing is that there's a door that the guy had painted with Jesus in front, but he didn't put a doorknob in for a reason. God's ready. He's there. He's ready to go in, but we have to open the door from the inside. We have to say yes to this. God is already willing. It's just crazy—it just blows my mind.

I love the fact that God's given me a new set of eyes through everything I've been through to appreciate what has been done for me. I would want everybody in heaven too—forever. I can see why God hasn't brought Jesus back, because He wants more and more. He doesn't want to end it where it ends. He wants more people, more people, more people. I can appreciate that because if he would have stopped a long time ago, I wouldn't be here. Yes, life is not perfect. Trust me, I could have done without a lot of the things I have gone through, but I also wouldn't be at this level of appreciating life and seeing God's hands at work every day, all day.

When you're at the end of your rope, just let go and jump in His arms. He wants to catch you and be there for you. Every time we get stressed out and freaked out, it's because we're trying to do it on our own. We're not trusting God. Trusting God does not have worry. If you're worried, you're not trusting Him. I've learned that more and more every single day.

Thanks for hanging in there. I know it's long. I love you guys. I just pray that you can really know that God loves us so unconditionally. (God) did watch His Son die on the cross for *our sins. He could have easily just said to forget it. He loved us so much that we didn't have to do what previously was done before getting to be in heaven. He made it easy, but it's still our choice. Yes, the things we do in our lives—we don't always have a choice with how we were born or whatever, but we do have a choice for eternity. I love that and hate it at the same time. I wish I could just make the decision, and then everything else would fall into place instead of having to still do life and still have a free choice. Oh, I remember this saying I used to say, "God, I pray that you'll just—this is what I want—I want you to lead my life and take away my free choice." I know He's up there saying, "I can't do that because it wouldn't be fair. Now you wouldn't want that really, to not have the choice." Just like a two-and-a-half-year-old doesn't like not having her choice. She wants to have her choices—I know, for my daughter anyway. I love you guys and I just pray that you really enjoy your trainings that He's giving you and that you use what you've learned. (Blows a kiss.) Love you!*

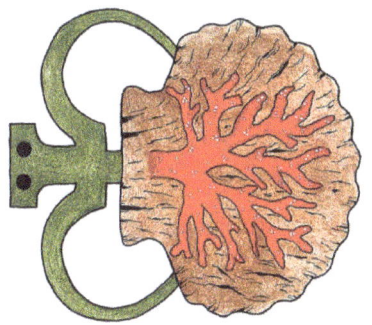

MAY 19, 2014

36 › Heaven or Bust

God is nuts, and I'm crazy—makes for a wild ride together!

I've heard lately how timing is everything. I sit here typing this, realizing that God's timing really is everything! I've had many plans from my controlling heart, but God has always been gracious in moving me toward His bigger and better plans. He has given me the desires of my heart over and over through jobs, the man of my dreams, children, church/mission, family/friends, and more. To say life is boring would be far off base for my life! Let's look at some fun bulleted points for some of the medical mountains in my life:

1995 (and previous years): Polycystic ovary syndrome (PCOS) with many cysts rupturing—lots of pain and agony along with hospital visits.

1996–2006: Horrible sickness with stomach problems and struggles that included diagnoses from Crohn's disease to irritable bowel syndrome—when it was really my lovely gallbladder leaking into my body for all those years. My first gallbladder attack was in December 1996—my senior year of high school.

2003: Abscess in my throat—I almost died. My husband (boyfriend at the time) rushed me to the hospital from Cassville, Missouri, to Stillwater, Oklahoma. I ended up getting the abscess and tonsils removed—followed by "the blues" from losing my tonsils (not normal)! I lost a ton of weight, which made me look super skinny for my wedding that December—bonus!

Fall 2005: I could eat only rice and drink water from all the allergies and reactions that almost killed me. Again, my lovely gallbladder was the culprit. I got to experience using a couple of EpiPens—scary and weird. I turned purple and my body shook continuously—good times!

January 2006: Finally, my bad gallbladder was discovered. I almost died. My husband carried me into the surgery center, thinking this was it. The doctor said my gallbladder fell apart in his hands after removal. It was full of marble-sized stones and infection. I was told that I was a superwoman—not too shabby! It only took something like ten doctors to solve the problem in over a decade's time. I'm reminded that doctors are humans and aren't God, who knows everything. Thank God for my allergist, who got me to the right person!

February 2006: More cysts ruptured, and I thought I was going to die.

May 2006: Horrible miscarriage where I held the fetus in my hands. I struggled in the dark with lots of therapy for two years. I was an overachiever and completely wore myself out!

June 2008: My appendix leaked into my body—my allergist, again, was smart and had an idea. I drove from Bixby, Oklahoma (camp supply pickup), to Ponca City, Oklahoma (4-H Camp), to Stillwater, Oklahoma (the voodoo village, a.k.a. University Health Services), to the final destination at Stillwater Medical Center (SMC) for emergency surgery. I almost died. I'm not sure how they let me drive from the voodoo village to SMC, but I must have been very persistent about no ambulance fees!

Spring 2008: We tried fertility treatments with no success.

April 2009: Not a bad thing—I finally got LASIK on my eyes since I thought I'd never get pregnant again. Bonus: I can really see perfectly when medical things aren't messing up my vision!

January 2009: Another miscarriage, but I didn't know for sure that I was pregnant. I got sick on a road trip, and my OBGYN said that I'd had another miscarriage. He did some counseling with us.

Spring/Summer 2009: We tried the fertility clinic again with more options but no success. The fertility clinic said that we had only a 0.05 percent chance of getting pregnant together. It would have to be by the grace of God for us to have children together. They wouldn't be able to treat us any longer.

July 2009: I had a seizure at 3D Nail in Sand Springs, Oklahoma, and got rushed to the hospital—probably the first signs of my tumor that was removed December 2013—by my awesome friend, Jeni Harbour, because again, I was persistent about no ambulance fees!

Fall 2009: We decided that we would try to adopt. We were going to do a private adoption with a family. On the day before we were going to do everything, the biological parents ran off with the baby without a medical release. To our surprise, on the very same day, I saw a positive pregnancy strip. I was pregnant with Lilian Grace Whitten!

January 2010: Since I had a nineteen centimeter cyst in my right ovary while pregnant with Lilian Grace, at seventeen to eighteen weeks' gestation, I had an emergency partial hysterectomy. If I hadn't done the surgery, both Lilian and I would have died. They removed the ginormous cyst, right ovary, and right fallopian tube. I lost a ton of blood post-surgery while in my room after I got really sick—violently vomiting. I'm not sure how many bags of blood they gave me, but it was a lot. I had to be monitored especially closely because I was allergic to the process—of course. Benadryl and some other drugs made the transfusions happen slowly but made them possible and successful. I ended up with C. diff for six to eight weeks. I lost a ton of weight. Though I wish it had been diarrhea, it was way worse—the smell killed. I thought I had died. At week twenty of gestation, we found out Lilian Grace had heart defects and that her first breath was more than likely going to be her last.

It seemed like each week the devil hit me harder and harder. I've always said that the devil hates me, but God loves me and needs me here. I started realizing that Job and I were kindred spirits—totally starting to understand how He could keep trusting God and not giving up!

April 2010: Emergency C-section with Lilian Grace. She wouldn't have survived if we hadn't delivered her eight weeks early. On day sixteen of her life, we found out she was a trisomy 18—Edward's Syndrome—baby, and she wouldn't live. We were to live it up until her last breath. We lived at the hospital for her first fifty-one days, then for the next fifty-two days we were in and out of the hospital. Thank God for St. Francis. They gave me 103 days with my precious Warrior Princess!

July 2010: A week before my first daughter earned her wings, I had a full stomach hernia repair. I was told again it was life threatening, and I could lose organs and my life. She lived a glorious 103 days in which we got to rock out her mission, and I wouldn't trade her, the experiences, or life changes for anything.

January/February 2011: We decided we'd start the adoption process again—this time with an organization. We found out that what seemed like an open window had closed. Not too long after the window closed, we found out that we were pregnant with our sweet baby girl number two, March 2011, the night before my hubby turned the big three-oh!

October 2011: Emergency C-section with our second daughter, Piper Allegra. We were in a wreck the week before, and I lost half my amniotic fluids. She came three weeks early.

November 2012–All of 2013: I dealt with major symptoms due to the walking/talking dead tumor. I could have been talking or walking and just keeled over. Michael found me so many times blacked out and not able to wake me up. Our baby girl got into a lot of messes when mommy was out! Needless to say, my husband is a rockstar. He has had to deal with the craziest of crazies with me!

December 2013: Emergency brain surgery to remove a deadly tumor in my pineal gland. If I didn't do it, then again, I would die. This time, I was ready to go. I was at peace like no other and had accepted that my second daughter's fate might be to grow up without me. I was surprised when I woke up to my doctor's face instead of Jesus's precious, glorious face. I've dealt with depression and the struggles of healing, but I'm here and working my way through it all. I realized God's not done with me yet—it reminds me of a kids' book I read to both my girls about a caterpillar. Thank God again for my allergist, who, almost a year before this, got me to the right person yet again. He's my guardian angel on earth!

January–March 2014: I have been still and wondered why I felt so stuck, but now I realize God was working for the good to prepare me for the year to come!

May 2014: This past month of April, I got my dream job back with OSU Extension working with teens as part of a special grant program as the program assistant. I met with a life coach from our church to get on track with what God has planned for my ministry. God has been giving me such huge desires in my heart, but I wasn't expecting the latest one we've discovered, which has been set in motion. My second daughter has been praying that she could be a big sissy, while my husband has wanted another child since Piper was six weeks old—God has answered both of their prayers. Yes, we are pregnant! Not only did we have a 0.05 percent chance of getting pregnant together when I had both my ovaries removed, I am recovering from brain surgery! I know you are about to pass out, your mind is blown, or you need to remember to breathe! GOD IS BIG!

HALLELUJAH! Like I stated before that God is nuts and I'm crazy—it makes for a wild journey. I wouldn't trade it for the world, except eternity will be really nice with no pain, suffering, sorrow, and any other bad thing we experience on this earth! It'll be nicer when I get to experience heaven with my large family who are in heaven waiting for us—three of our babies are there! I decided that He needed more perfect angels to help Him out!

I type all this not only to remind myself but to help you see that God helped me survive and thrive through these major mountains in my life. Any one of these could have destroyed me—a few almost did. There were many times when I didn't think I could do much more and questioned just what God thought I could handle. It had been far from perfect when it came to my medical health and mountains. There was pain beyond description, along with suffering, loss, sorrow, and depression. Each of the mountains I've faced has always prepared me for the next one. I have been more blessed than I could ever deserve from my point of view. I'm so glad He sees me differently and thinks I'm worth having it all. This life is not guaranteed to be painless, easy, or perfect—heaven is!

My plans are nothing compared to His. I seem to be trying to catch up too often, while being blown away and mesmerized by His handiwork. It goes to show you that life is going to suck while being hard many times. But God's grace, love, and mercy can make all those things beautiful and worth the journey, even if it doesn't feel like it at times! Remember that we can plan all we want, but He has the right plan for us. He knows what we are going to face in life, and He's here to provide the tools to help us survive and thrive through all of them.

He rocks my world, as well as many of yours. If this

doesn't blow your heart and mind into a giddy, crazy praise, I don't know what can. I'm proof that no matter what happens, He will make good of it all for His glory and kingdom purposes. At least that's what I signed up for all those years ago when I asked Him to come into my heart and lead me to His purpose for my life! I know that the timing of this is wild since I'm still recovering from (brain) surgery and starting my fabulous job, but God knows best. It wasn't my plan right now, but He decided it was in His! I am in awe and grateful that I get to do another mountain with Him!

No matter how this mountain looks, I know God has prepared me to climb it. I'm equipped and walking with Him by my side. I ask that all of you lift us up in prayer. I'm facing head pains, sickness, and exhaustion, but I love that I get to do this. It's still early, but my baby bump is already showing. We need all the prayers we can get for a healthy baby, pregnancy, and delivery. It makes coming back after surgery even sweeter. I'm super blessed with a wonderful OBGYN, specialist, and nurses who take care of me above and beyond the call of duty and pay grade! We should get to meet our next miracle that we get to borrow from God at the end of December 2014 or the first of January 2015! Thank you for always lifting us up! It means everything to me!

Heaven or bust! Until then, let's put on that armor of God and battle it out with God right by our side. He is my all in all and gets all the glory! He has won; therefore, I'm winning as long as I have Him leading! Here's a list of amazing songs that just gave me power and peace this past Sunday—thanks Shad (Foley), Rachel (Foley), Shanna (Santiago), and the rest of the praise team/band:

"Praise Him" by Hillsong
"The Lord Our God" by Passion featuring Kristian Stanfill
"Waiting Here for You" by Christy Nockols
"White Flag" by Chris Tomlin

Love you all! I couldn't have asked for a more perfect playlist to praise my God and remember my story and His plans for me and all of us. GOD, KEEP BLOWING ME AWAY! I LOVE YOU and LIFT YOU HIGHER THAN HIGH! God is good all the time, and all the time, God is good!

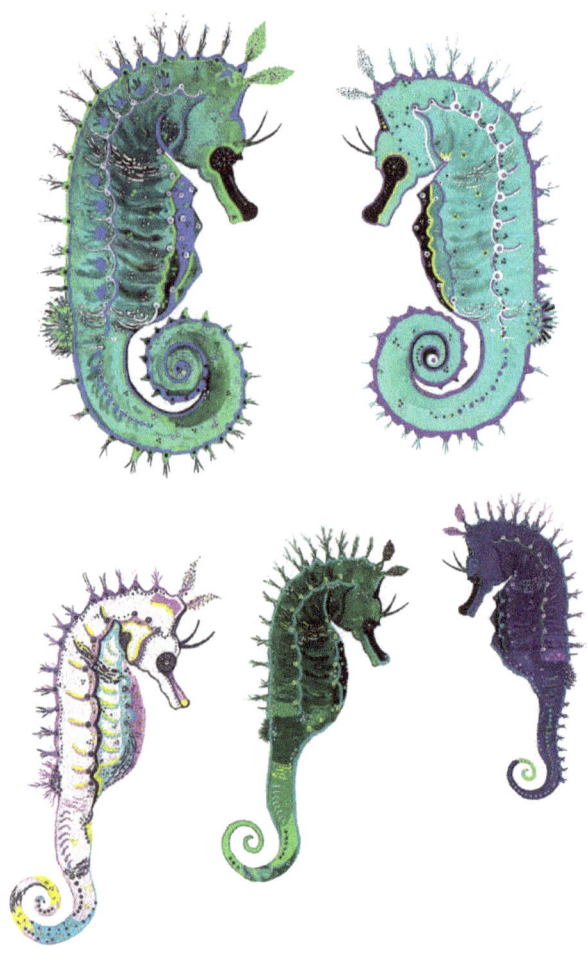

JUNE 2, 2014

37 › Both Sides

I've been shaken the past two weeks by friends who were pregnant alongside me. It was a happy time, yet the journey for my lovely girlfriends has ended. To be on this side of it all is surreal and devastating. I think back to all my fellow preggos who did my journey with me, experiencing my losses from miscarriages and the death of a child, while they continued to carry theirs. I never understood the fullness of their pain until now. I know many of you have gracefully walked your journey while being here for me in mine, and I thank God you have been strong enough to do it—just like my fellow brain tumor survivors.

This past week, I was fortunate enough to meet two brain tumor survivors and hear their stories. It made me appreciate mine even more. Each journey has two sides, and each side has its own battles to fight. Neither side escapes loss, but each side has a different type of loss to face. I lift all of us up in prayer, no matter which side of the journey we find ourselves on. It's never easy.

My pregnancy has made my post-brain surgery recovery not as fun. I praise God for the good moments and pray for His help through all the hard, tough ones. People ask me how I'm doing, but sometimes it's still hard for me to express myself. I think my husband has earned another badge trying to be an observer. I got upset last night because I let myself just blurt out all that's going on with me mentally, emotionally, and physically. He pretty much got an attitude and told me that he hadn't asked nor wanted to know at the time. Looking back, it makes sense because he has to watch me go through it all while not being able to fix or relieve anything for me. I think that's enough to deal with without me putting words to it, making it all too real and more traumatic.

He has walked this journey with me through it all, and I thank God He still manages to keep walking with me. Through my head pain, nausea—dry heaving a ton throughout the day, stomach pains—hoping it's just the stretching of old surgery sites, low energy, digestive problems, depression, and more—I thank God that I can function every day. I get to be here, be me, and take part in bringing another child into this world. There are definitely some days that are worse than others. Those days, I take a long nap to try to assist my body in its healing.

I had some wake-up calls last week that scared me and brought back old fears from my previous pregnancies. Also, I had some similar brain tumor-like symptoms, which rattled me, thinking I might have another tumor. It's funny and sad how quickly the past can instill fear in us through our current battles—trauma! I let worry and fear pour over me, but God reminded me of where I've been and where I am now—peace! He really has the ultimate plan. I completely trust Him to get me through this journey, no matter the outcome. I'm in better hands with Him! I decided that I could only do the best I could, and the rest was in God's hands. I'm small, and God is ginormous. He has plans for me and this baby growing inside me. My job is to step aside and let Him do His thing!

The fear is going to try to attack me, but I'm going to fight back with God's help. I don't want to live in fear. I want this pregnancy to be full of faith and trust in the One who holds my future. Life has never been a promise of no pain or struggle—only heaven can promise that! I think back to my (brain) surgery and remember that I was done, but God wasn't. He really knows what's best.

I don't want to live in fear. I want this pregnancy to be full of faith and trust in the One who holds my future.

I know at this point I would have missed out on wonderful moments with my family and friends since the (brain) surgery. There's been a ton of healing, changing, and growing for so many I've prayed for. I've witnessed a dozen answered prayers for my family and friends. No matter where you find yourself in any situation—no matter the side—please remember that both sides have their own loads to carry, process, and survive.

Natalie Grant's song "In Better Hands" reminds us that we are always in better hands with God! He will always make things good for those who trust Him. My hope is in Him. He moves mountains and makes the impossible possible. He is my rock!

JUNE 7, 2014

38 › Hope & Strength in the ER

The only hope that I have while He gives me strength...

On Friday, June 6, 2014, Michael and I had the opportunity to spend five hours and forty-five minutes in the ER at St. Francis Hospital in Tulsa, Oklahoma. After three days of suffering pain in my abdomen with more discharge for the third week in a row, it was time for me to get checked to see what our fate was going to be. Is there a word that's worse than stressed, tired, worn out, or fed up? No matter the words, I was exhausted and needed some answers. The hospital is my husband's least favorite place. This dislike started way before me. Sadly, he's had to visit almost every ER in Stillwater, Oklahoma; Tulsa, Oklahoma; and miscellaneous vacation spots across the United States. We can't forget about last summer when we made an emergency visit to the County Hospital in Seattle, Washington, while on vacation. Let's just say if we could ever use my percentages to win the lottery instead of ER visits, we'd be millionaires!

After such an extensive stay at the ER on a Friday night, I was able to get blood work testing, a liquid analysis (sounds better), a pelvic exam, and an ultrasound. Now, before we did this nice little visit, I had already come to peace with whatever and however this journey needed to go. I still really wanted God's kingdom purposes to be fulfilled. Being on major medications during the month this baby came to exist in my womb has had me concerned a time or two. I know God has the ultimate plan, and I trust

Him completely. No matter what happens at this point, I will either get time here on earth with this miracle or in eternity!

Being in the ultrasound room and waiting for the tech to do her thing, I bit my lip and held my breath. I waited to hear the baby's heartbeat, but no beats were heard. I remember thinking in my mind, *God, I have peace about this, but walking through this fire right now is not fun.* Thank God the tech had the sound off. I remember seeing Michael's eyes get really big, and I thought I might not make it. Come to find out the baby is measuring eight weeks and two days as of Friday, and there's a really strong heartbeat—PRAISE GOD! This still didn't help me know why I was in pain and didn't feel well at all. After all the results were pulled together, this is what was found out:

- I have a small subchorionic hemorrhage (hematoma) between my uterine wall and placenta.

- I have a bacterial infection that probably occurred after all the medications I've been on for the sinus infections that I've had every month since my brain surgery. I'm working on the imbalance and hoping this will help get my body more balanced.

- Both of these are cause for a threatened miscarriage.

I need all my fellow prayer warriors to stand up with me to fight this new battle. I know it always seems there is something, yet I trust God to provide and give me exactly what I need, no matter the journey. Though it feels unfair, I again find myself not being exempt from anything challenging in this life. I know my body has its work cut out for it, trying to heal my brain surgery sites and growing a baby at the same time. We shall battle and fight, yet again, with God leading us.

I am to rest as much as I can while not participating in tackle football or horseback riding—as both a doctor and nurse suggested. I'm not supposed to lift heavy things or climb any stairs. I thought that was hilarious since I couldn't do some of those anyway due to my post-brain surgery recovery. Though, if you remember, I did try to tackle a chair not too long ago!

My fears come and go. I have to keep remembering that God is with me now, like He was yesterday and today. He walks with me now—never leaving me. He is the only hope that I have and my lighthouse through this next storm. I know that as long as I look to Him, He is for me, and nothing can be against me. It doesn't mean everything will go my way every day. It does mean that I won't lose hope, come what may, in the good, bad, or indifferent along the journey. Losing hope is one of the worst places to go. I've sadly been on the edge of losing hope. Trust me, you don't ever want to get even close to that edge. It's lonely. Hope may be all you have when the journey plays out.

He is hope and love. He is the one you can always count on when you need Him to scoop you up in all the tears, pain, loss, joy, and life. He holds me more times than I wish He had to at times. I cling to Him tighter than a baby to their momma when they are scared. I sit here crying tears of joy, knowing that nothing and no one can take Him away from me. Nothing, not even myself, can get in the way! He continues to walk with me!

There are many times where we all have reached a point of weariness that feels like there may be no hope. There's a point where we can't understand the why, the how come, or the what for. No matter where I find myself or you find yourself, know that He will give the weary strength when we lift our eyes to Him, giving it all to Him while finding hope in Him. Trust Him, no matter what you feel like, how much you want to give up, how much you'd rather not be here walking this journey, and how many tears you shed with all the unanswered questions you cry out for Him to answer. HE WILL GIVE ME STRENGTH when I am weak—He is ALWAYS strong!

I was reminded tonight that God allows us to go through our trials and tribulations to make us shiny, new, and in His image. He pulls us out of it all—the fire—at a very specific time where He can see His own reflection as He looks at us! For Him to care this much—well—it means the world to me. I sometimes joke that I must need a lot of shining through all this fire I go through. Yet, if it takes me going through one fire after another so He can continue to see Himself in me, I'll walk through those fires every single day!

Here's a list of three songs by Ellie Holcolmb to help sum up what I've just shared. Ellie Holcomb has a beautiful, God-given talent. Please enjoy these songs after you look them up on YouTube—I promise they will bless you.
"With You Now"
"Only Hope I've Got"
"He Will Give the Weary Strength"

Ellie shared the following Scripture verses in her blog post about the songs. It all fits perfectly with this entry.

Memory Verses 46 & 47

"Therefore let all the faithful pray to you while you may be found; surely the rising of the mighty waters will not reach them. You are my hiding place; you will protect me from trouble

and surround me with songs of deliverance" (Psalm 32:6–7).

⚔ *"Come, let us return to the Lord. He has torn us to pieces but he will heal us; he has injured us but he will bind up our wounds" (Hosea 6:1).*

Ellie wrote about how the songs of deliverance from her album were a wonderful reminder that we are never alone, even in the worst situations. It's a blessing to know that God delivers His people in every situation. Even if you find yourself in the hardest place of your life, He will never leave you. The fires can be strong, but they will never consume you. His promises are provided by His songs of deliverance.

I pray that we all remember to never lose hope and sight of our heavenly Father. He will always use our trials and tribulations to glorify His name and kingdom if we can graciously step aside and let His light shine. It is so easy to wallow in our pain and suffering. I know because I did this a time or two in my life. My biggest rewards and successes have been when I gave it all to Him, stepped aside, and let His light shine—oh so bright (at least I hope I have more than not). None of us are perfect, but when we die and go to heaven—oh, we will be blessed with perfect, whole, healed bodies and minds, walking with Him!

I pray we each are successful in this journey—always with Him! Thank you for your prayers, and I appreciate that you are still a part of my wild ride. I know it's not easy riding this journey with me, but you are a blessing to me for continuing. I love you all and praise God for you!

My dad and his three kids on Father's Day

JUNE 16, 2014

39 › Quick Update

It's already been a week since I had a checkup with my OBGYN. My treatment plan with added probiotics into my diet has helped me make great strides in my recovery. I'm still learning that it doesn't take much for my body to start screaming at me to slow down. I had to miss some important events with family and friends this past Saturday. I had to rest way more than expected due to more discharge, swelling, and pain.

The hematoma is still giving me lots of wonderful memories—not! On the bright side of resting, I did get to catch up on some movie watching—sharing an "oldie but goodie" movie or two with friends. A couple of my friends and I have started a list of must-see movies from the "good old days" called the 80s for our future movie watching and rest parties! It's so much easier to rest when others join me, plus movies and girl talk help pass the time!

I slept a lot yesterday while trying to celebrate Father's Day with Michael's dad and my own. I'm sure my sawing logs aloud made for some interesting entertainment—proving to myself and others that I need more sleep. Why is it that when I rest more, the more tired I get? I'm assuming that it just proves that I was really relaxed and resting like the doctor intended for me to do.

I go back to my OBGYN at the end of June, so I'll have more updates by then. I'm hoping we don't have to see the hematoma or any signs of it anymore—amen! Many have said that they are sorry that I'm having to deal with more trials and rough times, but I think it's just normal for my life after looking back at everything. It's strange to have the attitude I do at this point. I'm not used to letting go and seeing what God has planned for all of this. It's easy to say but not as easy to live out at times.

I ended up buying the Ellie Holcomb CD this past week, and I love it. Between her and Mandisa, I'm keeping my spirits up. It's not fun thinking you might have miscarried on most days. I am really exhausted this go around. It could be that my body is just really overworked with healing my brain while growing a baby. A picture my sister posted of me with my siblings and dad on Father's Day has provided proof that I look extremely exhausted, plus it was right before I took my second nap for the day! I know this too shall pass. I've been fortunate to see God's hands at work for many of us. I just have to remember to keep trusting him on a daily basis.

I praise God for Zofran, ginger ale, club whole wheat crackers, cranberry juice, and probiotic drinks! They are helping me survive and thrive in the chaos—it's the littlest of things!

JULY 1, 2014

40 › Miracles Grow

I had a wonderful checkup this past Monday, June 30, 2014, with my OBGYN. I was at the doctor's office for an hour and twenty minutes. Plus, I had to sit in the lab downstairs for an additional forty minutes, which made for a crazy morning. At least I got a good report on the hematoma. It looks like the hematoma is healed—praise God, and continued prayers that it doesn't return! Thanks to all of you who have sent prayers up on my behalf and for those who have been a part of my care team over the last five weeks. It's working—God has heard and answered!

I'm still dealing with the fact that my body cannot make good bacteria right now, so probiotics are a necessity in my daily nutrition intake. This could be a side effect from my brain surgery in December. Hold up for a minute—thinking back, it has been just six-and-a-half months since my brain surgery. Well, it's crazy to think life rolls in all directions. I'm not sure my mind will ever be able to fully grasp this concept of brain surgery and getting pregnant three-and-a-half months into the recovery process. Even if I had tried, I don't think it would have turned out this way. I've always wanted to do life how God designed it, which makes for a very interesting life—totally blessed in the midst of all the storms.

Though I have been very sick this week, today seems to be turning around—PRAISE GOD! I try hard to not let it get to me, yet I'm human, and it does. It's such a blessing that God has given us technology like 3D imaging so we can see our little jelly bean/peanut—nicknames already given to our little one—a.k.a. third miracle growing. That picture is going to go a long way in helping me through the continued nausea and throwing up.

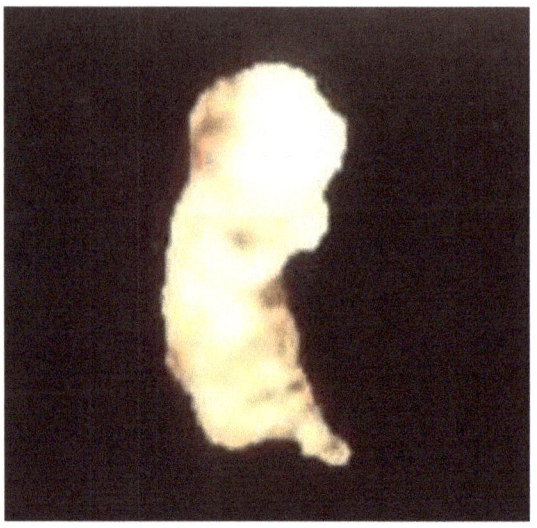

3D image of little jelly bean/peanut

It's funny to think that we were told in 2009 that we would only get pregnant together by the grace of God. I thank God that His grace is sufficient for us! Once this little miracle gets here, we need to make a fun visit to the fertility center so they can experience how wonderful and sufficient God's grace has been for us. It speaks volumes of how Big our God really can be. What's really wild is that this is only a small percentage of how Big He really is!

I need continued prayers for my bacterial infection. We are waiting for my blood work results. If the results are still positive for the bacteria, I will need an intense treatment to see if we can get my balances back to normal. I'm hoping that it's not necessary, but it seems my body is having difficulty recovering from brain surgery while growing a baby at the same time. It does make sense, but I'm hoping for the best.

God continues to blow me away—big time. I continue to be blessed watching answered prayers for people to be loved on, healed, and blessed by God. It has renewed my soul and spirit. Everything from relationship changes, healing of past hurts, baby adoption, and more. I just love getting to watch God's hands at work. He really loves us unconditionally! May we each get to see Him at work and know He wants the very best for us, no matter where we are in our journey!

Remember, this life is not meant to be perfect! Just because we follow a life after God does not mean we are exempt from suffering, heartache, and brokenness. I'm at a place in my life where I'm really understanding that each road I walk gives me the opportunity to step aside and let God do His glorious miracles and works by showing each of us who He really is. Don't get me wrong—it has its bad and ugly days. I'm just so thankful the good outweighs the bad and ugly ones.

"Do Life Big" by Jamie Grace is a wonderful inspiration in how I want to live my life. I need to work on slowing down to follow God's lead! Doing life big is living like God's example in loving, giving, and being. We just have to trust the Holy Spirit to guide us. Hope you enjoy while doing life bigger than you could ever imagine! Spread those wings and keep trusting Him on the daily.

JULY 16, 2014

41 › Reset & Reach Up

Resetting and reaching up to grab His hand . . .

As I continue this journey, I've discovered that the depression and post-traumatic stress disorder (PTSD) from my Lilian Grace experience has been running rampant every day. During my prayer time this morning, I had a wonderful talk with God. I've been reminded that I must keep giving it all to Him so this life, recovery, and pregnancy don't swallow me whole. As I finally got back to reading my *Jesus Calling* book again this morning, tears rolled down my cheeks while I laughed with joy, knowing God gets what I'm going through. I keep thinking I have this, but the reality is that I do not. I'm not a superwoman.

I'm Chrissy! I have a heart I wear on my shoulders. I get hurt too many times when I'm the one who should let go. I get disappointed in myself, people, and life. I work too hard. I care too much. I get misunderstood and quoted wrong. I don't live up to my own expectations or other people's. I don't always say the right things nor do other people. People get mad at me. I don't have the relationship I'd like to have with some people, but there is more for us. I do know that I keep trying and trusting God through it all. He can heal and change it all, no matter how stubborn we can all be!

Go read July 16 in the *Jesus Calling* devotional. It focuses on self-pity and depression. Sarah encourages you to reach up and look to God for help. She shares the following three Bible verses, and it was good for me to type them out here:

Memory Verses 48–50

🗡 *"He lifted me out of the slimy pit, out of the mud and mire; he set my feet on a rock and gave me a firm place to stand. He put a new song in my mouth, a hymn of praise to our God. Many will see and fear the LORD and put their trust in him" (Psalm 40:2–3).*

🗡 *"Why, my soul, are you downcast? Why so disturbed within me? Put your hope in God, for I will yet praise him, my Savior and my God" (Psalm 42:5).*

🗡 *"The LORD delights in those who fear him, who put their hope in his unfailing love" (Psalm 147:11).*

WOW! After reading the entry, I can see how good He is to me and others in my life. He just needs us to lean on Him daily. Life gets fast and furious. Life with trials and tribulations can beat us up so much that we don't even recognize ourselves or who we are supposed to be anymore: physically, mentally, emotionally, spiritually, and more! I sometimes don't know where the time goes, but I always seem to need more of it. I know that fighting my battles will not end nor will yours, but my strength to get through it all daily depends on my dependence on Him. Life is not fair. People, including myself, aren't going to be who you and I need them to be. It's not about what we've been dealt—it's how we survive and thrive through whatever comes our way.

I've found myself at my own pity party lately. I let what others are doing or have done, plus life not working out how I want it to be, overcome me. I've let too many past hurts and pains rule my life these days. I'm over it! I still want freedom from all that consumes me so my chains can't hold me back. What chains are you letting hold you down, keeping you from living out the life made just for you? You and I can put on the pity parties and play the blame games, but we are only going to go as far as the chains and bars will allow us to go. Last time I checked, it's not far at all! Let's face those hurts and disappointments to start living in the light! Here's to resetting myself and yourself once again so we can live the life God has intended for us to live—free and purpose-driven!

A post-brain surgery note: I'm working through not being able to produce good bacteria. It's still a struggle, but I'm working out a better eating plan that's focused around nutrition to help balance my body. Half my head still gets the feeling of hundreds, even thousands, of bees stinging me. I've learned to do my best at not overheating or getting as stressed. Those two things tend to increase the pain if I get too hot or stressed out.

A pregnancy note: I have a lot of pain in my right abdomen. If I remember correctly, I had the same issue with Piper. With her, part of my hernia repair sites ripped and stretched away from where they were surgically sewn. It feels worse when I cough or sneeze. I've discovered a few food items that make my nausea and throwing up worse, so I'm avoiding those like the plague. I think my body has a lot of the regular aches and pains that come along with trying to share one's body with another life source! I'm calling the doctor today to make sure that I don't need to be seen.

I know I've been hard on myself lately. I apologize to the select few of you who have had to hear my negative, self-pity talks. I try hard not to share too much of that. It was overwhelming, so some of you had to suffer through harder conversations. I love you for standing by me, no matter the state you find me in.

Today marks my double eighteenth birthday—thirty-six if you'd rather not do the math! I have seen more things than I'd like to see and experience, yet I am thankful I haven't seen worse things that exist. I have a good and blessed life. No matter how good I know I have it, I still find myself battling inside and out on a daily basis. Life happens—wearing us down. I just have to remember to keep putting it all at His feet, grabbing His hand, and letting Him do His thing that He does so beautifully.

On a positive note for my birthday: I love birthdays! I have always loved them, even though these past few years were not as fun. Birthdays have always meant the world to me. It's the anniversary of the one day people rejoiced that God brought you into this world. You were the reason for smiling faces and shouts of praise. That day will always be a miracle in that you were created in your mother's womb and given life—your first breath! The possibilities for you and your journey were unmarked and fresh, bringing so much hope that you could do anything. This is why I love birthdays. No matter what today brings, I know hope was born, and the day was made right when I entered the world.

Praying that we all can remember that it's never too late to restart. There's not a limit for resetting so we can live the life God intended for us to live. Praying we all find hope, love, and multitudes of blessings on a daily basis.

"Burn Bright" by Natalie Grant reminds us to keep burning brightly, even after we find ourselves dimming in this life. It's never too late to reach up and grab His hand. He never leaves us—not for a second. His arms are waiting for you. The world needs His bright light, so don't be afraid to burn bright in Him!

AUGUST 3, 2014

42 › Warrior Princess Angel Run

My faith is made stronger as He calls me out, and I answer . . .

The lyrics from "Oceans (Where Feet May Fail)" by Hillsong take me to the most wonderful holy place any time they are played. I imagine myself walking out on the waters toward Jesus as the waves crash over me, trying to swallow me up, yet never harming me. The storms rage around me as the strong winds try to take me out, yet I'm still standing. I always want to be in the presence of my Savior. He takes me deeper as He strengthens my trust and faith. He is everything.

As I walk through this life with God placing certain people on my heart and things I must get done, I sometimes wonder why. It doesn't take me long to discover that I should listen and trust Him, because both parties always seem to be blessed by it all. I've had many fabulous conversations lately with people whom God has placed on my heart and in my thoughts. He wants to heal and create a richer journey for each of them. It's been incredible to hear what comes from it all. There's so much healing and training that needs to take place in our lives. I'm glad He cares about each of us, and I hope we can step aside to let Him do such things.

I have to remember that I told God I wanted to be a vessel and to let Him do what He needs done. Too many of us are hurting and tired of just doing life—barely getting by. Circumstances can weigh us down. We tend to hold on to things way too long when, if we would let go and let God do what is needed, we'd be free! I love how He keeps blessing me with freedom from so much! Freedom is still my word for this year, and I love how God is making this happen.

Sadly, I have things that tend to weigh me down, though, and scars that get ripped open too quickly. I don't respond very well to how I should or need to be. I'm imperfect, and I get that. I just want to always do better by being a better version of what I was yesterday and today. It takes trying and doing, which sometimes isn't easy. Sometimes I don't want to do anything, but I know God won't let me live in that place for very long. Praising Him daily for such a thing! Also, I pray that He is with all who are in my path when I'm not who I need to be for Him or them.

Putting on the Fourth Annual Warrior Princess Angel Run over the weekend was exhausting. I got to the point, not too long ago, that I thought it would be better that I just quit. It seemed that my quitting would make many happy by bringing relief that they could finally forget and move on. The devil sure likes to get in there and mess with me. I'm thankful that God hasn't let me quit. He has brought several amazing people to re-energize me by fueling me with good soul food! They made sure I knew it wasn't just for me or them but for all of us! I praise God for each of you for your stories, thoughts, and prayers. All of you have touched my heart and soul! You are part of the reason I'm still in it!

Watching everyone show up and be a part of this cause to help T18/T13 babies and their families makes my heart happy. I see individuals who have sadly lost their babies come as a team to run/walk in honor and memory while raising awareness for others. I see supporters who have always been there in some way, shape, or form. All have played an important role in our lives. I see God through all of it, even in the twists and turns that make me sad, angry, and tearful at times. It wears me out, but it also energizes me.

Having to organize a race with post-brain surgery recovery and another pregnancy has not been my idea of a good time. I have dealt with short-term memory loss, which I combatted by writing lots of notes to make sure I don't forget. I always have certain types of people that I deal with who are good, bad, and ugly. Yet I am grateful to all who are huge blessings to me, my family, and all our T18/T13 families. It matters—you all matter!

God calls me to do many things, and my faith truly has been made stronger. There have been many assignments that I have not wanted to do. I've begged Him to take some away. I'm glad He knows what I need and that He didn't take these things at times, because I wouldn't know Him like I do. I love Him so much and appreciate that I get to have a relationship with him 24/7. I may finally reach perfection the day I die, but until then, I'll keep striving to be more like Him. I will rest in Him when I'm not being stubborn and trying to do it on my own!

I was so blessed with many special guests that traveled from afar to be with us on race day. Many happy tears were shed seeing them. We got to have Bruce Noblett, Michael's boss during Lily's life here, all the way from Texas, along with his family. He was the last person outside the hospital we spoke to before removing Lilian Grace from life support. He holds a special place in our hearts.

We were super blessed to have our OBGYN specialist, Dr. Christine Blake, come and make our very special gender reveal announcement at the race awards ceremony! I love that I got to share these special guests with the participants and supporters. If you haven't heard or seen the news, we are happy to announce that the next miracle to join our family is another sweet baby girl. Her name will be Daphne Mae. I love that we will be adding another girl—no offense, boys!

One of two cowboy legacies

AUGUST 4, 2014

43 › My Celebration of Life Wishes

Inspired by the movie The Fault in Our Stars

My sister and I got excited today about having some sister time, so we went to watch a movie with recliners and blankets at the fabulous AMC theatre. I neglected to think about the choice of movie we were going to see on the eve of my sweet Lilian Grace's death. Let's just say *The Fault in Our Stars* is an incredible movie, but it's a major tear-jerker, especially with the timing of my life events and Lily's angelversary.

I was going to type all my thoughts out, then chose to do a video—forgive my voice and appearance. I have cried many tears tonight, plus I'm recovering from major events that happened in the past couple of weeks. It's a well-deserved look, if I say so myself. Love you all, and I hope you enjoy! I'm thanking God that I'm still here and get to share what would have been done if God had called me home!

Happy fourth angelversary to my sweet baby girl, Lilian Grace! We love being your mommy and daddy, no matter where you are or how long we will be apart!

Note: To see the video, visit https://youtu.be/iuJj7-vP4Gw.

So if you know me, you know that I have talked a lot about God's timing and that He's here all the time. Today was—actually, tonight—was an incredible night. My sister and I ended up taking a break. We watched a movie called The Fault in Our Stars. This video is inspired by that movie. I wasn't thinking about it being Lilian's angelversary in the morning. She passed away four years ago tomorrow, August fifth.

Here I am watching a movie about cancer and the people going through that struggle. It's sad because there is death in it. I cried a lot, so forgive the beauty here because I was crying like crazy. It was really good for me. But this inspired me to share something that I had to write—really, the night before I had to go to the hospital to get ready for the eighteenth of (December 2013) to get the tumor taken out. I had to have brain surgery.

Here it is—I was told that this (exercise) would be good for me to plan out my celebration of life. I'm going to read straight from the piece of paper, so forgive me, I'm not going to be looking at the camera.

Chrissy Larie' Whitten's celebration of life—my song number one, "Call Me Higher" by All Sons & Daughters—my singers would be Shad and Rachel Foley. My speaker number one was Kaye Sanders Schooley—her topic would be the full armor of God. Song number two, "I Will Never Be the Same Again" by Hillsong that everyone would sing—it would be on the big screen. My speaker number two would be Marsha Gonzaga Johnson—her topic would be God's will lived out in a life. Song number three, "Come to Jesus" by Chris Rice—Chuck Burton was going to be the singer. Speaker number three was my sister-in-law, Leslie Hall—her topic was supposed to be grace plus comfort plus peace plus death equals assignment is completed. Song number four, "God of This City" by Chris Tomlin—again, my singers were going to be Shad and Rachel Foley. Speaker number four would be pastor Matt Blair—God is Big and how to live out your purpose, trusting Him all the way.

I wanted to share my prayer cards that I had through the time leading through Lily's life and through a lot of my mountains—even ones I added from other people. I wanted a slideshow because there are so many pictures. If you know me, we take a lot of pictures. I always wanted to have moments where you have to get those down, just in case your brain forgets. With Lily, we took thousands of pictures, or so it seemed like (that many). I put on a note to make sure they are action pics because my daddy always said that he needs action pics. He doesn't just want us standing there, just looking all like, "Hey!" I thought that was really funny. I put a big smiley face (on the paper).

I said that I'd love for there to be a praise and worship section with these songs:
"Mighty to Save"
"How Great Is Our God"
"You Never Let Go"
"Your Love Never Fails"
"How He Loves"
"Shout to the Lord"

I put down that you could do some in the beginning and the end (of my celebration). It's my favorite way to worship—to sing to Jesus. Another note: I put that I don't want there to be negativity. I want there to be praising and worshiping. I want people to be filled up so they can be poured out. My other note: I hand wrote a letter that's two pages, front and back, for you to read. I never put who (would read it)—I just have that. Here I am, because of The Fault in Our Stars. *I decided, who better to read this than me.*

Maybe someone could benefit from this—at this very time. Hmm (clears throat)—forgive my voice because I'm still recovering from the race, my end of summer work period, pregnancy, and brain surgery. Here we go:

Dear Fellow Brothers and Sisters in Faith:

It's surreal to sit here on Tuesday, December 17, at 12:40 a.m., writing out my celebration of life wishes and now this letter to you. I just feel really led to do this. If you are having this read to you—well—it means my heavenly Father has decided to call me home. He has always known the very second that my life would begin and end.

I have enjoyed an abundant life full of rain—followed by rainbows. God has always brought me to and through all the trials of life. Know that I'm sitting here writing to you not knowing if I will be healed here on earth or on the other side of heaven. I just know that God has an amazing plan and mission for each of us. Are you living the life He has planned for you?

He sees the whole picture! If I could do this life again, I'd choose—every time—I'd choose Jesus and follow Him. Though my life has been filled and full of giant mountains. They could have always been worse, and I really believe that. God always provided in each trial and tribulation. He never left me nor failed me. He gave me exactly what, who, and how I needed it all to conquer and pull through. Yes, things would be bad. I'd think, "How in the world can I do this?" But I'd stop and remember I just needed to trust Him. He is the answer to conquering!

Put on the full armor of God and live out His will in your life to further His kingdom. You will not regret it! Yes, it will be hard. Tears and pain will exist. The devil will hit you from every direction. You will get tired, but you will be blessed beyond measure. The ultimate gift is eternal life and knowing that you have a purpose. You get to be used and make His kingdom grow.

I love you all! Each of you has played a role in my walk. I could not have done it without you. Some of you were right by my side, battling with all we had been equipped with in our lives. Some of you were prayer warriors, near and far away. No matter what role, I thank you for your faith. I appreciate your trust. I praise God for placing you in my life to help shape and mold me into who He needed me to be.

I'll leave you all with this: live a life that's God-driven. Live a life full of unconditional love and forgiveness. I did not always get it right. I hurt people along the way, and I made peace with all that I could. Life is too short—we don't have forever to do what needs to be done. We have free will, so choose wisely in how you live it out. Don't be stagnant! Live a life that produces much fruit for God.

Soli Deo Gloria,
Chrissy Whitten

PS: I hope to see you in heaven!

I hadn't read this since—you know—forever. It seems like it hasn't been that long—we are on eight months or nine since brain surgery. But I'll be honest, whenever—if you know me, you know already that I struggled right after brain surgery. I was really in a good place (before surgery). I was at peace. I was ready to go, and God brought me back. Then—now, He's got me pregnant, and I'm getting to do this craziness again. I love it!

There are some days I wish I could take away, but I can't. It wouldn't be good to take it away because it's helping me be who I need to be for my children and for other people—most importantly, for God. I just want—I just know so many people are struggling right now in their lives. They are just trying to get by, or they just don't care anymore. But know this, no matter where you are, just trust Him. Drop to your knees. Put your head on the floor, and just say, "God, I don't know anymore. I don't know how I feel. I don't know how to act. I don't know how to be."

At 3:00 a.m. tomorrow, August fifth, it will have been four years since Lilian passed away. At 3:00 a.m. was when she first coded, and I remember being cuddled up, hearing the "No Air" song by Jordin Sparks and Chris Brown. I bawled my eyes out because I knew this was it. This was going to be the last day of her life.

But I also knew that was the day I realized what I thought I knew, who I thought I was, and who I thought everybody else was—that kind of died with her. But what was good about that is I got to see people differently, and my expectations have changed. I still have to work on some of that because those scars are still there from those time periods in life. But I've seen people change and be bigger and better. I've seen others struggle—not to forgive, deal, and move forward. I'm just praying for each of us, that no matter what hits us or no matter what we carry with us, that we remember God wants to heal us. He wants to make us whole.

So thanks to The Fault in Our Stars. It's surreal, and it helped me remember some things and helped me pull out some important stuff I needed—I guess—to share. I love you all! Know this, you just gotta try. I love you!

Happy angelversary, sweet baby girl! I can't believe it's been four years. But I'm so lucky to be your mama and to keep living out your legacy while I get to do mine and help some other people get to do theirs.

I'm very blessed and honored that no matter how many pity parties I throw—how bad or whiny I am—God can still do stuff. He can still produce fruit in all this mess that's me. I love you all! Bye!

AUGUST 27, 2014

44 › It's Time!

Worry can pour down on you and consume every part of your existence. I'm not worried about what my future holds, but I do get scared of what my walk will be on a daily basis, trying to get to the other side of each mountain that I face. I know fire will come, but it's not fun walking through it all the time. I know my life is built on the solid rock—the One and Only! I trust Him completely. I just don't trust what this life will throw at me on any given day. That fire can hurt and wear on you!

I've been watching so many of us face our own mountains. All look very different, yet we are still fighting the good fight by climbing each mountain we face. Even if we think we are failing, God is succeeding and making a way for us. We just have to let Him take the lead! He's the number one guide in mountain climbing—in trials and tribulations! He can give us peace like no other and provides for our every need for the entire time we're climbing.

If you want to look at it as a storm, He is the perfect weatherman and rescuer! He knows what the storm is going to do and places help along the way. Yes, I've been stressed about today. Today is our twenty-week scan. Why is it so scary? This is the scan where our hopes and dreams for Lilian Grace were shattered and destroyed. It's the timing in a pregnancy where we found out her predicted fate. I remember when it came time for Piper's twenty-week scan; I overate and spent money just like I have with Daphne this go around.

I had my regular OBGYN check-up on Monday. Sadly, I gained weight too quickly, so I immediately went on the low-carb diet like my doctor directed at the appointment. I knew I was getting out of control, especially with the timing of everything. So here I am listening to "Worried" by Jonas Woods—praising God because He has my back! Whatever comes of today's scan is going to go one way or the other—a fifty-fifty shot. God's wonderful at reminding me that He's got this, and I need to let go once again.

Please send some prayers up! The appointment is at ten in the morning. Life is going to be what it is going to be. I live for Him and want to do His will—so let's do this! I pray I can keep stepping aside and letting God shine! Daphne Mae has her own mission in life. I pray that I'm ready to help her live it out loud, like I'm getting to do with my other two girls. I'll do an update later today. Thank you so much for the continuous support! Go listen to Jonas Woods's song—it's incredible!

Radiating happiness

AUGUST 27, 2014

45 › Twenty-Week Scan Praise

Memory Verses 51 & 52

🗡 *"Because you are my help, I sing in the shadow of your wings. I cling to you; your right hand upholds me" (Psalm 63:7–8).*

🗡 *"Your word is a lamp for my feet, a light on my path" (Psalm 119:105).*

Praising God! We had to be at the doctor's office for almost two hours since Dr. Blake was a very busy lady and got behind today. God is so good! All is normal from the scans today. This is a huge relief!

Now I'm getting some delicious food in my belly as I celebrate making it through this point. It's never fun going through the waiting game. The Bible verses above remind me to keep singing His praises as He guides me through the darkest times with His glorious light.

Be praying for my anesthesiologist, brain surgeon, and/or neurologist in making sure we get a safe plan for my C-section. It's the only concern now at this point.

Love you all, and thanks for everything! This ride is never boring! Praise God!

Hello Piper's 3rd birthday

NOVEMBER 13, 2014

46 › Gestational Diabetes

Sorry, it's been way too long since I updated everyone on here. I've had many good days, yet I still struggle with headaches, depression, and pregnancy symptoms on other days. I've been feeling not so well, even when I have followed a low-carb diet like the doctor suggested. It's not a surprise that I got a call from the nurse this morning letting me know that I failed my three-hour glucose tolerance test. I have gestational diabetes. At least it explains why I've struggled so much with not feeling well and the drastic weight gain/loss.

What now? Well, I pick up my kit and start testing my blood sugar four times a day while being on a very strict low-carb diet to see if we can balance it out. If this doesn't work, I'll more than likely be doing insulin. I don't have a long way to go. But I do know that how I've been able to control my headaches and pain from post-brain surgery has been through certain foods, which are not approved on my low-carb diet.

I need prayers for the headaches and swelling to go away, plus the ability to balance my diet for the blood sugars. I don't want this to affect Daphne Mae at all. I remember having gestational diabetes with Lilian Grace. I wasn't sure if it was all the stress I was dealing with or all the post-surgery recoveries. It's crazy how things can throw you right back. I've been super emotional this past week, but now I see why. It feels like I got thrown back to all the stuff with Lily, which was far from easy or fun.

I met with the anesthesiology department at the hospital yesterday. I know that I more than likely entertained them with all my medical craziness. I'm hoping that when they get to talk to my neurosurgeon that they can all come up with a plan to safely deliver Daphne Mae while protecting both of us. I know diabetes was brought up yesterday, so I'm not sure how that will affect everything on surgery day. Pray that there's a perfect timing that God will reveal for when to perform the C-section.

I know that many are concerned about my high-risk status. I knew the risks from day one when I found out four months post-brain surgery that we had been blessed with another miracle growing inside me. It wasn't my plan, but I trust Him in His plans always—even if I shed a few tears and might breakdown for a minute! He will make it good! So here's to winning medically in the not-so-fun things of life! If I could just channel this luck I have in the medical world into winning that lottery, I'd be mega rich!

Here's to eating a perfect diet and feeling better than I have been—especially during the holiday season! At least I know that I won't go past December 29. I'm just not sure if we'll have her sooner than that until everyone gets together to make those decisions. Thanks for always praying and reading my craziness. Love to you all!

NOVEMBER 22, 2014

47 › Update & Baby Sprinkle

Update: My low-carb diet has been awesome for my blood sugar readings. Last Tuesday night, I spent some time with my girlfriends and thought I'd let myself snack on all the delicious goodness that everyone brought. I had thought that maybe I really didn't have gestational diabetes, but I was mistaken. When I got home and the two-hour post-snacking mark hit, I checked my blood sugar. It was—drumroll, please—almost double what my good numbers had been. So I proved that being on my strict low-carb diet mattered. It was good for this stubborn girl to see this. If I hadn't done it, I may or may not have quit checking my blood sugar.

My other event was last night with my Cooper family in Cushing, Oklahoma. I measured food portions out precisely and kept track of everything. I saved up my carbs to eat a heavenly carb-loaded meal. I didn't go crazy. I didn't go over half a cup on things, yet two hours later, post-eating heavenly food, showed that I was twenty-eight points over where I should have been. Saving up carbs doesn't matter. In fact, it's how much you eat at one time that matters! I knew this, but it was wishful thinking! It wasn't like the forty-eight points over from Tuesday night, but it still was higher. I'm proud of myself for not eating one dessert, even if it almost killed me!

Life can throw many things at us. I'm just glad God keeps preparing, molding, and shaping me into something better than I've been. I wish it didn't have to be some of the things

I've dealt with, but it wouldn't be my journey without it all. Here's to me cutting back, letting go, and adjusting in large amounts!

Another update: My neurosurgeon is good with the anesthesiologist for my C-section. I go to my specialist in less than three weeks, and hopefully, we will get a game plan that day—no promises though. I know we are all anticipating this sweet miracle. I'm tired of being pregnant, and I would love for my body to get some relief. Plus, I'm just so ready to hold her and love her. To think that God decided I get to do this for a third time blows my mind, especially since we were told we wouldn't have any kids together, but by the grace of God! Praising Him that His Grace remains sufficient!

Parenting is really hard. There are tough days iced with the sweetest moments. Sometimes, I feel like I am failing miserably while I drown in the ocean of life. Thank God for the army in my life, especially my prayer warriors! I know I'm not alone in the battles that we face every day.

---

*Parenting is really hard.
There are tough days iced
with the sweetest moments.*

Keep praying that Daphne Mae and I both are healthy and ready to go when her arrival time comes. Pray for all the staff, from the janitor to the surgeon. Pray that all are prepared and do their jobs better than they have ever been able to do—stepping aside and letting God's team do their thing!

I appreciate all the prayers and support. It keeps me

going. I know there are many of you walking, running, and dealing with your own journeys. God's got us always! He is the number one weapon to help us be victorious through each battle. Don't ever give up! I could have, but I didn't! God isn't finished with me yet, and He's not finished with you either. Love you all!

For those who do not have Facebook, I didn't want you to miss out on a celebration we are doing. Here's the post from my Facebook page:

I have finally agreed to do a baby shower that we are calling a baby sprinkle. I don't want anyone left out, so if you haven't gotten an invitation via Facebook, let me know. I will make sure to get you added. Ever since Lilian Grace, it's been tough to do these. Poor Piper didn't get one because I was so afraid of celebrating and that it would all come crashing down. I trust God, but I still have things that hold me back. I'm looking forward to the baby sprinkle and celebrating with everyone! Time has given me strength and healing thanks to God above!

Also, please do not feel obligated to come if you receive an invitation. I just didn't want to miss someone. If you did get an invitation and notice someone hasn't but would care to join us, please invite them. It's an open invitation! Love you all!

Please make sure to officially RSVP, if you are coming, to Shanna Santiago—info is in the invite!

Celebrate!

Baby Sprinkle!

Hostesses: *Rachel Foley, Shanna Santiago, Kris Ramsay, Karen Marquis, & Debbie Cooper*

We are having a baby sprinkle for Michael Whitten and Chrissy 'Cooper' Whitten to celebrate their third miracle, Daphne Mae.

Time: *2:30–4:30 p.m.*
Come & go party with a dessert buffet & drinks (Make sure to RSVP to make sure we have enough goodies.)

Location: *Solace Church Lobby, 7314 W 41st St, Tulsa, OK 74107 (across from TCC West Campus)*

Needs: *Awesome double jogging stroller & car seat (It's being suggested that people make a $5 contribution or whatever amount you'd like to go toward this in lieu of gifts.)*

Please feel free to include others who are not on the current invite list. Chrissy doesn't want anyone left out. It's been a crazy ride, and she appreciates all the prayers and support throughout the years from Lilian Grace until now! We just ask that everyone RSVPs in order for us to have plenty of desserts and drinks!

RSVP to Shanna Santiago via email by Monday, December 1, 2014.

Nursery Theme: *Foxes, hedgehogs, and air balloons!*

NOVEMBER 22, 2014

48 › Car Wreck

Second update of the day: Well, life definitely doesn't stop! Praising God that He's got my back because the devil has a target on me. Michael and I went for a breakfast date this morning after I gave my first update of the day on here to let those without Facebook know about the upcoming baby sprinkle. Post-breakfast, we proceeded with shopping for Piper's new bedroom set since Daphne gets Piper and Lilian's old set. It's Piper's Christmas present—a *Frozen* room with big girl furniture! After getting an antique dresser and a cookie, we headed on to a furniture store in Tulsa Hills.

We decided to look at Target next before making a decision on a bed. Lo and behold, on our way, the unbelievable happened. Now before I say this, here's some important information: Lilian Grace came at thirty-two weeks gestation due to complications of her trisomy 18. Piper came three weeks early because we were in a car accident and I lost half of my amniotic fluid a week later.

That being said—I'll carry on with the story. Michael was driving, and I thank God he was trained and knows how to handle any situation, because if I had been driving, things might have gone differently.

A lady wasn't paying attention at all while on her phone and flew across all the lanes where we were going to turn. I'm not sure how the other cars missed her, but we were not so lucky. Since there was nowhere for us to go, Michael slowed down as much as he could, but we ended up fishtailing into her with the driver-side front of our vehicle. I was trying not to freak out, but I said very loudly, "Are you freakin' kidding me?" Here I am at almost thirty-three weeks gestation and now in another wreck while pregnant. It's insane. I can't make my crazy, ridiculous story up that by the grace of God gets to have some wonderful things come from all the bad.

After getting her info and calming down, we headed to labor and delivery to make sure that the baby and I were all good. St. Francis is my sanctuary, with angels working there. They were so good with me and very patient with a post-traumatic, stressed-out momma. I was surprisingly calmer on the outside than on the inside. I was hurting, but I think it was more because of tensing up during the wreck—nerves and stress happening with it all.

We were at the hospital today for over six hours. They checked everything and captured my amniotic fluid because I didn't want to go through what I did with Piper. Since we were there so long, I did get my absolute favorite meal from there that I used to eat when Lilian Grace lived there for over fifty-one days. It consists of a chicken quesadilla (no onions), mashed sweet potatoes, green beans, cottage cheese, a side salad (no tomatoes), and tea. I refrained from ordering my favorite dessert of chocolate cake or pecan pie—gestational diabetes—but it made up for not getting to eat from ten in the morning to seven at night—not good for a pregnant lady or Chrissy. I tend to get angry when hungry, so I try to feed myself every two to three hours with a meal or snack.

All my blood tests, stress test, ultrasounds, and everything else looked good. I'm glad we know where all my numbers are so we can compare when I follow up with my other doctors. This will help me sleep better.

I will say that I'm not a normal person. It felt good to be in that hospital room being taken care of by certified professionals. I thank God for them and their training. Ever since Lilian Grace, I don't mind if I have to be there. Trust me, I'm not trying to get there, but I don't hate it. It's a weird feeling of peace. It may have something to do with Lilian passing away there. When really stressed, I have found myself going to the cafeteria to eat my favorite chicken caesar wrap from time to time.

We are now home, and I'm just trying to de-stress and calm down from the chaos of today. I'm not going to lie—I split a piece of Italian butter cake with Michael to help with this process. My nerves are shot. I'm tired, but I know God knew what was up and took care of me. Here's a fun twist: My next-door neighbor's wife is an RN at the hospital. I just met her this week after living here for over two years because Piper locked me out of the house—yes, it's been a rough week, to say the least. I don't think any of this was a coincidence but a divine appointment. It gives me great peace knowing she is next door. When Lilian and Piper were born, I had two pastors living right next door and across the street. God is really cool in how He takes care of me!

Anyway, pray that things are good like all my test results showed. Forgive me for not completely trusting the results, because Piper's all had come back great too, and it wasn't. I am more experienced now and know what to get checked out so we can compare. See, training really does pay off. I'm hoping I have no more drama for this pregnancy or year. This momma is worn out. God can have all of it because I'm finished! Praying Daphne comes when she is fully baked and ready to come out healthy, whole, and happy.

Life keeps throwing so much at us. I'm thankful I have a

wonderful support system who prays for me and loves me unconditionally. I finally shed some tears tonight while I sat in the car waiting for my husband to get his to-go order for supper. Tears are a blessing, because it means God is helping me release it all. I needed that more than I thought.

During the car ride home, Michael switched from the football game to my Crowder CD. "Come as You Are" played first in the car. I have grown to really love this song. It makes me think of so many who need hope and healing from their brokenness, wandering, burdens, and hurts. I love how God loves us unconditionally, wanting us to come as we are. We are never too far to come to Him. I know my struggles of fear and bitterness are in His hands. I've come a long way. I'm thankful for His loving grace. I'm a perfect example of His grace at work. It's always sufficient!

The famous hospital meal

NOVEMBER 28, 2014

49 › Thankful

As I reflect on 2014 and my past, I am blown away by what God has helped me overcome all these years. Thank God for my stubbornness and strong-willed spirit. I do think God has used these two crazy traits to get me through each mountain I have faced and will come up against in the future. There are times I wish I could erase 80 percent of it all or make it different, yet it wouldn't be as sweet! I know I joke that I couldn't make this stuff up if I tried, but I really couldn't. It's been a lot on this journey, yet I know I'd rather have gone through mine than someone else's. I pray for everyone as you conquer your own mountains! God is here to help you climb and succeed through them. Just let go and let Him take care of you.

The days I struggle most are the days I try to pick it all up and charge forward without a thought of letting Him lead the way. Thank God I don't last long and finally get my priorities straight, because I truly am only successful when I step aside and let Him lead. We only have three to four weeks left before Daphne Mae will join us in this world to let her light shine brightly for us all. I'm updating my nutty nesting to-do lists and making sure that I'm caught up to the point of getting to relax and feel more freedom from the chains that procrastination can have over one's self. Trust me, I know I'll never get caught up. I just want to get to a point where I'm not overwhelmed by it all.

Both girls' rooms are painted—thanks to our cousin! Daphne's room will glow and knock people off their feet with sparkling apple—bright green—instead of the Sunkist Orange that Lilian Grace and Piper had in their nursery in our previous home. Piper's room is a gorgeous purple gladiola—lavender—in which she will have a *Frozen* theme, as per her request to Santa Claus this year. I wasn't sure about doing a major theme surrounding a cartoon, but my memory served me correctly when I realized that the most memorable bedroom theme I had growing up was my Strawberry Shortcake one. I'll never forget that theme. It brings lots of happy memories with it, so I caved easily by letting go and getting the *Frozen* theme ready to unveil to Piper for her Christmas present!

My checkup this past Wednesday went well with my regular OBGYN. I talked to my specialist that day as well. I'll have more specifics to update when I go back in the next couple of weeks. I think I got some information mistranslated from my neurosurgeon's nurse, so I want to verify again before sharing and asking for specific prayers. I may be out for the C-section for a safer delivery. It makes me sad because I was awake for my other girls' deliveries. I'll be okay if it means I'll have a better chance of pulling through the surgery and having our sweet third baby girl join us safely.

My blood sugar, even when eating the right amounts, has been mostly good with some ridiculous spikes once in a while. I'm learning that, even if I eat lower carbs, I still have to increase my protein intake to balance it out. I feel for everyone who fights gestational diabetes—actually, diabetes period! It is not fun at all. When your numbers are off, you feel terrible. I'm praying that I will return to normal like I did after I gave birth to Lilian Grace. I really don't want to live with this forever. Since I am facing this on a daily basis, it may mean I need to have Daphne a week sooner. I will not argue with that! We should have a date set by December 11—PRAYING! I really do want Daphne Mae to be ready for this world. Pray for the doctors to pick the right timing. I completely trust them.

For now, I've marked on my calendar when I need and want my to-do list completed. I want to be ready for whatever and whenever so I can alleviate as much of the I-feel-so-behind feelings. I started to do this with Piper but had her early due to the wreck. Thankfully, I had pushed us to do most of the to-do list early. I decided to make enough room for any surprises this time, so we are getting the bigger items on the to-do list completed by Monday. I'm thankful my hubby is on board with the plan. He's getting to go hunting every morning, so it's a win-win for us both!

Speaking of Monday, December 1, 2014, I cannot believe it's been thirteen years ago that Michael took me on our first date—lucky thirteen! I wasn't convinced at first that Michael was "the one." I'm glad he was persistent and kept making sure we spent time together on dates and on the phone. He can get me more than frustrated and angry at times, but he truly is the one for me. I don't know anyone else who could put up with me and my chaotic, unbelievable-at-times medical journeys. I love him more than I could ever love another human being—plus my girls.

I am thankful that he gets it together more times than not. I'm thankful for our crazy, stubborn three-year-old who never stops. They both can exhaust me to no limit, but I couldn't live without them. It's going to be a wild ride adding Daphne Mae to our mix. I've been praying extra for the addition! I can't wait to see what God has in store for her. Watching my two other girls live out their purpose has been the greatest honor. Lilian's purpose was short-lived here on earth, but I get to watch her legacy continue with her purpose everywhere. Piper's purpose is nonstop and beautiful to watch—even through the trying threes! I am super blessed to get to be part of their journeys. I pray that I step aside and let God prepare them for all the mountains they will face.

I'm thankful that God's helped me to be successful in climbing all my mountains, though some haven't looked as pretty as others. I think back to the moment before I went under for brain surgery, thinking I would be waking up to Jesus. I know I struggled more than I wish I would have post-brain surgery. I hated walking with depression, and at times, I still fight it. I think about how I wondered why God brought me back this time, and then I feel Daphne Mae kick me. I'm back because He needs her here. I get goosebumps thinking about it all. To think that she wouldn't be here if I had left this earth back on December 18, 2013, blows my mind. I'm beyond excited to meet her and see how this family will merge into a new journey together.

Praying for us all as we face shifts and changes in our journey. I know we wish we could erase a percentage of it all, but we wouldn't be growing and going where He needs us to be. He has the whole picture before Him. He's setting it all up because He already knows our future. Don't cheat yourself by thinking you know best. The days I wish I could take away are the days I learned more than I ever could have if I hadn't walked this journey. Trust Him! He has us in His hands!

I am thankful to my family and friends. We aren't perfect, but we do get to be a part of each other's lives, and I am grateful even for the good, bad, and ugly! Thanks for being in my life in any part that you play—big or small. You matter and make a difference even if we don't get to talk. I love you all!

PS: If you haven't RSVP'd to Shanna Santiago for the baby sprinkle (Sunday, December 7, 2014), please do so by Monday, December 1! We need final numbers to order dessert and miscellaneous items.

Can't stop, won't stop

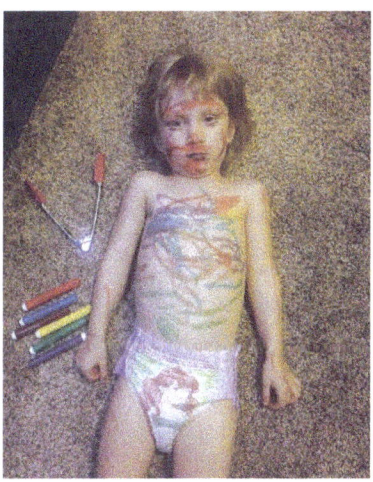

Piper's "Trying Threes" proof

My copy cat

DECEMBER 20, 2014

50 › One-Year Post-Brain Surgery

Update: I absolutely love "Forever Reign" by Hillsong. I'm holding on tight to it these days. God rises above all the bad because He is good. He's the light in the darkness. He brings peace to the storms. It seems like I keep facing one thing after another, and I'm worn out! I know that in my life, I have only God to hold me tight and help me through it all. I don't want to downplay all my amazing prayer warriors and supporters—it's just that He is my true strength in the battles! He forever reigns in my heart. He is more than I could ever be, say, or write.

Since a food poisoning episode, I have been dealing with shocks to my brain, which disorient me for a minute or two. It's scary because it started happening while I was driving. I'm limiting my driving and doing it only if I have to. Plus, my kidneys have been really hurting, so the doctor sent a sample off to check my numbers. I haven't heard back yet.

This past week, I got myself to labor and delivery for a checkup because I had a bad rash and swelling on the sides of my legs and butt. I decided to look it up, and it was ridiculous what it said. The gist was that it could be my liver, which could cause death to the baby. Needless to say, I loaded myself up at one in the morning and headed to the hospital. Things checked out okay for the baby, so they gave me the option to head home or stay until morning so that Dr. Razdan could see me. Sadly, I had some major things—not that major, but it was important to me—going on Thursday during the day. I decided I'd call in the morning and headed home. Dr. Razdan decided I needed to fast Thursday night and get blood drawn Friday morning to check my liver—I'm waiting for the results.

Friday, I did acupuncture to help with the head and kidney pain. I asked for his opinion on my rash, and he's thinking it's a hot, angry liver. So I'm glad my doctor is ahead of it and we can see if it's okay. Plus, I have a horrible sinus infection that I'm dealing with. Thank God for my allergist, because I have meds I'm taking to nip it in the bud. I feel like I'm not winning on the health-side. Plus, I need major attitude adjustments periodically. I am winning, though, because I decided God can have it all. We did our own little family Christmas last night. I loved every minute of it, even if I felt like crap. God really blessed us!

I think back to last night, watching Piper open presents, and I'm giddy thinking about my two of three girls getting to grow up together in this life. I'm so glad Piper will get to have a sissy here on earth. It's going to be a wild ride, and I've been more than scared thinking about it. God is crazy thinking that I can handle all of this—being the mom my girls need me to be. God is so good at calming me down, though, and helping me see that He makes no mistakes. He knows exactly what He's doing. I pray that I step aside always and let Him do His thing like I try to do. I think on my tombstone it will have "try" as my middle name, which is all that God asks for us to do.

On another note: my neurosurgeon is sending my OBGYN a dictated letter about my shocks and what they mean. I hope with all that's been going on that we can finally book the C-section sooner rather than later. My body is shouting out loud that it's finished. I trust God's timing in it all though. I'm trying to be at peace as best as one can be at thirty-six or thirty-seven weeks preggo! Not many out there are rational thinkers at the end of one's pregnancy. On the positive side, at least, I'm not an elephant. I can't even imagine growing a baby for three years.

Please lift me and my family up in prayer. I need an extra hedge of protection from all the attacks on my body, mind, and spirit. I'm exhausted, but not too exhausted to jump into my Father's arms for a rest.

Another positive: Thanks to everyone who sprinkled us with money for our stroller and car seat fund. We went on a date Thursday night and ordered/purchased it! I'm so pumped about having such a nice one to take my girls around and make memories in while getting back to my running life, which I have totally missed.

By the way, Thursday, December 18, marked my one-year anniversary since my brain surgery. Michael took me on a date, including a steak dinner and shopping. We were able to mark more things off my to-do list, which I love! It's crazy what a year later can bring in adventures, trials, and lessons. I thought a year ago that I was getting to head to heaven, but God had a wonderful plan instead to keep me here longer. It hasn't been easy, but nothing worth it really is for me! My heart sings His name, loud and proud. I will always run into His arms for safekeeping. I couldn't ask for anything more.

Thank you all for hanging in there with me. Major props and appreciation for always lifting me up in prayer—it matters! Love you all!

FYI: I highly recommend the *Waiting Here for You, An Advent Journey of Hope* plan by Louie Giglio from the YouVersion Holy Bible app. It's really good while being short and sweet for the spirit!

Christmas 2014

DECEMBER 26, 2014

51 › C-section Date

After dealing with two more trips to labor and delivery, Christmas celebrations with family at five different places, and three church services, I had my last checkup with Dr. Razdan. Since Daphne needed more time to grow, her delivery date got pushed back one week. My luck keeps coming because my doctor will be on vacation that week. This makes us push back even further, but we do finally have a C-section date scheduled!

As long as the baby girl stays put and content, we are looking at Tuesday, January 6, 2015, as Miss Daphne Mae's arrival date into this world via C-section! Keep those prayers going as she grows and that everyone involved will step aside and let God do His work! I'm so thankful we have a plan!

Since my depression (post-brain surgery) and PTSD have been wearing me out, I feel better after getting a date scheduled today. I'm mentally and physically ready when it comes to not being pregnant anymore. I'm ready to meet our third baby girl! The reason for my tears this pregnancy has been different than my last two. Lily's pregnancy brought me sad tears. Piper's pregnancy brought me stressed-out tears. Daphne's pregnancy has brought me upset tears. No matter the good, bad, or ugly of a pregnancy, there are always tears when it comes to me. Pregnancy is not for the weak. It's crazy what we go through over almost ten months of pregnancy!

I want to thank everyone again for being here for

another crazy turn in the journey. Pray my brain surgery side effects don't interfere and cause complications for giving birth. I know my shocks to the brain have been increasing, but I could just be exhausted. Plus, I'm still not good at being out during surgery—yet I don't have a choice. After three dry runs these past two weeks to labor and delivery, I finally decided I need to get back to my to-do list—getting my act together! I've said so many times lately that God won't let me climb the next mountain until I do my work or training to get ready for the climb!

Today, Michael jumped on board, once again, to help me chisel away at my to-do list! We were able to get all Christmas decor down, organized, and put away; four loads of laundry washed, folded, and put away; dishes unloaded and reloaded; first run to Goodwill after cleaning out and decluttering four areas of the house; and making a plan for tomorrow's tackling of the list! Praising God because He knows me well!

I hope everyone had a Merry Christmas! Even among all the contractions, harder than a rock stomach, back pains, shocks to the brain, headaches, nausea, infections, and more, we were still able to celebrate Christ's birth with all our families at different times this past week. We are very blessed!

JANUARY 2, 2015

52 › Looking Back

As I look back at this year recovering from brain surgery, I'm overwhelmed with emotions. I would stick to my guns on not recommending a woman get pregnant four-months post-brain surgery. Though it was not a goal or plan of mine, God knew this would be my twist on the journey and set it up where I would be able to survive and thrive through all the ups and downs. The first four months of recovery were not like other people's—mine could have been worse. I mostly dealt with depression, short-term memory loss, bee-sting-like headaches on one half of my head, and gaining twenty-plus pounds.

I didn't realize how active I was in the adventure world, but I was reminded throughout the year that I was not able to participate in lots of sports and adventurous activities. They were off limits for post-brain surgery recovery and pregnancy. I remember the doctor telling me that I wouldn't get to do activities where I could hit my head because it could cause death. It's funny how almost exactly a year later, I just have to wait six to eight weeks post-pregnancy to jump right back in to participate in so much of life that I took for granted. God is good at making sure I followed through on the nos. If I hadn't gotten pregnant—well—sadly, I might not have listened too well. If you haven't already gathered, I'm very stubborn. I do a much better job when I am accountable for another human life.

I remember the moment I woke up from brain surgery, I thought, *I'm not dead? How did that happen? I'm alive? I get to stay?* I thought when I went into brain surgery that I would not be rejoining you all. I had accepted whatever God needed my journey to be. Part of me was very sad to leave, but the other part that misses Lilian Grace was ecstatic that I'd get to join her. I know it's twisted, but it's a state-of-mind that I live in periodically. I don't want to die. I just want the ability to be in two places at once. Missing Lilian Grace has never gone away. Being a mother is the hardest thing I've ever had to do at this point. It's beautiful, scary, and the greatest gift wrapped into one! Meeting Lilian Grace was powerful. She lit my lightboard up, and it's been glowing brightly ever since—without ever going out.

When Piper Allegra came into this world, I wasn't sure how it would play out. I was scared she would be taken away at any moment. Surely I wouldn't be happy forever. That, of course, is my broken heart and loss talking. I've trusted God through it all, yet I know there's reality and life. God prepares us, yet we still have to walk it out. He knows our future, thankfully, and trains us to climb. Piper has been wonderful for my healing process. She is my rainbow baby.

By having her in my life, I've been able to understand why and how I am, because I'm a rainbow baby myself. God has a purpose for rainbow babies. I'm glad I've been blessed to see one in action! She rocks all our worlds and amazes me every day, even through all the chaos she brings by just being a kid and learning, pushing, and growing. She is compassionate and full of empathy and sympathy. She can sense something is wrong with you and will give you a hug to make it all better.

I am looking forward to meeting our third Warrior Princess from heaven above! She's a different kind of rainbow baby. Piper came after the storm of our first baby girl dying. Daphne Mae is coming after a physical and mental health storm. I can't wait to see her full purpose.

I'm praying and hoping that surgery goes well, especially with me going under. I hope I wake up here on earth. I know we will get plenty of time with Lilian Grace in eternity, so I want life here on earth with my two other girls and hubby. I am excited to see what life can be like without restrictions from my post-brain surgery and pregnancy. There's so much life to live, and I can't wait. I'm hoping we get a life free of crazy surgeries and recoveries. I've had my fill and would love a break!

Even trying not to take things for granted, I still find myself doing just that—taking it for granted. Life can weigh us down and get in our way. I want to keep enjoying this fabulous life God has blessed us with. Eternity is forever, so why rush it when we have plenty of time? Tonight, I watched a movie called *One Day*. I bawled my eyes out then and am still crying as I try to get my emotions together to write this journal entry. It's been good for me to cry it out, preparing for Tuesday when Daphne is scheduled to join this world. My training is ongoing, and the healing is constant. I knew I was due for another crying and healing session because I've been trained to recognize these points. I've been feeling overwhelmed and full as can be. I'm breathing better, knowing I'm not too stubborn to let my Father release what's building up inside. Tears are a true blessing. I'm starting to feel renewed and refreshed already.

I'm so thankful that God gives me these raw moments where the floodgates open, pour out, and empty so that He can fill me back up. I love that He does this, even if it can be exhausting. If you find yourself not understanding why things are happening (or not), buckle up and give it all to God. He will reveal it all to you in time because we can't handle it all at once. If He would have shown me just the last five years, I don't think I would have taken it so well. I probably would have had a heart attack. It needed to play out slowly. I have been blessed to see so many people's journeys change by being a part of ours. I love being used by my heavenly Father.

Natalie Grant has a necklace I just purchased online tonight that says All Things New and reflects the verse below. I'm all about God renewing, remaking, and restoring, as the website states!

Memory Verse 53

"See, I am doing a new thing! Now it springs up; do you not perceive it? I am making a way in the wilderness and streams in the wasteland" (Isaiah 43:19).

I always wanted to be a youth pastor or missionary overseas. I never thought my mission work would mean living life out and trusting Him daily. Trust me, I do not get it right so many times. I am short tempered and impatient with the craziest of them. I never thought I'd be journaling like I have with Lilian Grace's CaringBridge site or mine. The glorious moments and memories I've made through my pain, suffering, and loss have been priceless. There have been so many times I whined and didn't like the limbo phases, but God has been gracious and loving to me, no matter my state. I really couldn't change it because He wouldn't have the reach in my journey as much as He does without all the pieces. He doesn't make bad things happen, but He knows what's going to happen and sets up what we allow Him to so He can help us get through it all.

I can't talk too much about life being short. I'm going into surgery, not knowing if I get to wake up or leave this life next week. I do know that whatever happens, God's got my back. He has a plan and purpose, so I'm leaving all the fears, unknowns, what-ifs, and insecurities at His feet. I'm picking up the armor of God and marching into the next battle! I'm climbing and fighting with His strength and not my own—this is my constant prayer that I ask the Holy Spirit to speak on my behalf 24/7!

Whatever battles you are facing—especially the ones where you are not getting the desires of your heart—step back, drop to your knees, put your face to the ground, give Him all the mess that's inside—the turmoil—let the tears pour out, and let Him bless you with His plans and not your own. Our plans are empty and fall short. His plans are grand and purposeful!

I love you all and pray God blows you away in 2015. I pray that we all step aside and let Him work. Just think what our journey and others will look like if we let Him be in charge. It'll be like nothing we've experienced. Happy New Year, and here's to more adventure and mission work!

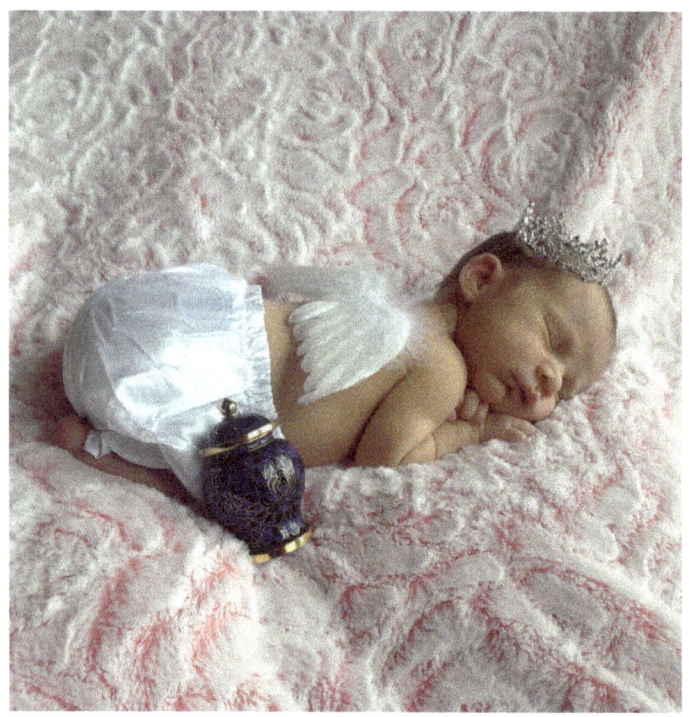

Daphne and her big sissy's urn

JANUARY 12, 2015

53 › Rainbow Baby #2

Memory Verse 54

🗡 *"Who comforts us in all our troubles, so that we can comfort those in any trouble with the comfort we ourselves receive from God. For just as we share abundantly in the sufferings of Christ, so also our comfort abounds through Christ. If we are distressed, it is for your comfort and salvation; if we are comforted, it is for your comfort, which produces in you patient endurance of the same sufferings we suffer" (2 Corinthians 1:4–6).*

In the YouVersion Holy Bible app, my devotional plan, *How to Get Through What You Are Going Through,* hit dead on for my life. The title, "Your Pain Often Reveals God's Purpose," gave me hope. I don't mind suffering when it's for God's purpose. As I read the daily plan, God highlighted how He won't waste any of my story. He has a purpose for what has been allowed. The author of the plan spoke about redemptive suffering, which gave me peace like no other. To go through all these troubles, heartaches, pains, sufferings, and loss to benefit others is an honor.

He won't waste any of my story.

Many will say to themselves that it's not fair what we've been through. They even question how my family can endure one more thing. I know this is true: God is good all the time, and all the time God is good! He is my comforter and provider for anything that is against me on the battlefield of life. If He brings me to it, He will get me through it.

Last week, we had Daphne Mae at 3:11 p.m. on January 6, 2015, weighing 6 lbs., 13 oz. and measuring 19 3/4 inches long. I was doing awesome after surgery at first. It was amazing! I'm not sure what changed, but I started feeling horrible and threw up multiple times on three different occasions. Some things that weren't fun happened, and needless to say, my mindset was not awesome. Since then and even after coming home, I've dealt with major swelling, pain, engorgement, and sore nipples. It's not been fun, but these aren't the worst parts.

The day after Daphne was born, I was breastfeeding her late at night. I was exhausted. I wish I would have taken precautions, knowing how tired I was. I fell asleep, and Daphne rolled off the hospital bed. I saw her on the floor, and I was devastated! It was awful. The worst feeling a parent can feel, especially not knowing if their child is okay or not!

They took her to the nursery for a full checkup, and they said everything was fine. So with nothing more to look for, we were sent home on Friday. I was glad, because this time around I got to count my blessings from the first two births compared to this nightmare! Let's just say, I don't want to repeat last week, and I'm praying for many to be renewed and regenerated! Over the weekend, we dealt with all my stuff while Daphne rocked breastfeeding, sleeping, and just being plain cute as can be. Piper loves her Daphne, but we can tell bringing another child into the home is going to have its challenges.

Last night, my mom was admiring Daphne's head and noticed a bump. She showed me, and I immediately remembered the incident at the hospital while trying not to freak out. I wanted to go to the children's ER, but my husband reminded me we were going to her first pediatrician appointment the next day. This still did not satisfy me, so I prayed that if anything was wrong, God would make Michael uncomfortable. I found out later that Michael prayed three times and never got comfort. So we loaded Daphne up and headed to St. Francis Children's ER!

They are amazing here—guided by God. I've never gotten in faster. We even had her CT scan done before the check-in nurse had completed her vitals. God had it already set up for us. They did find a linear fracture and a small bleed where the bump was located. It breaks my heart, but we've been in amazing hands marked by God.

We had to stay at the PICU overnight, and if you know our story from our first daughter, this was the last place she was before she earned her wings. To get even closer to tears flowing, we are actually right next door to the room where our Lilian Grace passed away. I've cried a lot of tears and beaten myself up. I know what happened last week was an accident, but I hate that it happened. God has been gracious in giving me peace and comfort. I'm just glad God revealed it to us so we could catch it early.

I did get comfort from one of my dearest prayer warriors who has had to battle with me in the spiritual realm too many times. But I'm glad God gave me her. Also, I got a personal call from our wonderful pediatrician, Dr. Gordon. His gut feeling has always been wonderful, and I'm praying it holds true to this day that everything is going to work out. In fact, I need Daphne to heal with no damages! Pray this with me, because I believe in the power of prayer!

Lindy, from Pastoral Care, was phenomenal during our one-hour visit. She gave me so many treasures of perspective. One of my favorites and most cherished was her telling me that Lilian was without sin, which makes her a saint. Where a saint passes away becomes holy ground! My heart leaped for joy over this! Praise God for taking care of my heart and soul, letting me be near holy ground!

She also reminded me about airtime and who I should and should not give it to. So I'm choosing to give God all the airtime. He knew that we would be going through this. He knew how crafty things were being coordinated against us, and He has stepped up in big, ginormous ways all over our story. He's battling for us!

Though I've kept playing in my mind what I could have done to not be in this situation, God keeps giving me beautiful pieces of how we are going to survive and thrive. He wants to show all of us that He gets us through one thing after another. God uses it for good to help others who may not know how they can believe and trust Him! I'm one of the luckiest, I know, even if the story doesn't always look so good at the beginning of each chapter. God uses all things for good!

If you find yourself facing more trials, tribulations, storms, or whatever you call it, remember that God is our strength, and He holds our future. He's working it out for the good, even if we are tired, frustrated, and losing our minds. Hang on to His truth and grace. Let Him give you a renewal of the mind, body, and soul. He's who we need to put our trust in!

Please lift us up with more prayers! Pray that Daphne and I will heal. She needs the fracture to heal completely and blood (fluid) to absorb with no damage done at all to her mentally, physically, emotionally, or anything else! We love you all and want to thank you all ahead of time for the continuous prayers you lift up along with your love and support!

We will not be taking visitors this week as we monitor Daphne. Please keep those prayers going up! I'm a huge believer in the power of prayer! God's in this all the way. I know we've had several ask if they can bring a meal. We will let you know. My sister-in-law will be using a calendar online for us. We just need to get through some hurdles before us.

Always remember that God wants to use your story. Be still and know He's working everything out for the good! I'm thankful He helps me with my perspective. I knew we were going to be battling again, because two different churches, several people's own battles, and my devotionals were training me for such a time as this! God's armor is on, and all of me is in His hands!

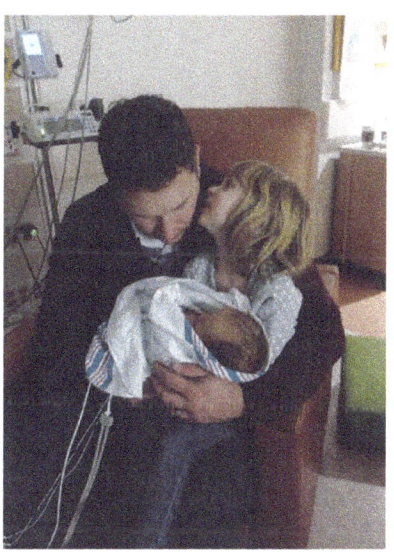

Sweet whispers

Rainbow babies united

JANUARY 14, 2015

54 › He Makes Me Brave

First of all, thanks to all of you, our supporters and prayer warriors, for always dropping to your knees in prayers on our behalf! I truly believe God hears us when we go to Him in large numbers. I don't know what I'd do without you all! I'm praying this beautiful verse below over you.

Memory Verse 55

⚔ *"May the Lord repay you for what you have done. May you be richly rewarded by the LORD, the God of Israel, under whose wings you have come to take refuge" (Ruth 2:12).*

God has been so gracious to me and my family! This adventure and mission has given us a new perspective on our past, present, and future hurts. More healing has been completed on our grieving journey. We've reconnected with people from Lilian's time. I've gotten to talk about God every day. We've met new people who get to hear great things about God. I can't complain. Thanks to one of my best prayer warriors, best friends, and sister!

"You Make Me Brave" by Bethel is a perfect song for such a time as this. God makes me brave to climb all my mountains! Whether I find myself swimming in the deepest ocean waters or walking on the beach side by side with Him, God reminds me that He is always for me. The waves can get nasty and powerful, crashing over me, yet His strength brings me renewal and energy.

He has always made me brave in the good, bad, and ugly

of life. That doesn't mean I have been perfect, because I say and think the wrong things, worry about the little things, and overdo everything. Without Him, I truly would fail miserably at climbing each mountain. My Father blesses me and brings me out of each storm, helping me soar high like an eagle. He makes me successful as soon as I step aside.

Now it's time to share some good news for us all to send praises up, yet keeping in mind that each journey is a rollercoaster ride. Daphne still has healing to do. I'm lifting this up with praise, as well as praying it all holds true and continues in a positive direction.

Yesterday (1.13.15), the doctor ordered a second CT scan, which showed the bleeding has stopped—praise God! Her jaundice levels were higher, which is a crazy praise. Yet it means her body is starting to absorb and process the fluid. We just need this all to hold true. We need her little body to keep processing the jaundice out and there to be no more bleeding. Since there's a good-sized pocket of blood from the small bleed, we don't want her jaundice level to climb to an unwarranted number. We got a report a couple hours ago that jaundice levels are down to a 10.8—praising God again! Plus, we need to pray that no damage has been done.

Daphne has been tanning like her oldest sister, Lilian, with light therapy and sunglasses. It's crazy that she's been on two of the floors, like Lilian was on her final days on earth. God just keeps rewriting our story to replace memories with different ones that don't hurt.

We are getting released from the hospital in just a bit. I have been so blessed by St Francis Children's Hospital. No offense to the other side of the hospital, but staying at both places is compared to staying at a Howard Johnson Motel (adult side) and the Hyatt Regency Hotel (children's). I love getting to see my peeps from Lilian's time. I'm super proud of one of our nurse techs from Lilian's time working hard to become an RN here. It's so cool! I remember praying for her.

I'm feeling much better. My swelling is working itself out. I've been taking inflammatory and pain meds, and they're making me feel better. My head pain has lessened. My engorgement is evening out, and my soreness, blistering, and bleeding is starting to heal. All praise to God the highest!

I've loved eating here. It's almost like a mini vacation without having to rush and get to all those places in the crowds. I've gotten the peace and relaxation parts of vacation! Though our time here is coming to a close, I am glad to be heading home in a better mood and experience this week versus last week. Last week was more than just things being bad—I was being attacked. What was meant for bad God used for good. Praise God to the highest on that one, especially that He knows what's ahead and lines it all up so we can win!

Thank you to all the mommas who were humble and gracious in sharing their horror stories about their babies falling. I pray for all of us—parents, children, and anyone involved in their lives. It's so easy for something bad to happen! Some of your stories really got to me, yet they helped me know that I'm not alone at all. Here's to all of us having drama-free days with peace and comfort, knowing that no matter what, God is always going to be here—praises to infinity! I really can't thank you enough for the prayers, support, and love. I am super blessed and glad you are in my life and part of this crazy, wild journey!

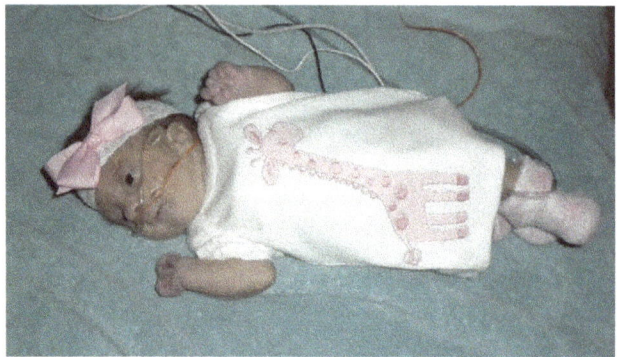

Sister Project: Lilian Grace

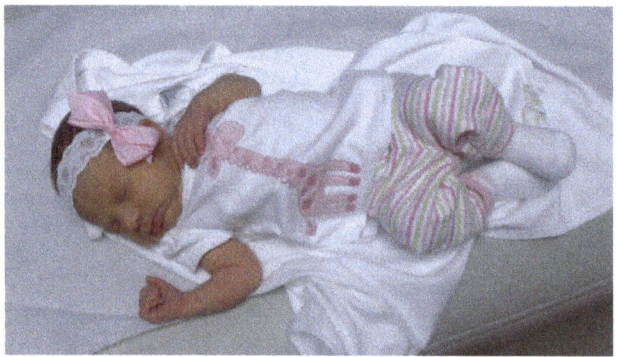

Sister Project: Piper Allegra

Sister Project: Daphne Mae

APRIL 1, 2015

55 › Time Flies

I can't believe it's been seventy-seven days since I last updated you all! I have a major praise God about my post-brain surgery with my one-year post-surgery MRI and some information about our Warrior Princess Foundation. Daphne Mae, our third miracle baby girl, will be three months old on April 6, 2015. It's a little crazy!

I get weird with numbers and wanted to see how old Daphne will be on Lilian's fifth birthday anniversary. It blows my mind that on Lilian's birthday, Daphne will be three months and twenty days old—only seven days older than the time we had with Lilian Grace on this earth at three months and twelve days when she earned her wings. Lily lived 103 days, and Daphne will be 110 days old on her big sister's birthday. It really puts the time into perspective about how much of life we lived with Lilian Grace.

God is amazing in His timing! Seeing these numbers reassures me that God has this vast plan, and I'm lucky and blessed enough to be a part of it. I am so undeserving, yet He thinks I'm worth it all! I praise God for sending His Son to die on the cross so that we could be forgiven and live for eternity with Him. I love my life with my two other precious baby girls and husband here on earth, but I so look forward to living with them all for eternity, where there is no pain, sorrow, or tears.

Make sure to see the video I made this morning (transcription included below). And yes, I got over four inches of my hair cut off and brought back my blondness! It was time to reset and renew, just as I have been working on my eating and workouts. God gave me this body and life. I don't want to waste it! I'm continuing to praise God that my depression has stayed away since Daphne and I were in the PICU! Hallelujah!

Register online for the Vintage Shadow Run at https://www.eventbrite.com/e/warrior-princess-vintage-shadow-run-tickets-12418619425 [22] by eleven thirty this evening. We will open registration for the Fifth Annual Warrior Princess Angel Run on Lilian's birthday, April 25, 2015.

Thanks for keeping up! May God bless you immensely!

Love *en theos*,
Chrissy

Note: To see the video, visit https://youtu.be/K_ZBXhl9-4g.

Hey, everybody! It's been a while since I've updated you on life. God has been phenomenal in answering so many prayers, not only for me and my family but for friends. It's been an incredible ride. I feel like God has just swept me off my feet. I know so many who have so many more prayers and needs, and I'm lifting you up in prayer.

I have awesome news! Number one: For my brain surgery stuff, I had my MRI, and I got the results back. Because it was so good, I don't have to have another scan for two years. They had originally told me I'd have to do one every year for the next five years. I'm getting to wait two years, so I'm pretty pumped about it.

---

[22] Note from author: This link is no longer active.

I finally had Daphne Mae, my sweet little baby girl number three. My body's starting to heal more than it was with the brain surgery. I still have half of my brain here where the surgery sites are, where I have the thousand bee stings, but it's not as bad. I've noticed that if I don't get as much sleep that it is worse. I'm trying to work on that.

I've been getting super vegetables in—for probably—I want to say the last ten days while getting seven to nine servings. That's been really good. I've started walking again. Now I'm really kicking it up. I've been walking every day. My wonderful husband has walked with me. I know it's not his favorite probably, but he's been really nice to walk with me with the kids in the jogging stroller. So I look forward to seeing where that's going to take me eventually.

I have other news about the Warrior Princess Foundation. I promised I'd do it for five years. Lily's birthday is April twenty-fifth, and it's been five years since she was born. In August, it will be five years since I started the foundation. I feel like I have walked this path that has helped me and been very healing, but because of it being detrimental to my husband and some other people, we will no longer have the Warrior Princess Foundation as of December 31, 2015.

I know to some people it's a shock, but it's actually a good thing, and it is time to do something different. It doesn't mean I'll be out of the T18 to T13 community. It just means I won't be running a whole foundation by myself. We don't pay anybody. Even our accountant, who has been wonderful, has never taken any (payment) of the money these past years to do our taxes and keep up with our business. I try to do a lot of this stuff so he doesn't have to. But I do know in the last month since I made the decision—because I've prayed a lot about it—it's time.

Today is the deadline for the Vintage Shadow Run. It's your chance to get past race shirts that we've had from all the other races—and medals. There's also a new shirt if you have all the shirts. I know I have quite a few people who collect every single shirt. It makes me happy because I love the shirts too.

But then the fall race—we've had to move it from August first to August eighth. Registration will open on Lily's birthday, April twenty-fifth. We will have the race on August eighth. It will be at Chandler Park—August eighth. This will be your last chance to donate and race, so just be aware of that. I wanted you guys to know from my mouth what's going on, because I just appreciate all of you for your prayers and for participating.

I know a lot of you couldn't participate, but knowing that you're praying for us and that you've supported us just by being here has really meant a lot. For those who have gone way above the call of duty when I know you didn't even have it, you still participated, and that brings so much joy to my heart, knowing that you sacrificed so much for a great cause. I know Lily changed our lives, and I just thank you so much for being part of this journey. It has been a wild ride, and it continues to be.

I saw my allergist yesterday because we were trying to make sure I'm up on everything—my EpiPen and my emergency kit. Just kind of remembering I started with him when all the chaos really started with my gallbladder back in 2005, so that's a ten-year run of crazy craziness. I just praise God for everything. He has gotten me so far. He's brought so many of you wonderful people into my life. I hope I can give back to many of you if I haven't already. I just want to tell you that I love you.

Thank God for your prayers! I am here! I shouldn't be here. So many times, I should have been gone, and I'm still here. God had a plan, and I'm so glad I've gotten to be a part of it, no matter how crazy it's gotten or no matter how I wish it were something different. In the end, it's exactly what I was supposed to have. It was exactly what other people were supposed to have. It's been a blessing. I am going to miss running the Warrior Princess Foundation, of course. But it doesn't mean we won't still do stuff in memory of Lily. It just means I won't be running a big thing.

I'm excited, though, because we have twenty grand in the bank, and we do have a special cause that we're going to contribute to. Trishtan, to whom I donated my breast milk after Lily passed away, just turned five recently—which is phenomenal. She and Lily were almost the same age, exactly. To be able to help her now with a feeding program that's going to help her with her life—it's like God's helping me come full circle. He's done that with so many things. He's rewritten a lot of my stories with people, healing a lot of paths. I still have a long way to go, but I feel like we've gotten there.

I'm really excited! Any money we raise over what we need for her, and I'll be able to help some of our other T18 and T13 friends, which I'm really excited about. We've helped so many with thousands and thousands of dollars, and it's all because of you giving and participating. You just helped heal my heart—it's been wonderful. I owe you so much. Thanks, and I pray for so many blessings for you. Love you guys![23]

---

[23] Note from author: Entry 55 was also an update on Lilian's CaringBridge website (April 1, 2015, entry 221).

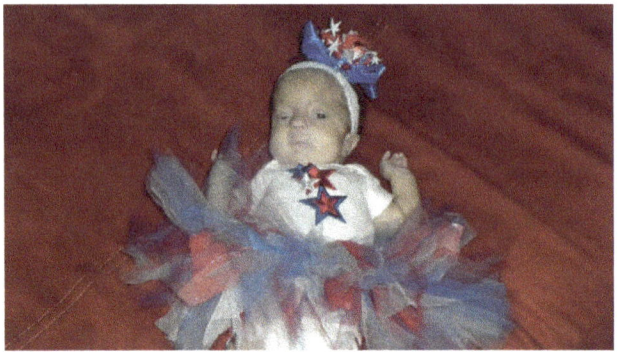

Firecracker Lilian

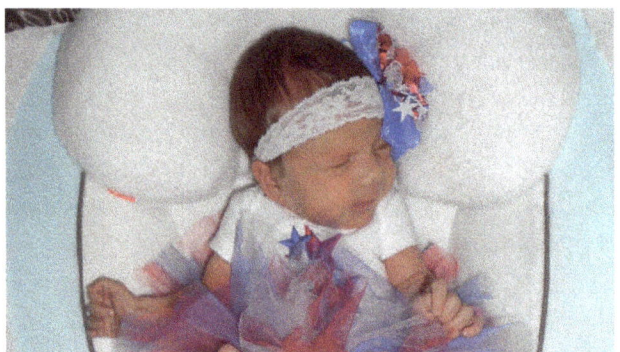

Firecracker Piper

Firecracker Daphne

APRIL 3, 2015

56 › Extended Deadline

Since we've had quite a few people who missed the deadline, we are opening online registration back up. The extended registration deadline for our newest shirt pictured here is this Monday, April 6, at 10:00 a.m. Extended registration for past race shirts is Thursday, April 16, at 11:30 p.m. Thank you to everyone who has registered! A big thank you to our donors for giving to our cause![24]

https://www.eventbrite.com/e/warrior-princess-vintage-shadow-run-tickets-12418619425[25]

---

[24] Note from author: Entry 56 was also an update on Lilian's CaringBridge website (April 3, 2015, entry 222).
[25] Note from author: This link is no longer active.

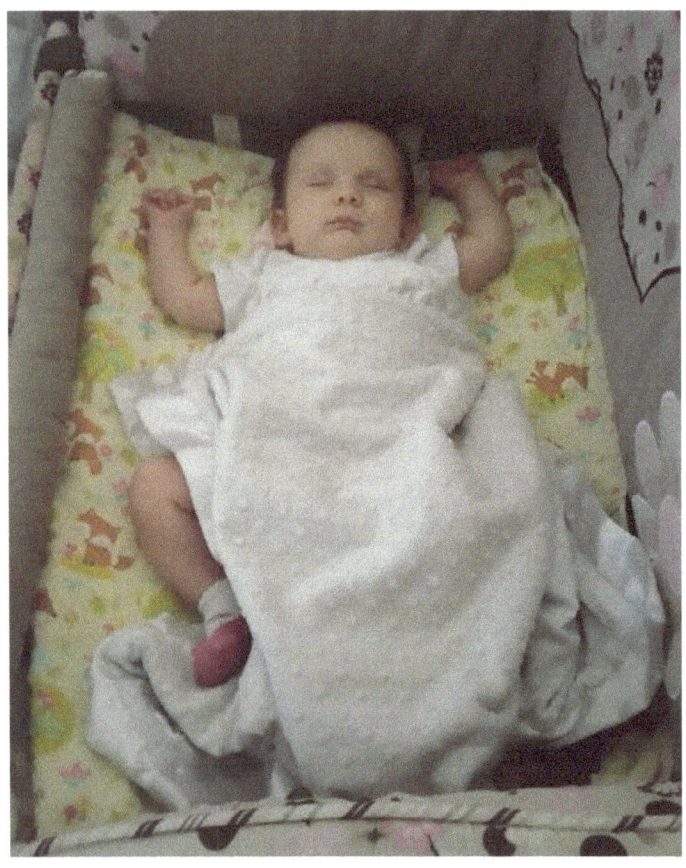

Daphne's 103rd day

APRIL 21, 2015

57 › Daphne's 103-Day Milestone

This past week, I caught myself being lazy about smoothing out my schedule and watching my food allergies. This has really ramped up my post-brain surgery problems with bee-sting headaches and weight changes. I'm learning once again that letting my guard down, as well as ignoring the information God has given me, only results in being exhausted and sick more than usual.

I learned last week another very valuable lesson about being a vessel. I've said too many times lately that I feel like a ghost in my life. If I were to walk away, it would look like all my hard work, effort, and energy wouldn't change much. I've been marking off my to do lists and accomplishing goals, yet I felt as if I didn't really exist. It sounds crazy, but it's what I've been going through. Thank God, He knew I needed a different perspective. He revealed to me that it's not a bad thing to feel like a ghost. It's actually good.

I'm a vessel for Him. When we are a vessel, we step aside and let God do His thing. I always want to be used by Him. Instead of feeling like I'm a ghost, I can now see myself as a vessel that has stepped aside. It's not about me but about God and His mission and purpose for His kingdom. I want everyone in eternity where there is no pain, suffering, confusion, and fire. To be on fire for eternity, burning and hurting, doesn't settle with me. I want us all to experience the glory of God, instead of the alternative. Being a ghost has been replaced with being a vessel. I love this perspective much better!

Sunday, April 19, marked Daphne Mae's 103 days on this earth. It blows my mind how our subconscious can run rampant behind the scenes. I was reminded that this milestone would be reached after I was preparing for my University of Tulsa (TU) lecture about Lilian Grace and our grieving journey last Thursday, April 16, 2015. Speaking to the students at TU has become a treasured experience for me. This was my fourth year to speak, and having my two other girls there with me brought giggles of joy. We've been through trial after trial, adventure after adventure, and storm after storm, followed by rainbows of blessings. In a photo taken right before the lecture (below), you can see my pure joy with my two rainbow babies and Lilian's picture.

God's miracles!

Let's just say that my mental exhaustion from it and the timing of the year (Lily's birthday is this Saturday, April 25, 2015) has caught up with me. To add to it, we got home Sunday from a jam-packed weekend, and I couldn't stay awake. I slept for over four hours while Piper let our house be her playground. I didn't get to see it, but my husband cleaned it because he thought it was terrible. Thanks again to him for stepping up!

My allergies have turned into a sinus infection. I went back to sleep for another seven hours after moving from the couch to the bed. I'm reminded that I am not a superwoman, plus taking care of myself—especially in traumatic times—is more important with two kids here. I must not be lazy when it comes to being strict on my diet and scheduling events, even if it means letting go of events I really want to go to.

It seems that, though I have lots of time during the day, everything always seems to happen at once. I'm reminded I can't cut myself into multiple pieces to be at all of them. I've been getting my lists updated and deadlines set so I'm not over doing it—at least as best I can. It may seem like I don't say no, yet I really do.

Back to Daphne being 103 days old, plus a couple of days now. I can't help but look back at Lily and Piper at their 103-day milestones. The most important thing is reflecting on what God accomplished in such a short time. We were able to live and experience so much life with cherished memories. They remind me to keep life in perspective and focus. You never know how the journey will turn, so it's vital to own the moment and be content.

My word of the year has been *renew*! It fits perfectly with my journey at this point. God is constantly renewing me with my life adventures, which helps get me through the calm and storms of life. I'm starting to cut myself some slack, even if I catch myself tearing myself down. I have high expectations for myself—and lots of things in my life. God knows me and never forgets me. I'm a work in progress, and so are you. I'm glad He takes care of me when I am weaker than weak—rundown.

Remember that we are precious vessels for Him! We are worth everything. He has an ultimate plan. If you know me, my three daughters, and our lives, you know God truly can make the impossible possible. I have to remember that milestones, storms, and more are imprinted on my heart and my soul. The busy schedule may be a distraction, yet my subconscious doesn't forget. I have to buckle up and embrace the journey in the past, present, and future!

God has continuously used my storms, trials, and brokenness for good. I hope He continues to use my weaknesses and brokenness to help others. Though I will be celebrating Lilian's fifth birthday anniversary this Saturday without her, I get to celebrate in praise of who, what, and how God continues to be in all areas of my life, as well as those around me!

My bee-sting headaches, sinus infection, and emotional eating are running rampant right now. I'm stepping up and taking action to help reduce these common symptoms. The above are my warning signs that I'm trying to step back in. Here's to stepping aside. Thank you for taking the time to read up on me and our story. Your thoughts, prayers, and support are appreciated. Lots of love and blessings to you!

Fifth Annual Warrior Princess Angel Run Update: Our last race registration will open this Saturday on Lily's birthday. The first twenty-five registered runners will receive a free Warrior Princess water bottle with registration. I'll be posting details in the next couple of days.

A NOTE FROM THE AUTHOR

Thank you for reading the third installment of my story. I published these journal entries for readers of my first and second books and for people who battle depression. I felt like I was drowning on most days, yet God kept showing up in the harshest of waves. I hope you can see that God blesses us with rainbows after every storm as a promise He will work everything for good.

If you found *Rainbows & Brainstorms* helpful or healing, please recommend it by leaving a review on Amazon, Goodreads, or wherever you browse for books online. Who do you know who is going through a storm or struggling with depression? Please consider lending or gifting a copy of this book to them. You can also donate a copy to your local library or church. I pray this book reaches those who need it most.

To see book three come to life is rewarding and proof that rainbows do follow storms. There is beauty in life if you take time to be still and acknowledge God's goodness. May God's infinite ways and wondrous orchestration help you persevere. Swim strong and don't give up.

You are meant to be a vessel of the Holy Spirit who can weather storms and help guide others to safety. Trust God to give you the strength you need in each season. He's the reason I haven't drowned!

If you're currently in a storm, I promise you there is a rainbow shining brightly ahead. Keep trusting the process and know you are loved. God's plans are mind blowing!

Blessings,
Chrissy

"You will travel in a land of marvels."

Jules Verne

BOOK COVER LEGEND

Circle Window

God knows our future. He created us in His image with a beginning and an ending to our story that brings us full circle. It's not a smooth, round circle; the curves represent the bumps, turns, and twists on our journey.

› **Clamshell:** Despite two rainbow babies, a rhythm of grief continued through book three when health storms raged on top of everything else. The clamshell represents strength and God's protection and safety from adversities and elements.
› **Colors/Edging:** The driftwood edging represents phases of my life when new beginnings and self-sacrificing challenges occurred. The weathered appearance of the driftwood, after facing adversities and being washed up on the shoreline, is a tactile symbol of what our spirit and self look like beyond the aftermath of storms. This piece of driftwood on the beach is the tree that stood on the covers of book one and two showcasing different seasons of our journey. Each was used to glorify God, no matter the state of the sky.
› **Sea Slugs:** These beautiful sea creatures symbolize positive energy. They've been associated with teaching someone to be more spiritually aware. God wants us to let go of control in difficult times and rely on Him. Trust His plan. These two sea slugs represent the book artist and her husband. They've both helped me become more spiritually aware through shared stories of our strength in God when

adversity hits us.

› **Lily Flower:** Our daughter's name, along with this mesmerizing mix of fuchsia and aquamarine, fuse a description of her with symbolism associated with the lily flower and these colors: unique, certain, individual, strong, accepting, well-intentioned, confident, mature, supportive, and instinctive.

› **Sapphire Trilliant Gemstone:** This trilliant gemstone reminds me of the Father, the Son, and the Holy Spirit. The sapphire color calms the mind and assists with focus. If you find yourself overthinking or overanalyzing like I do, sapphire can ease mental tension. It has a peaceful and restorative effect. When rough waters raged around me, God reminded me that turning to Him can calm the storm. Depression plagued me for a year, but God healed me over time. The six stones divided by the lily flower represent the six years and three-and-a-half months it took to get Lilian here from our wedding date to her birth!

› **Multicolored Wave:** This rainbow wave contains colors of adversity mixed with colors of joy. Our joy in having two miraculous rainbow babies followed two giant storms: losing Lilian Grace and brain surgery. Waves are unpredictable. They come and go to wash away impurities and surpluses that no longer serve us.

› **Sun and Rays of Light:** Today might be dark, but tomorrow is a new day. The light of God's Word burns bright and helps guide us through life. Joy is on the horizon. Part of Psalm 30:5 states, *"weeping may stay for the night, but rejoicing comes in the morning."*

› **Storm in the Sky:** The storm represents trials, trauma, messes, and hardships like death and depression. These experiences renew, strengthen, transform, and cleanse us.

› **Cliff:** In book two, I began climbing a metaphorical

mountain beyond the valley of heartbreak and loss. Imagine that I journey toward the shore. Lilian is there on the beach below. I come to a cliff. I'm tempted to jump—to take a shortcut to her. That was how my depression felt at times. But I knew it wasn't God's plan for me. I'm choosing to stand in faith, hope, love, and joy with my remaining family until God calls me home.

› **Starfish:** A starfish is linked to divine love, inspiration, and brilliance. This perfectly matches who God is to me. Without His unconditional love, constant inspiration, and immaculate brilliance, I'd be lost in dark times. His love never fails!

› **Conch Shell:** The conch shell was in book one. We were awakened to appreciate the present as we overcame adversity, which remained a theme in our lives through book three. The swirling shape of the shell illustrates a point. As humans, we can become jaded and settle for a one-dimensional outlook. I want a three-dimensional view of life, reality (that which is visible and invisible), and truth.

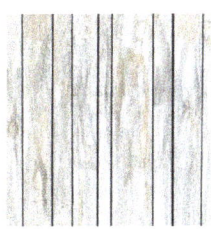
Door Background

God opens and closes doors while guiding and helping us fulfill our purposes in life, especially when adversity hits.

› **Whitewashed Wood:** The white-washed wood color represents the light around us when we're grieving. It's a reminder to keep looking up while swimming, so the storm doesn't consume us. The waters we went through were dark and unknown. At times the wind was so strong, I thought it would overtake me. But God didn't sway. His steadfastness has calmed me through every wave and storm. *"When you pass through the waters, I will be with you" (Isaiah 43:2).*

Conch Shell Doorknob

A doorknob allows everyone to open and close doors to other possibilities and adventures. If you don't try to open the door, the unknown remains a mystery. You may or may not fail when you walk through a door. God gently leads us to places where He can always rescue us. We are safe. The conch shell is a sign of victory over suffering. With God battling for us in the storms, we are able to prosper and live for another day.

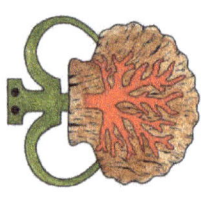

Door Hinge

A combination of driftwood, clamshell, and red coral, the door's hinges symbolize transformation and protection through a storm. We evolve after each experience. It's important to consider our family and our community. As long as we're alive, we still have purpose. A hinge signifies flexibility between healing and happiness. Cracks in the driftwood represent our wounds and scars. Healing is ongoing and circumstantial—winning and losing as we go. As long as we do the work, we will progress toward a wiser and healthier version of ourselves.

Door Knocker

God loves us unconditionally and wants to give us good gifts. In Matthew 7:7, Jesus reminds us to ask, seek, and knock on doors that will lead us onward toward rainbows.

› **Anchor:** The anchor stands for the cross, which gives us confidence and stability in Christ. He grounds us daily when we seek Him. He offers us salvation and security—a solid rock to stand on. With Him, we can have unwavering determination in the face of challenges. He is our constant source of strength.

› **Red Coral:** God's power gives us courage to wake up and persevere each day. All we have to do is lean on Him. There have been endless days when I've been worn and broken. The red coral signifies my strength in Him. *"He gives strength to the weary and increases the power of the weak"* *(Isaiah 40:29).*

› **Clamshell:** The clamshell represents strength and God's protection and safety from adversities and elements. God will never leave us.

› **Starfish:** A starfish is linked to divine love, inspiration, and brilliance. This perfectly matches who God is to me. Without His unconditional love, constant inspiration, and immaculate brilliance, I'd be lost in dark times. His love never fails!

› **Seaweed:** This plant grows in abundance and symbolizes nourishment, fertility, and motherhood. Our chances of having children were less than one percent, but God—He had different plans. Those setbacks became our greatest comebacks. We are eternally grateful that God blessed us with two more miracles following the loss of Lilian.

Keyhole Plate

As seasons of life change, we pass through door after door. Trusting in God's eternal perspective while seeking His light keeps me moving forward. When I'm hesitant, God unlocks the door in front of me and holds it open so I can safely cross through. His love and guidance help me maneuver through the storms in each season.

› **Red Coral:** God's strength is available to anyone who believes in Him. No matter if the season you are in is up or down, you will be strongest on your knees in prayer. *"Remain in me, as I also remain in you. No branch can bear fruit by itself; it must remain in the vine. Neither can you bear fruit unless you remain in me" (John 15:4).*

› **Sea Slug:** A sea slug is attracted to light, and Jesus is the light of the world. As we grow closer to Him and give our circumstances to God, we enter a better environment to grow. Like the slug, our path is not straightforward or quick. We become stronger through determination and perseverance in storms as we shift and adapt to change.

› **Bubbles:** The bubbles signify healing, renewal, and clarity. When we release a breath underwater, bubbles rise. It's like letting go of our insecurities, disappointments, and bitterness to find peace. Above water, we breathe continuously and rely on God for oxygen. Each breath is a gift from Him meant for a purpose.

› **Glowing Light within the Keyhole:** God will be with us wherever we go, and His light within us illuminates His goodness and grace in the surrounding darkness. Are you allowing God to shine brightly in your circumstances? It's easy to overlook the positive in a hard situation, but people take notice when you allow His light to shine through your brokenness.

› **Clamshells:** Though there are other clamshells on our cover, these two clamshells symbolize resurrection and new life. Dying to self and being born again in Christ is the key to heaven. Jesus's resurrection is the greatest gift—He conquered death to give us eternal life. Everyone who seeks Him and asks Him into their heart will be saved.

Skeleton Key

God provides perfectly molded keys that are unique to each door we come to in life. When the time is right, He gives us what we need to transition to the next season. Progress and purpose await us on the other side of a door.

› **Mermaid (bow and stem):** This is Sereita. She's named after my grandmother, Sereita Cooper. Mermaids are thought to be independent, playful, wise, and insightful. There's always hope, no matter the circumstance. We must accept what we cannot change. When we embrace and explore what's new, we experience the magical moments God orchestrates for us!

› **Sapphire Trilliant Gemstone (bottom of bow)**: Lilian's third-month birthday color was blue. It represents the sea of support for our little Warrior Princess. On her three-month birthday, we were joyful because the ocean decor on the second floor of St. Francis Children's hospital matched the theme of Lilian's monthly birthday celebration. The stone's trilliant shape reminds me of the Father, the Son, and the Holy Spirit.

› **Trident (in the key ward):** The trident symbolizes God's immense power. God is the all-powerful master of the universe and heavens. The three prongs also represent book three in the Journals from a Warrior's Mother series.

› **Driftwood (instead of metal):** Every piece of driftwood has a story—birth from a seed, growth into a tree, transformation as it's used to construct something useful, and a life of service to mankind. It's highly possible it will be damaged at some point by abuse or a storm. But that will result in a new purpose. Like driftwood, storms change and weather us. But as we float onward from heartache, we move closer to our heavenly home.

› **Waves:** Waves are referred to as the sea's heartbeat. The ocean is never truly calm, because currents always exist. When there's no wind, the water ripples. When the wind twirls and moves, waves roll to various heights and depths. This depiction of the wave is showing its infinite power when challenged.

› **Bubbles:** The three bubbles represent my three gorgeous girls. They bring me connection, joy, and life.

› **Sea Life (bottom of stem):** Sea life in the ocean is out of sight and mysterious unless you look for it. But the truth is sea life is amazing and beautiful—a whole new world. Above water, people and places can also surprise and delight. If we stop and take a minute to look around at the surrounding beauty of life, we're likely to be more joyful and grateful for what we have. Life is a gift, but our time to live it is not guaranteed. Own your moments, especially when your circumstances are beyond your control or comfort level.

Fairy Fern

The fairy fern on the spine invites you to spread your wings and fly. You'll gain new perspectives and broaden your horizons when you take leaps of faith. My grief could have paralyzed me, but God didn't let it. He pushed me to fly and do bigger things so I could experience His goodness.

Back Cover

› **Seahorses:** These creatures have incredible balance. They'll curl their tail around a limp plant and somehow withstand the ocean currents while balancing—a much-needed skill in my life. Seahorses are calming to observe as they navigate through the ever-changing waters of the sea. Words associated with this unique sea creature are protection, perspective, persistence, contentment, and generosity. Thirteen years after Lilian's departure, our family of five is depicted as a herd of seahorses in the release of book three. We love keeping Lilian's memory alive as we live out our purposes here on earth.

    🐴 **Michael:** As Dad, he helps carry the loads and burdens as seasons come and go. Fun fact: male seahorses actually give birth because they have a special pouch that allows the fries to survive their environment. Michael continues to protect us as he grinds away to provide for our basic needs and beyond. His blue and lime green seahorse represents hard truth and safety. Michael is loyal, generous, confident, responsible, and trustworthy. He orchestrates our adventures.

    🐴 **Chrissy:** As Mom, she must persist and endure indefinitely. Chrissy doesn't give up easily. She's teaching her fries to adapt and adjust as needed. Her teal, purple, and yellow seahorse is symbolic of her motivation, intuition, protective nature, and commitment to her family. Chrissy is communicative, truthful, faithful, compassionate, spiritual, supportive, imaginative, and intentional. She encourages people to process their feelings. Circumstances help shape us, but they don't define us. She believes joy can be found in any circumstance when you stop, pray, and give God the chance to reveal His grace and goodness.

Lilian: Our firstborn fry swims with us in spirit. She fought a good fight and finished her race. Her pink, yellow, teal, and purple seahorse radiates peace and joy. We see her life and legacy in light of God's unconditional love and eternal plan. For He is *"the way and the truth and the life" (John 14:6).*

Piper: Our middle fry is adventurous and flourishing. She loves animals and takes care of four at our house: Luna June—a bearded dragon, Elvis—a hairless guinea pig, Lucky—the leopard gecko, and Daisy Sueanne—our guinea pig. Piper is helpful, trustworthy, dependable, sweet, loving, and brave. Her emerald green, lime green, teal, and yellow seahorse hint that she is insightful, compassionate, courageous, joyful, creative, and sincere. As our first rainbow baby, she infused our family with more love, harmony, and hope when we needed it. She arrived the year following Lilian Grace's death.

Daphne: Our youngest fry dances to her own tune. She is empathetic, determined, eager, sweet, and adventurous. The dark purple, teal, pearly pink, and lime green colors characterize our third daughter and second rainbow baby. Daphne has a mind of her own and captures your heart when you look into her eyes. She arrived one year after my brain surgery. Her birth helped me heal after battling clinical depression for a year post-brain surgery.

Dragonfly

Dragonflies symbolize change. Change is inevitable. We can't stop change from happening; it's a natural process as we learn, grow, and evolve. Without change, we can't become the person God created us to be or make the world around us a better place. To change is to level up in the game of life and grow wiser because of our experiences.

› **Sand Dollars (end of top wings):** The sand dollars represent Jesus Christ's birth, death, and resurrection. His wounds from the cross are like slits on the surface of sand dollars. I love that you can break one open and tiny pieces that look like doves fall out, which symbolize peace and the Spirit. Jesus's sacrifices freed me to persevere, grow, and experience life's beauty despite my brokenness.
› **Colors (purple, sapphire, coral orange, sunrise yellow, pearly pink, and teal):** The colors of this dragonfly represent love, royalty, acceptance, support, sympathy, growth, balance, energy, optimism, extravagance, tranquility, wisdom, and empowerment. God knows what He's doing. Let Him lead and carry you.
› **Fiery Flames:** The flames on the top wings signify the fires that have refined me. This is a nod to the silversmith story in chapter 83 of book one. God uses the fires of hard seasons

to purify and refine us. *"For you, God, tested us; you refined us like silver. You brought us into prison and laid burdens on our backs. You let people ride over our heads; we went through fire and water, but you brought us to a place of abundance"* (Psalm 66:10–12).

› **Flying Position:** Before Lilian earned her wings, a light radiated from within her. Now Lilian's legacy is laced with God's glory! God helps us heal with reminders of her beautiful heart.

› **Pearly Pink Heart:** Since Lilian passed away, we've felt God's healing powers flood our hearts and spirits with His love and compassion. We will always grieve to a degree, but He continues to bring joy in the aftermath of loss. *"The LORD is close to the brokenhearted and saves those who are crushed in spirit"* (Psalm 34:18).

› **Amethyst Lilies:** Lilian's journey, like these amethyst lilies, sparked spiritual enlightenment. God showed us the world through His eyes and purposes. Remembering her draws me back to God and His kingdom's work.

› **Sapphire Double Triangles:** The sapphire double triangles represent the Father, the Son, and the Holy Spirit along with the body, mind, and spirit. We are at peace when we are connected and balanced. The triangle shape is also related to the past, present, and future. God has given me understanding about these nine points.

› **Mermaid Print (tail):** The mermaid scales look like tiny rainbows representing both my rainbow babies. The colors entail bravery, freedom, strength, and protection. We overcome the struggles of life as we lean into God. We can handle any situation with Him in our hearts. The scales are a reminder to trust His promises and stay strong.

› **Waves (tail):** The waves on the dragonfly pay homage to Hillsong UNITED's "Oceans (Where Feet May Fail)." This sacred song has become my anthem. It was inspired by Matthew 14:22–32. I want to go "deeper than my feet could ever wander" with Jesus—unafraid to walk out on the water with Him. It's scary, but He always calms the storm.

› **Blue Circle:** The blue circle replaced the upside-down teardrop of book one and two's dragonfly. Why? God has given me a multitude of full circle moments since I glanced at Lilian's pupils shaped like upside down teardrops. Our world once felt upside down, but we now own the fact that we can't go back to what we thought was normal. Our new reality has a broader perspective from each closed door and full-circle moment. We've received much-needed closure about the past, and our family is living in the present.

› **W:** The letter W in the blue circle represents winning. *"But thanks be to God, who always leads us as captives in Christ's triumphal procession and uses us to spread the aroma of the knowledge of him everywhere" (2 Corinthians 2:14).* We testify to His strength by surviving and thriving in all circumstances. It may take us time to adjust, but God leads us to the joy in all things.

MEMORY VERSES

🗡 "It is God who arms me with strength and keeps my way secure" (2 Samuel 22:33).

🗡 "Praise the LORD, my soul; all my inmost being, praise his holy name. Praise the LORD, my soul, and forget not all his benefits—who forgives all your sins and heals all your diseases, who redeems your life from the pit and crowns you with love and compassion, who satisfies your desires with good things so that your youth is renewed like the eagle's. The LORD works righteousness and justice for all the oppressed. He made known his ways to Moses, his deeds to the people of Israel: The LORD is compassionate and gracious, slow to anger, abounding in love. He will not always accuse, nor will he harbor his anger forever; he does not treat us as our sins deserve or repay us according to our iniquities. For as high as the heavens are above the earth, so great is his love for those who fear him; as far as the east is from the west, so far has he removed our transgressions from us. As a father has compassion on his children, so the LORD has compassion on those who fear him; for he knows how we are formed, he remembers that we are dust. The life of mortals is like grass, they flourish like a flower of the field; the wind blows over it and it is gone, and its place remembers it no more. But from everlasting to everlasting the LORD's love is with those who fear him, and his righteousness with their children's children—with those who keep his covenant and remember to obey his precepts. The LORD has established his throne in heaven, and his kingdom rules over all. Praise the LORD, you his angels, you mighty ones who do his bidding, who obey his word. Praise the LORD, all his heavenly hosts, you his servants who do his will. Praise the LORD, all his works everywhere in his dominion. Praise the LORD, my soul" (Psalm 103).

🗡 *"So that Christ may dwell in your hearts through faith. And I pray that you, being rooted and established in love, may have power, together with all the Lord's holy people, to grasp how wide and long and high and deep is the love of Christ, and to know this love that surpasses knowledge—that you may be filled to the measure of all the fullness of God" (Ephesians 3:17–19).*

🗡 *"When you pass through the waters, I will be with you; and when you pass through the rivers, they will not sweep over you. When you walk through the fire, you will not be burned; the flames will not set you ablaze" (Isaiah 43:2).*

🗡 *"Finally, be strong in the Lord and in his mighty power. Put on the full armor of God, so that you can take your stand against the devil's schemes. For our struggle is not against flesh and blood, but against the rulers, against the authorities, against the powers of this dark world and against the spiritual forces of evil in the heavenly realms. Therefore put on the full armor of God, so that when the day of evil comes, you may be able to stand your ground, and after you have done everything, to stand. Stand firm then, with the belt of truth buckled around your waist, with the breastplate of righteousness in place, and with your feet fitted with the readiness that comes from the gospel of peace. In addition to all this, take up the shield of faith, with which you can extinguish all the flaming arrows of the evil one. Take the helmet of salvation and the sword of the Spirit, which is the word of God. And pray in the Spirit on all occasions with all kinds of prayers and requests. With this in mind, be alert and always keep on praying for all the Lord's people" (Ephesians 6:10–18).*

⚔ *"Shout for joy to the LORD, all the earth. Worship the LORD with gladness; come before him with joyful songs. Know that the LORD is God. It is he who made us, and we are his; we are his people, the sheep of his pasture. Enter his gates with thanksgiving and his courts with praise; give thanks to him and praise his name. For the LORD is good and his love endures forever; his faithfulness continues through all generations" (Psalm 100).*

⚔ *"Carry each other's burdens, and in this way you will fulfill the law of Christ" (Galatians 6:2).*

⚔ *"So do not fear, for I am with you; do not be dismayed, for I am your God. I will strengthen you and help you; I will uphold you with my righteous right hand" (Isaiah 41:10).*

⚔ *"The LORD is my rock, my fortress and my deliverer; my God is my rock, in whom I take refuge, my shield and the horn of my salvation, my stronghold" (Psalm 18:2).*

⚔ *"The LORD is close to the brokenhearted and saves those who are crushed in spirit" (Psalm 34:18).*

⚔ *"Let us not become weary in doing good, for at the proper time we will reap a harvest if we do not give up" (Galatians 6:9).*

⚔ *"The LORD is my shepherd, I lack nothing. He makes me*

lie down in green pastures, he leads me beside quiet waters, he refreshes my soul. He guides me along the right paths for his name's sake. Even though I walk through the darkest valley, I will fear no evil, for you are with me; your rod and your staff, they comfort me. You prepare a table before me in the presence of my enemies. You anoint my head with oil; my cup overflows. Surely your goodness and love will follow me all the days of my life, and I will dwell in the house of the LORD forever" (Psalm 23).

"Wait for the LORD; be strong and take heart and wait for the LORD" (Psalm 27:14).

"For I know the plans I have for you," declares the LORD, "plans to prosper you and not to harm you, plans to give you hope and a future. Then you will call on me and come and pray to me, and I will listen to you" (Jeremiah 29:11–12).

"Peace I leave with you; my peace I give you. I do not give to you as the world gives. Do not let your hearts be troubled and do not be afraid" (John 14:27).

"He will wipe every tear from their eyes. There will be no more death or mourning or crying or pain, for the old order of things has passed away" (Revelation 21:4).

"Blessed is the one who perseveres under trial because, having stood the test, that person will receive the crown of life that the Lord has promised to those who love him" (James 1:12).

"Be strong and courageous. Do not be afraid or terrified

because of them, for the LORD your God goes with you; he will never leave you nor forsake you" (Deuteronomy 31:6).

⚔ "When I called, you answered me; you greatly emboldened me" (Psalm 138:3).

⚔ "Trust in the LORD with all your heart and lean not on your own understanding; in all your ways submit to him, and he will make your paths straight" (Proverbs 3:5–6).

⚔ "Come to me, all you who are weary and burdened, and I will give you rest. Take my yoke upon you and learn from me, for I am gentle and humble in heart, and you will find rest for your souls" (Matthew 11:28–29).

⚔ "Blessed be the God and Father of our Lord Jesus Christ, the Father of compassion and the God of all comfort, who comforts us in all our troubles, so that we can comfort those who are in any trouble with the comfort we ourselves receive from God" (2 Corinthians 1:3–4).

⚔ "In my distress I called to the LORD; I cried to my God for help. From his temple he heard my voice; my cry came before him, into his ears" (Psalm 18:6).

⚔ "We wait in hope for the LORD; he is our help and our shield. In him our hearts rejoice, for we trust in his holy name. May your unfailing love be with us, LORD, even as we put our hope in you" (Psalm 33:20–22).

⚔ "Being confident of this, that he who began a good work in you will carry it on to completion until the day of Christ Jesus"

(Philippians 1:6).

⚔ *"Do not be anxious about anything, but in every situation, by prayer and petition, with thanksgiving, present your requests to God. And the peace of God, which transcends all understanding, will guard your hearts and your minds in Christ Jesus" (Philippians 4:6–7).*

⚔ *"Humble yourselves, therefore, under God's mighty hand, that he may lift you up in due time. Cast all your anxiety on him because he cares for you" (1 Peter 5:6–7).*

⚔ *"There is a time for everything, and a season for every activity under the heavens" (Ecclesiastes 3:1).*

⚔ *"Do not let your hearts be troubled. You believe in God; believe also in me. My Father's house has many rooms; if that were not so, would I have told you that I am going there to prepare a place for you? And if I go and prepare a place for you, I will come back and take you to be with me that you also may be where I am" (John 14:1–3).*

⚔ *"The Spirit himself testifies with our spirit that we are God's children. Now if we are children, then we are heirs—heirs of God and co-heirs with Christ, if indeed we share in his sufferings in order that we may also share in his glory" (Romans 8:16–17).*

⚔ *"For in this hope we were saved. But hope that is seen is no hope at all. Who hopes for what they already have? But if we hope for what we do not yet have, we wait for it patiently" (Romans 8:24–25).*

⚔ *"For I am convinced that neither death nor life, neither angels nor demons, neither the present nor the future, nor any powers, neither height nor depth, nor anything else in all creation, will be able to separate us from the love of God that is in Christ Jesus our Lord" (Romans 8:38–39).*

⚔ *"Praise be to the God and Father of our Lord Jesus Christ! In his great mercy he has given us new birth into a living hope through the resurrection of Jesus Christ from the dead" (1 Peter 1:3).*

⚔ *"For we do not have a high priest who is unable to empathize with our weaknesses, but we have one who has been tempted in every way, just as we are—yet he did not sin. Let us then approach God's throne of grace with confidence, so that we may receive mercy and find grace to help us in our time of need" (Hebrews 4:15–16).*

⚔ *"Review the past for me, let us argue the matter together; state the case for your innocence" (Isaiah 43:26).*

⚔ *"Praise the LORD, my soul; all my inmost being, praise his holy name. Praise the LORD, my soul, and forget not all his benefits—who forgives all your sins and heals all your diseases" (Psalm 103:1–3).*

⚔ *"When Jesus landed and saw a large crowd, he had compassion on them and healed their sick" (Matthew 14:14).*

⚔ *"Jesus Christ is the same yesterday and today and forever" (Hebrews 13:8).*

🗡 "The thief comes only to steal and kill and destroy; I have come that they may have life, and have it to the full" (John 10:10).

🗡 "Never will I leave you; never will I forsake you" (Hebrews 13:5).

🗡 "What, then, shall we say in response to these things? If God is for us, who can be against us?" (Romans 8:31).

🗡 "God is our refuge and strength, an ever-present help in trouble. Therefore we will not fear, though the earth give way and the mountains fall into the heart of the sea, though its waters roar and foam and the mountains quake with their surging" (Psalm 46:1–3).

🗡 "For no word from God will ever fail" (Luke 1:37).

🗡 "The eternal God is your refuge, and underneath are the everlasting arms. He will drive out your enemies before you, saying, 'Destroy them!'" (Deuteronomy 33:27).

🗡 "Neither height nor depth, nor anything else in all creation, will be able to separate us from the love of God that is in Christ Jesus our Lord" (Romans 8:39).

🗡 "Therefore let all the faithful pray to you while you may be found; surely the rising of the mighty waters will not reach them. You are my hiding place; you will protect me from trouble and surround me with songs of deliverance" (Psalm 32:6–7).

⚔ *"Come, let us return to the Lord. He has torn us to pieces but he will heal us; he has injured us but he will bind up our wounds" (Hosea 6:1).*

⚔ *"He lifted me out of the slimy pit, out of the mud and mire; he set my feet on a rock and gave me a firm place to stand. He put a new song in my mouth, a hymn of praise to our God. Many will see and fear the LORD and put their trust in him" (Psalm 40:2–3).*

⚔ *"Why, my soul, are you downcast? Why so disturbed within me? Put your hope in God, for I will yet praise him, my Savior and my God" (Psalm 42:5).*

⚔ *"The LORD delights in those who fear him, who put their hope in his unfailing love" (Psalm 147:11).*

⚔ *"Because you are my help, I sing in the shadow of your wings. I cling to you; your right hand upholds me" (Psalm 63:7–8).*

⚔ *"Your word is a lamp for my feet, a light on my path" (Psalm 119:105).*

⚔ *"See, I am doing a new thing! Now it springs up; do you not perceive it? I am making a way in the wilderness and streams in the wasteland" (Isaiah 43:19).*

⚔ *"Who comforts us in all our troubles, so that we can comfort those in any trouble with the comfort we ourselves receive from God. For just as we share abundantly in the sufferings of Christ, so also our comfort abounds through Christ. If we are distressed, it is for your comfort and salvation; if we are comforted, it is for your comfort, which produces in you patient endurance of the same sufferings we suffer"* (2 Corinthians 1:4–6).

⚔ *"May the Lord repay you for what you have done. May you be richly rewarded by the LORD, the God of Israel, under whose wings you have come to take refuge" (Ruth 2:12).*

PLAYLIST

- ♪ "What If We Were Real" by Mandisa
- ♪ "Human" by Natalie Grant and Jordin Sparks
- ♪ "With Everything" by Hillsong
- ♪ "I Look to You" by Selah
- ♪ "Jar of Hearts" by Christina Perri
- ♪ "I Lift My Hands" by Chris Tomlin
- ♪ "The Story of Your Life" by Matthew West
- ♪ "Please Be My Strength" by Gungor
- ♪ "Hold My Heart" by Tenth Avenue North
- ♪ "Not Alone" by Jamie Grace
- ♪ "Fall Apart" by Josh Wilson
- ♪ "Survivors" by Matthew West
- ♪ "Strong Enough" by Matthew West
- ♪ "Change This Heart" by Sidewalk Prophets
- ♪ "Angel by Your Side" by Francessca Battistelli
- ♪ "Love Is Gonna Break Through" by Chris Rice
- ♪ "Broken for Love's Sake" by Tricia Brock
- ♪ "Weeps for You" by Johny Diaz
- ♪ "God of This City" by Chris Tomlin
- ♪ "So Small" by Carrie Underwood
- ♪ "Footprints in the Sand" by Leona Lewis
- ♪ "A New Day Has Come" by Celine Dion
- ♪ "Somebody That I Used to Know" by Gotye
- ♪ "Powerful Stuff" by Sean Hayes
- ♪ "When It Rains" by Eli Young Band
- ♪ "When I Get Where I'm Going" by Brad Paisley and

Dolly Parton
- ♪ "The Hurt and the Healer" by Mercy Me
- ♪ "Beam Me Up" by P¡NK
- ♪ "Overcomer" by Mandisa
- ♪ "Worn" by Tenth Avenue North
- ♪ "Called Me Higher" by All Sons and Daughters
- ♪ "What Scars Are For" by Mandisa
- ♪ "Amazing Grace"
- ♪ "Born for This (Esther)" by Mandisa
- ♪ "O Holy Night" by Celine Dion
- ♪ "I Hold On" by Dierks Bentley
- ♪ "You Never Let Go" by Matt Redman
- ♪ "Wake Up" by All Sons & Daughters
- ♪ "In the End" by Natalie Grant
- ♪ "Walk on the Water" by Britt Nicole
- ♪ "Press On" by Mandisa
- ♪ "Say Something" by the Great Big World and Christina Aguilera
- ♪ "Healing Begins" by Tenth Avenue North
- ♪ "Your Love" by Brandon Heath
- ♪ "Sound of Your Voice" by Third Day
- ♪ "Even If" by Kutless
- ♪ "I Can Just Be Me" by Laura Story
- ♪ "Whom Shall I Fear (God of Angel Armies)" by Chris Tomlin
- ♪ "Praise Him" by Hillsong
- ♪ "The Lord Our God" by Passion featuring Kristian Stanfill

♪ "Waiting Here for You" by Christy Nockols
♪ "White Flag" by Chris Tomlin
♪ "In Better Hands" by Natalie Grant
♪ "With You Now" by Ellie Holcomb
♪ "Only Hope I've Got" by Ellie Holcomb
♪ "He Will Give the Weary Strength" by Ellie Holcomb
♪ "Do Life Big" by Jamie Grace
♪ "Burn Bright" by Natalie Grant
♪ "Oceans (Where Feet May Fail)" by Hillsong
♪ "Worried" by Jonas Woods
♪ "Come as You Are" by Crowder
♪ "Forever Reign" by Hillsong
♪ "You Make Me Brave" by Bethel

https://open.spotify.com/playlist/6Ok1QIfzQfGehwj6ufSnWw?si=488de6d201d14886

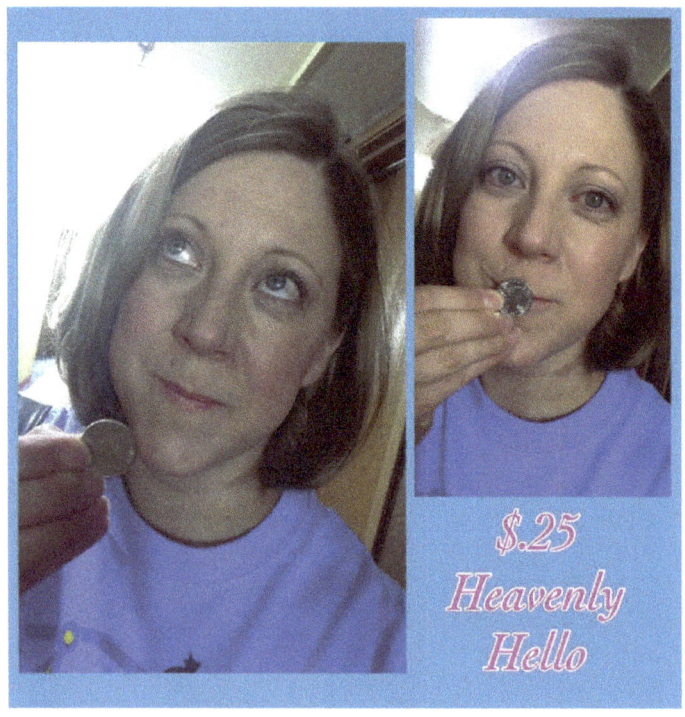

Blessings from above always find me.

ACKNOWLEDGEMENTS

To my family: We've been through multiple storms together, but we keep swimming. God led us through deep waters, but I love where we're floating now as a family.

To my friends: Thank you for your nonstop support! You've attended my book signings and speaking events, prayed for me through sickness, and listened to me process life. I love my tribe that spreads across the United States.

To my team (the warrior tribe): Despite the enemy's attacks and in between everyday life, you keep plugging away to help me publish my journals. I can't thank you enough for your commitment to each project we work on together. God has woven our talents into three beautiful tapestries now. Your gifts, passion, and follow through impress me to no end. Thank you for not giving up!

To everyone in my life: Our paths have crossed for a reason. If you've attended a book signing or speaking event, read my story, or supported me at any point in my journey, I thank you from the bottom of my heart. My life is amazing because God purposefully placed all of you in it. I wouldn't have made it through the hardest times of my life without your help and love.

May God guide, direct, and protect each of you. He is our Healer and Lord of Heaven's Armies. Look to Him in battle. He'll not only bring you through it, He'll harvest goodness from the very things that brought you pain. Don't give up. I'm proof that you can survive and thrive. I love you all and hope the best is yet to come for you and your family!

ABOUT THE AUTHOR

Chrissy L. Whitten holds a bachelor of science in leisure service management and a master of interdisciplinary studies in educational psychology, REMS, and leisure service management from Oklahoma State University (OSU). She has over thirty years' experience working in youth programming and teaching fitness. She grew up in the Cushing and Stillwater, Oklahoma, communities before marrying her husband, Michael, in December 2003.

She lived in Sand Springs, Oklahoma, for fourteen years, where Chrissy was the Tulsa County 4-H extension educator for five years and Juntos 4-H educator for over a year and a half. She founded the Warrior Princess Foundation after Lilian passed away and ran it for five years to raise money for trisomy 13 and 18 children. She organized seven races with Ken TZ Childress and numerous donors and volunteers who helped with fundraising efforts. It was a healing experience.

Michael's work moved them to Tuttle, Oklahoma, with their two children (on earth), Piper and Daphne. Chrissy enjoys going on adventures around the world with her family, discovering and exploring together. She loves getting involved with her church and volunteering for her girls' schools and extracurricular activities where needed.

Chrissy continues to deal with health issues but owns the fact that it's part of her journey. She loves to run but is presently taking a break from that. However, she enjoys working out with some of her warrior tribe. Family activities fill most of her days.

She facilitates Calm Waters grief student support groups in schools in the communities of Blanchard, Bridge Creek, Mustang, Moore, Newcastle, and Tuttle. She teaches local fitness classes—barre, Pilates, PiYo, kickboxing, yoga, and fitness mix at Steppin Out Dance Studio.

Chrissy's been working on this book project for over thirteen years. She wrote her first journal entry shortly after her firstborn entered the world on April 25, 2010. Since then, storms have slowed her work, but she is determined to persevere and finish this project. She's overjoyed to see the third book out and is working on the fourth. She's grateful to be on this side of it all.

MORE FROM CHRISSY L. WHITTEN

The Fight (Book One)

How does a parent cope through days, weeks, or months in a hospital with their baby? Are you worn from fighting your own battle? Where is God in it all, and what is the purpose of your pain? If you need empathy and hope or simply want to gain perspective from a little warrior's mother, *The Fight* is for you. *The Fight* (book one) is available on Kindle, in paperback, and as an audiobook. Illustrations by artist Tammy Edwards and photos of the Whitten family are printed in color in the Collector's Edition.

The Fall to the Climb (Book Two)

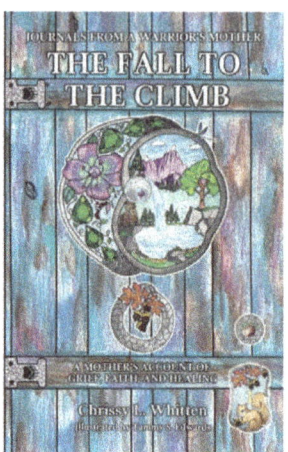 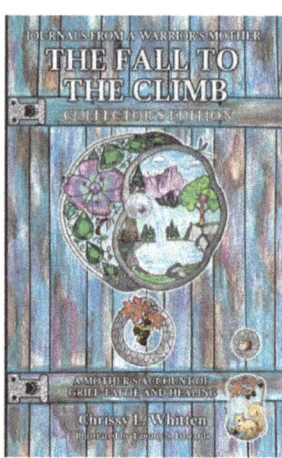

How does a mother get through the days and months following the loss of her child? In *The Fall to the Climb,* Chrissy continues to chronicle her journey through a valley of loss and grief in 2010 before beginning the climb to a higher hope-filled perspective in 2011. If you've experienced loss of any kind, reading Chrissy's CaringBridge posts feels like finding a friend who understands. *The Fall to the Climb* (book two) is available on Kindle or in paperback. Illustrations by artist Tammy Edwards and photos of the Whitten family are printed in color in the Collector's Edition.

REVIEW PLEA

Thank you for reading *Rainbows and Brainstorms*! I hope you enjoyed it. I would love to know if this book resonated with you and how you found it helpful. Your feedback will make the study guides and my future books better. Please take two minutes now to leave a helpful review on Amazon and Goodreads. Wishing you many rainbows!

Chrissy L. Whitten

COMING SOON

The Fight Study Guide
Triumph over an Aching Heart (Book Four)

To learn more about Chrissy, visit
https://chrissylwhitten.com.

www.ingramcontent.com/pod-product-compliance
Lightning Source LLC
Chambersburg PA
CBHW042123100526
44587CB00026B/4164